PEOPLE'S BIBLE COMMENTARY

JOB

RUDOLPH E. HONSEY

PBC

CONCORDIA PUBLISHING HOUSE · SAINT LOUIS

Revised edition first printed in 2004.
Copyright © 1993 Concordia Publishing House
3558 S. Jefferson Ave., St. Louis, MO 63118-3968
1-800-325-3040 • www.cph.org

Commentary and pictures are reprinted from JOB (The People's Bible Series), copyright © 1992 by Northwestern Publishing House. Used by permission.

Interior illustrations by Glenn Myers.

Manufactured in the United States of America
ISBN 0-7586-0426-2

1 2 3 4 5 6 7 8 9 10   13 12 11 10 09 08 07 06 05 04

CONTENTS

ILLUSTRATIONS

EDITOR'S PREFACE

The *People's Bible Commentary* is just what the name implies—a Bible and commentary for the people. It includes the complete text of the Holy Scriptures in the popular New International Version. The commentary following the Scripture sections contains personal applications as well as historical background and explanations of the text.

The authors of the *People's Bible Commentary* are men of scholarship and practical insight gained from years of experience in the teaching and preaching ministries. They have tried to avoid the technical jargon which limits so many commentary series to professional Bible scholars.

The most important feature of these books is that they are Christ-centered. Speaking of the Old Testament Scriptures, Jesus himself declared, "These are the Scriptures that testify about me" (John 5:39). Each volume of the *People's Bible Commentary* directs our attention to Jesus Christ. He is the center of the entire Bible. He is our only Savior.

We dedicate these volumes to the glory of God and to the good of his people.

The Publishers

Job and his family

vi

INTRODUCTION TO JOB

Title

The book of Job receives its title from its principal character, the only person in the Bible who bears the name *Job*. The name of the son of Issachar mentioned in Genesis 46:13, although given in the King James Version as "Job," is a different name in the original Hebrew. The precise etymology and meaning of the name of Job are uncertain.

Many modern scholars have questioned the historicity of the people and events related in the book. They regard the book as a fictitious account of a man who experiences great suffering and who stands as a supreme example for others to follow. They deny, however, that there ever was a real person named Job who lived and experienced the severe afflictions that are ascribed to him.

But there is no indication from the book of Job itself that this is merely a story or a poem or a drama using fictitious characters. On the contrary, Job is introduced in the opening verse as a man who lived in the land of Uz. Throughout the book he acts and speaks as a real human being.

Two other passages in the Bible refer to Job: Ezekiel 14:14-20 and James 5:11. The prophet Ezekiel lists Job along with Noah and Daniel. In two of those verses God declares that his people Israel had sinned against him to such a degree that even the prayers of those three great men would not avail to save the people or their children from the consequences of their sins. In the New Testament, the writer James refers to Job as a historical character when he says, "You have heard of Job's perseverance and have seen what the

Lord finally brought about." Somehow Job had learned to know and worship the true God.

Date of events

Since the book of Job makes no specific reference to other books or people of the Old Testament, we cannot give a specific date for the events of the book. There are, however, several indications of an early date. While we do not maintain that the inspired writer borrowed from literary works of ancient Egypt, Sumer, Assyria, Babylonia, and Ugarit, there are striking similarities between the heroes in some of those accounts and the person Job. All of those stories had ancient settings and describe ancient customs. The description of the behemoth and the leviathan also suggest an early date, as we will see from our discussion of chapters 40 and 41.

The book of Job also has a patriarchal flavor, with Job assuming the responsibility of offering sacrifices for his grown children. That appears to indicate a period earlier than that of the priesthood of Aaron. There are no direct references to the people of Israel. From that we might assume that Job lived before the descendants of Jacob became a nation.

Furthermore, the advanced ages of the people mentioned in the book of Job point to an early time, as early as Abraham or possibly even earlier. Job, the father of ten children, was no youngster. Yet his friend Eliphaz told him, "The gray-haired and the aged are on our side, men even older than your father" (15:10). In the closing words of the book, we are told, "After this, Job lived a hundred and forty years; he saw his children and their children to the fourth generation. And so he died, old and full of years" (42:16,17). Even the most conservative estimate would compel us to conclude that Job's total life span must have been between 180 and 200 years, even longer than that of Abraham or Isaac. All these considerations seem to point to an early period in which people lived to a ripe old age.

Place of events

In the opening verse of the book of Job we find two clues to the locale of the events and speeches described in the book. Verse 1 informs us, "In the land of Uz there lived a man whose name was Job."

The name *Uz* occurs only a few times in the Bible. There are a number of references to people named Uz. The land of Uz is mentioned in Jeremiah 25:20 along with other lands in the Middle East. The passage that most strongly suggests the location for the events of Job is Lamentations 4:21, in which the author exclaims, "Rejoice and be glad, O Daughter of Edom, you who live in the land of Uz." The parallel structure of those two lines identifies Uz with Edom, a land lying southeast of Israel and bordering on the southern shore of the Dead Sea. The location east of Israel is in harmony with Job 1:3, in which Job is described as "the greatest man among all the people of the East." Furthermore, the first-named of Job's three friends, Eliphaz, is called "the Temanite"; Teman is a place associated with Edom. The places from which his other two friends, Bildad and Zophar, came cannot be clearly identified, but the context suggests the general area to the east of the land of Israel.

Author

We need not assume that the book of Job was written at the time of the events it portrays. It may very well have been written several centuries later. There is no conclusive evidence pointing to the time or the identity of the author. As people who accept the Bible as God's Word, we believe that Job and the other speakers in the book spoke the words that are recorded, and that God inspired someone to record them. That may have taken place soon after they were spoken, but it is also possible that many centuries passed before the words were recorded in this book.

As is the case with several books of the Old Testament, neither the book itself nor the rest of the Bible tells us who the author was. Some have suggested Job himself; others, Moses or some other individual. Some contemporary Old Testament scholars are of the opinion that the book was written after the time of Solomon.

Martin Luther, along with many other conservative Bible scholars, has suggested Solomon as the author. There are similarities between Job and two biblical books of which we believe Solomon to be the author: Proverbs and Ecclesiastes. All three can be classified as *wisdom literature*. Particularly, Job chapter 28 bears a striking resemblance to Proverbs chapters 1, 8, and 9, both in vocabulary and in content.

We cannot, however, with any degree of certainty state who the human author of the book of Job was. Like certain other books of the Old Testament, the book of Job itself does not name the human author. While it would be interesting for us to know who the human author was, it is more important that we know who the divine author was. It was God himself who inspired the human writer, whoever he was, to give us this book.

We speak of the "author" of the book of Job rather than the "authors." Some critical commentators do not believe that the book of Job is a unit, a single literary work. They regard the chapters written in prose (chapters 1,2,42) and the chapters written in verse (chapters 3–41) as separate works written by different authors. They feel that, in spirit as well as in style, these sections describe two different men and situations. Furthermore, they claim different authors wrote various portions of the long middle section, in particular the chapter on wisdom (chapter 28), the speeches of Elihu (chapters 32–37) and the speeches of the Lord (chapters 38–41). Yet it was not unusual for ancient writers to use prose and poetry alternately. We have a number of documents from ancient Egyptian and mideastern literature written in this style which are acknowledged as literary units composed by the same author. Moreover, the plan of the book of Job is so carefully constructed that it makes the idea of multiple authorship highly improbable. The book is indeed a unit.

From ancient times until relatively modern times, the book of Job has been acknowledged to be a literary unit written by a single author. While we cannot say definitely who that person was, we can confidently believe that God the Holy Spirit inspired him to write this remarkable book. If we were deprived of the book of Job, our loss would be great. This book has served as a source of comfort to untold numbers of believers throughout the centuries.

Literary qualities

Despite a wide difference of opinion among scholars regarding the authorship and unity of the book of Job, there is essential agreement that the book is a literary masterpiece. It is highly poetic, abounding in striking figures of speech and bold imagery. The format of this volume of sacred Scripture resembles a book with its two covers (chapters 1,2 and chapter 42) enclosing the major portion of the book, the poetic section (chapters 3–41). It is surely appropriate that the prologue (chapters 1,2) and the epilogue (chapter 42) are written in prose and that the extended discourses in which there are six speakers (Job, Eliphaz, Bildad, Zophar, Elihu, and the Lord) form the central part.

The prologue and epilogue are written in stately prose that has an individualistic narrative style. The discourses that form the heart and center of the book are marked by a style that is distinctive in many respects. The verses are very brief, averaging only about seven or eight words in the Hebrew. There are also many words in the book of Job that are found in the Hebrew Bible only here and serve as a challenge to the translator. There are also many difficult grammatical constructions. When Martin Luther and his coworkers were hard at work translating the book into German, Luther remarked that it was difficult to make Job speak German and that Job was probably as impatient with the translators as he was with his three friends who scolded him when they visited him.

In the book of Job there are many vivid pictures drawn from nature. Such imagery is found throughout the poetic section, but especially in chapter 28, the great wisdom chapter, and in chapters 38 to 41, the two speeches of the Lord. Those chapters are also filled with questions that require no answer, since the answer is obvious. In the speeches of the Lord, the reader is reminded of the majestic greatness of the wisdom and power of God. As with Job, the reader must also be brought to his or her knees and acknowledge that God is the great Creator of this vast universe who also has a vital interest and true concern for us human beings. There is a striking similarity between these chapters and Isaiah 40:12-31 and following. In profound eloquence these chapters are unsurpassed and probably unequaled in all literature.

Theme

In order to understand and profit from a study of Job, we must come to grips with the question, What is the theme? Many suggestions have been given. A common one is

"Patience in suffering." A more specific theme is "Why does a righteous God permit a good man to suffer so intensely?" A three-part theme is suggested by Gleason L. Archer, Jr. in *A Survey of Old Testament Introduction:* "(1) God is worthy of love even apart from the blessings He bestows; (2) God may permit suffering as a means of purifying and strengthening the soul in godliness; (3) God's thoughts and ways are moved by considerations too vast for the puny mind of man to comprehend" (page 462).

All of these suggested themes are prominently set forth in the book of Job. Job surely suffered severely, and the troubles he experienced must have taxed his patience to the limit. But we must not overlook the important conversation between God and Satan in the two opening chapters of the book. When God commended Job and referred to him as a God-fearing man, Satan challenged God and asked permission to test Job to the limit with severe afflictions. God consented to allow Satan to afflict Job but added the condition that Satan must spare his life. God was confident that Job would not lose faith in him even though Job would be severely tried. Job's faith in God might frequently falter and waver, but in the end it would stand up even against the strongest assaults of Satan.

We must not forget that in the opening verse Job is described as a man who was "blameless and upright" and who "feared God and shunned evil." In his great suffering and pain, Job said things he should not have said and would not have said under other circumstances. His spiritual condition had its ups and downs. But in the end Job humbled himself before God and submitted to God's will. He was truly a man of faith, and God later blessed him even more richly than he had earlier been blessed.

Continuing significance

Although Job's message was originally proclaimed centuries ago, it is a message that continues to fit the conditions of mankind. We can benefit from reading and rereading this book.

Ever since our first parents fell into sin in the Garden of Eden, sin has been very much a part of our experiences. Sin has brought with it many consequences: misunderstandings, troubles, grief, pain, sickness, death. All of us as sinners are inclined to be judgmental and to point a finger at others as did the three friends of Job. Like them, we may be tempted to draw the conclusion that great suffering is a direct consequence of some special sin, which is not necessarily the case. All of us are tempted to make ourselves look better by making others look worse. While it is often true that a person who commits a certain sin may have to suffer the consequences (for example, a drunken driver who has an accident and maims or kills himself), it is also true that God uses troubles and afflictions to test and strengthen the faith of a Christian. That was pointed out by the young man Elihu, who spoke after Job's other three friends had stopped speaking. We will note this in our comments on chapter 33.

For Christians today as well as for Old Testament believers, the afflictions that God permits us to endure are not punishment but wholesome chastisement, a disciplining exercise to strengthen our faith.

In this volume of The People's Bible, we will attempt to show that there is much more to the book of Job than the story of a good man who suffered many things and was engaged in a prolonged dialogue with three friends who actually did more harm than good in their attempts to comfort him. This book also has a messianic content, in a number of passages that point to the coming Savior, Jesus Christ. The most notable of these is the great "Redeemer" passage (19:23-27), but there are also other passages that point forward to our Savior. We will note them as they appear in this commentary.

The book of Job, as does all of the Old Testament, points forward to Jesus Christ, who not only frequently quoted from the Old Testament but also stated that those Scriptures testified about him (John 5:39). Apart from God's love for us in Jesus Christ, we will be unable to grasp the real message of this book. Franz Delitzsch is not guilty of overstating the case when he writes, "The real contents of the book of Job is the mystery of the Cross: the Cross on Golgotha is the solution of the enigma of every cross; and the book of Job is a prophecy of this final solution" (page 32).

It is our hope and prayer that God the Holy Spirit will work in our hearts as we read this precious book, a book that is not read as thoroughly or as frequently as it deserves. The apostle Paul's words about the Old Testament are true also of the book of Job: "Everything that was written in the past was written to teach us, so that through endurance and the encouragement of the Scriptures we might have hope" (Romans 15:4).

Outline

I. Prologue (1:1–2:13)

II. The discourses of Job and the three friends (3:1–31:40)

   A. The first round of discourses (3:1–14:22)

      1. Job's opening complaint (3:1-26)

      2. Eliphaz's first speech (4:1–5:27)

      3. Job's reply to Eliphaz (6:1–7:21)

      4. Bildad's first speech (8:1-22)

      5. Job's reply to Bildad (9:1–10:22)

PART ONE

Prologue
(1:1–2:13)

Job is godly in the midst of his great prosperity

1 In the land of Uz there lived a man whose name was Job. This man was blameless and upright; he feared God and shunned evil. ²He had seven sons and three daughters, ³and he owned seven thousand sheep, three thousand camels, five hundred yoke of oxen and five hundred donkeys, and had a large number of servants. He was the greatest man among all the people of the East.

⁴His sons used to take turns holding feasts in their homes, and they would invite their three sisters to eat and drink with them. ⁵When a period of feasting had run its course, Job would send and have them purified. Early in the morning he would sacrifice a burnt offering for each of them, thinking, "Perhaps my children have sinned and cursed God in their hearts." This was Job's regular custom.

The book of Job begins with a statement that is straight forward and factual. It tells us about a man who really existed. This account is not dependent upon or connected to a previous biblical narrative but immediately introduces the central character of the book, a man named Job. No reference is made to his parents or earlier ancestors. He is presented as a man who lived in the land of Uz, located somewhere in the ancient Near East.

With just a few well-chosen words, the sacred writer describes Job: "This man was blameless and upright, he feared God and shunned evil." The word "blameless" can more literally be translated as "whole" or "complete." Job was a mature believer; his heart was right with God. He was also genuine and forthright, completely honest in his dealings with others, not a hypocrite. Shame and duplicity were not a part of his nature. He was "upright," genuinely righteous. Like Noah, who is similarly described in Genesis 6:9, Job was righteous through faith in God. Later in this chapter, in a dialogue with Satan, God attests to Job's blamelessness and uprightness. That fact is essential for a proper understanding of the discussion that later takes place in the book.

However, we must not confuse blamelessness and uprightness with sinlessness. No human being except the perfect God-man, Jesus Christ, is sinless. Francis Anderson correctly states, "Job is not considered to be perfect or sinless. All the speakers in the book, including Job himself, are convinced that all men are sinful. Job's first recorded act is to offer sacrifices for sin" (*Job,* page 79).

Job feared God. He stood in awe of God's holy will and tried to conduct his life accordingly. He shunned and hated evil because God hates evil. God gave this remarkable man and his wife ten children. The Bible regards children as a great blessing. In two consecutive psalms (Psalm 127 and Psalm 128) that truth is beautifully expressed. We would suggest that you read those psalms. Job was blessed with seven sons and three daughters. Several commentators have mentioned that the numbers seven (sons), three (daughters), and ten (children) suggest a complete number, making up an ideal family. As we will see in later verses, the ten children lived on close and friendly terms.

Verse 3 enumerates Job's livestock. To us the number of animals seems almost incredible: seven thousand sheep, three thousand camels, five hundred yoke of oxen (actually one thousand oxen, since a "yoke" implies two) and five hundred donkeys. The Hebrew word tells us they were female donkeys. The females were more valuable than the males since they could bear foals and give milk. They were also better for riding than the male donkeys. In those days people reckoned their wealth in real estate and livestock. Instead of having a bank account in the modern sense, they had a "bank account on the hoof."

To take care of the many animals, Job needed "a large number of servants." This suggests that Job was not a nomad who moved from place to place but a farmer with much land and a large number of cattle. As we learn from a later passage in this book (29:7-17), Job was also a prominent and active man in the city. When the writer says "He was the greatest man among all the people of the East," he includes Job's wealth and influence as well as character and reputation in the expression "greatest." In chapter 29 Job reminisces about his earlier prosperity before he fell victim to his many afflictions.

Verses 4 and 5 describe the ten children of Job: "His sons used to take turns holding feasts in their homes, and they would invite their three sisters to eat and drink with them." We are not told how often or how long they would have these get-togethers. Their gatherings may have been birthday parties. Some have suggested a prolonged annual feast, religious or national. Others think that the feasts were harvest festivals. In any case, we are told that the brothers took turns serving as hosts and also invited their sisters. Whether all of the brothers and sisters were married, we do not know. At any rate, there was a close and loving relationship among all of the ten children of Job.

In those days as well as today, it was unusual to find a large family in which brothers and sisters got along so well and enjoyed one another's company so much. Unfortunately, we often see the opposite: disharmony and wrangling, particularly over estates at the death of the parents. Some brothers and sisters have borne grudges and refused to speak with one another for years. How different were Job's children!

Yet they too were sinners, and Job knew it. With true fatherly concern, he would sacrifice a burnt offering for each of his children. He thought they might have feasted too much, drunk too much wine, not conducted themselves in keeping with God's will, or even cursed God in their hearts. He realized that it is very easy for people to indulge in frivolous conversation, and the frivolous can readily lead to the sinful.

Job is an excellent example of how parents should conduct themselves with regard to their adult children. The context strongly suggests that Job's sons were adults, since they had their own homes. His daughters also had very likely passed childhood. Job did not meddle. He neither planned their parties nor did he interfere with them, but he did have a true fatherly concern for their spiritual welfare. True Christian parents will also show such concern.

The relationship between parents and children changes when the children reach adulthood. Parents ought to avoid meddling and interfering with the plans and activities of their grown children. But they should never forget that as parents they should have a true concern for the welfare of their children, keep in touch with them, and continue to pray for them. Although our society is different from that in which Job lived, the parent-child relationship is still there. Even when children move away and establish their own households, that relationship can continue as a beautiful and enduring one.

Satan challenges God to test Job

⁶**One day the angels came to present themselves before the Lord, and Satan also came with them. ⁷The Lord said to Satan, "Where have you come from?"**

Satan answered the Lord, "From roaming through the earth and going back and forth in it."

⁸Then the LORD said to Satan, "Have you considered my servant Job? There is no one on earth like him; he is blameless and upright, a man who fears God and shuns evil."
⁹"Does Job fear God for nothing?" Satan replied. ¹⁰"Have you not put a hedge around him and his household and everything he has? You have blessed the work of his hands, so that his flocks and herds are spread throughout the land. ¹¹But stretch out your hand and strike everything he has, and he will surely curse you to your face."
¹²The LORD said to Satan, "Very well, then, everything he has is in your hands, but on the man himself do not lay a finger."
Then Satan went out from the presence of the LORD.

These verses are important for a proper understanding of the theme of the book of Job. This is the first of two appearances of Satan among the other angels (literally, "sons of God") when they stood before God. To us it seems strange that the evil one, the prince of darkness, would appear before God, but with God's permission he did so. In the two sections that record his appearances (1:6-12; 2:1-7), the word "Satan" is found 14 times. In each instance the definite article is used in the Hebrew, so it is really a title rather than a name: "the Satan," which means "the adversary," the great opponent and enemy. There is a reference to Satan in Revelation 12:9 in which John uses many terms to describe the devil: "The great dragon was hurled down—that ancient serpent called the devil, or Satan, who leads the whole world astray."

In his *Popular Commentary of the Bible,* P. E. Kretzmann explains Satan's strange appearance before God: "Although condemned to the chains of hell, the devil, as the prince of this world, has as much freedom as the Lord permits him to have, not only in governing his own subjects, but also in afflicting the children of God and leading them into temptation" (Old Testament, Volume 2, page 2).

When the L and asked Satan, "Where have you come from?" he first implied that Satan was an intruder who really had no business being there. Yet the L and did acknowledge his presence and gave Satan the opportunity to reply, "From roaming through the earth and going back and forth in it." Peter undoubtedly refers to this passage when he warns us, "Be self-controlled and alert. Your enemy the devil prowls around like a roaring lion looking for someone to devour" (1 Peter 5:8). The word "enemy" in that passage may also be translated as "adversary," as in the King James Version. That is exactly what *Satan* means. He was against Job, and he is against us. He is rightly called *the devil,* which means "slanderer" or "accuser." He accused Job, as we read in verses 9 to 11, and he accuses us.

In verse 8 God states the theme of this book. First he honors Job by calling him his "servant." Then he commends Job for his blamelessness and uprightness, using the same expressions as in the opening verse of the book. As we study and sometimes puzzle over the arguments of the various speakers in the long poetic part of this book, we must not forget that God spoke of Job as being a righteous man. Although Job's faith wavered and at times came close to the breaking point when he was tested, he remained a child of God and a man of faith.

After God had commended Job, Satan had the audacity to contradict God. He cynically asked, "Does Job fear God for nothing?" The Hebrew word translated as "for nothing" is related to the precious word meaning "grace," the free, undeserved favor of God. The expression "for nothing" literally means "relying completely on God's grace." In his childlike faith, Job implicitly trusted in God and loved him for his (God's) sake alone, without any consideration of material reward. Satan not only questioned this but denied it. The form of Satan's question really implies that Job did not fear God for nothing. Satan suggested that Job was a phony; he feared God only because God had greatly blessed him with wealth and honor.

Indirectly, Satan also accused and blamed God, telling him in effect, "God, you've been too good to Job; you've spoiled him." He maliciously accused God of having "put a hedge around him," having shielded him from dangers and calamities that had come upon others. He further stated that God had so arranged things that Job's flocks and herds had multiplied and grown far beyond those of other men. He then challenged God to stretch out his hand and strike everything Job owned. Satan predicted that if God did so, Job would curse him to his face. That last statement is given in the form of an oath and can be expressed, "I swear that he (Job) will curse you to your face."

God accepted Satan's challenge and placed everything Job had into Satan's hands. As we will see from the verses that immediately follow, that included Job's animals, his servants, and his children. Only then was Satan satisfied, and he left to carry out his diabolical scheme.

Verse 12 is important for a proper understanding of the book. If we fail to keep in mind that God permitted Satan to test Job and that God commended Job whereas Satan condemned him, we miss the main point of the book. In both the prologue (1:8; 2:3) and the epilogue (42:7-9), God held up Job as an exemplary, God-fearing man. In the end he blessed him even more richly than in the beginning. Although God repeatedly permitted Job to be severely afflicted during the course of his great trials so that at times Job bitterly complained, and although God later rebuked and humbled Job, he still regarded Job as his child. In this contest with Satan, God prevailed.

The four messengers report misfortunes to Job

¹³One day when Job's sons and daughters were feasting and drinking wine at the oldest brother's house, ¹⁴a messenger came to Job and said, "The oxen were plowing and the donkeys were grazing nearby, ¹⁵and the Sabeans attacked and carried them off. They put the servants to the sword, and I am the only one who has escaped to tell you!"

¹⁶While he was still speaking, another messenger came and said, "The fire of God fell from the sky and burned up the sheep and the servants, and I am the only one who has escaped to tell you!"

¹⁷While he was still speaking, another messenger came and said, "The Chaldeans formed three raiding parties and swept down on your camels and carried them off. They put the servants to the sword, and I am the only one who has escaped to tell you!"

¹⁸While he was still speaking, yet another messenger came and said, "Your sons and daughters were feasting and drinking wine at the oldest brother's house, ¹⁹when suddenly a mighty wind swept in from the desert and struck the four corners of the house. It collapsed on them and they are dead, and I am the only one who has escaped to tell you!"

In rapid succession, disasters overtook Job. These calamities, which came without any warning, like a bolt of lightning out of the sky, shocked Job and left him stunned. They must also have posed a great problem to Job, for he knew that God is in control of the universe. He must have asked himself why God, who had been so good to him, now permitted such calamities to overtake him. He was not aware of the fact that God had permitted Satan to put Job to a severe test of faith.

Job's children had been together feasting and drinking wine in the oldest brother's house. There is no indication that they were overindulging. Rather, as a closely-knit family, they were enjoying one another's company when, all at once, calamity struck.

On Job's large estate, many of his servants were busy plowing with oxen while the female donkeys were grazing nearby. Suddenly, a band of Sabeans from Arabia attacked them, seized the valuable animals, and killed the servants. Only one person was able to escape and report the catastrophe to Job.

Before this servant had finished giving Job the bad news, another hurried to tell Job of a second disaster that had just struck. He began by saying, "The fire of God fell from the sky." Some commentators have interpreted that to be lightning. Now, it is true that lightning has caused many deaths, more than tornadoes and hurricanes combined; however, since the disaster burned up all those sheep and servants, it seems more likely that "the fire of God" here refers to a special raining of fire and sulfur from heaven similar to the one God sent upon Sodom and Gomorrah. In an instant Job lost his valuable sheep, as well as his faithful servants.

As Job was hearing that bad news, a third messenger reported still another calamity. Three raiding parties of Chaldeans swept down on Job's camels, animals that were particularly valuable because they were able to travel great distances. As a big farmer and businessman, Job probably used camels in somewhat the same way businessmen today use automobiles and airplanes. While camels are much slower than cars and planes, they were probably more dependable and less accident-prone. Now Job had lost them and the servants that attended them.

The "Chaldeans" mentioned in verse 17 bear the same name as the cruel and heartless people the prophet Habakkuk later described in his book. Many translations call those people "Chaldeans" in Habakkuk 1:6. The New

Job hears tragic news

International Version calls them "Babylonians" in the text but has "Chaldeans" in the footnote. Whether or not the Chaldeans of Job were related to the people described by Habakkuk, they do show a striking similarity in their impulsiveness and cruelty.

When the fourth messenger hurriedly arrived, Job must have asked himself "What next?" He hardly had time to suspect it would involve his children. God had been so good to him and them, and Job had regularly been praying and offering sacrifices for his children. But now as a climax in this tragic series of disasters came the worst news of all. In the midst of their happy festivities, a mighty wind, probably a tornado, had demolished the house of the oldest son and killed all of Job's children. That was surely his greatest loss. It would have been enough to break and shatter almost anyone else. But Job was a man of such unusual faith and character that he did not break down. The next three verses picture Job as a remarkable man of courage and faith in God.

Job reacts to his misfortunes

²⁰At this, Job got up and tore his robe and shaved his head. Then he fell to the ground in worship ²¹and said:

"Naked I came from my mother's womb,
and naked I will depart.
The LORD gave and the LORD has taken away;
may the name of the LORD be praised."

²²In all this, Job did not sin by charging God with wrongdoing.

We need not wonder how most people would react if they should find themselves in a situation like Job's. Wouldn't they vent their anger and curse the bandits who stole their animals and killed their servants? Wouldn't they complain bitterly and even curse God for having sent fire and storm to destroy their property and kill their children? Wouldn't they be tempted to do something drastic to others and themselves and say, "I've had enough! I just can't go on!"

But not Job. Although he was churning inside and almost shattered by the terrible news, he got up and tore his robe and shaved his head as a symbol of his great grief. Yet he didn't do any physical harm to his body nor did he attempt suicide as many would if they found themselves in such a situation.

Rather, Job worshiped and praised God. In his deep sorrow he yielded to God's will and showed gratitude instead of resentment. He uttered some of the most profound words ever spoken by any human being, words that on many occasions have been used as a funeral text at the death of people who have been suddenly snatched from this life. There is great comfort for surviving parents or spouses in the words of Job:

> "Naked I came from my mother's womb,
>   and naked I will depart.
> The LORD gave and the LORD has taken away;
>   may the name of the LORD be praised."

Job believed in the one true God, Jehovah, or as it was probably pronounced, Yahweh. Whenever LORD is written in four capital letters in most English translations, it represents the name of God, Yahweh, not the title *Lord*. Although we're not told Job was an Israelite, he had learned to know and worship the true God. Three times in this verse Job refers to the true God by his name. In the poetic part of the book, the word *God* is usually used, and the God in whom Job believed was the one true God.

Without a word of complaint, Job accepted his great affliction. God had given him everything, and Job was willing to yield it all back to God, even his children, and he added "May the name of the Lord be praised." Job did not commit the sin of blaming God for his troubles.

In his patient submission to the will of God during his deep affliction, Job gives us an Old Testament preview of that person who suffered even more and not for his own sin—our Savior Jesus Christ. As that sinless man was struggling under the burden of the sins of all people and awaiting his deepest humiliation, suffering, and crucifixion, he earnestly prayed to his heavenly Father in the Garden of Gethsemane. Our Savior's prayer was a true prayer of resignation to his Father's will: "My Father, if it is not possible for this cup to be taken away unless I drink it, may your will be done" (Matthew 26:42). Like Jesus, Job also yielded to the will of his heavenly Father and praised God even in his deep sorrow and affliction. What an example he is to all of us!

Satan again challenges God to test Job

2 On another day the angels came to present themselves before the LORD, and Satan also came with them to present himself before him. ²And the LORD said to Satan, "Where have you come from?"

Satan answered the LORD, "From roaming through the earth and going back and forth in it."

³Then the LORD said to Satan, "Have you considered my servant Job? There is no one on earth like him; he is blameless and upright, a man who fears God and shuns evil. And he still maintains his integrity, though you incited me against him to ruin him without any reason."

⁴"Skin for skin!" Satan replied. "A man will give all he has for his own life. ⁵But stretch out your hand and strike his flesh and bones, and he will surely curse you to your face."

⁶The LORD said to Satan, "Very well, then, he is in your hands; but you must spare his life."

In spite of the severe afflictions he had brought upon Job, Satan had not succeeded in making Job curse God or renounce his faith. But Satan was not about to give up. Again he appeared before the LORD, and the conversation began in the same way that the original conversation went in 1:7,8. This time, speaking of Job, the LORD added, "And he still maintains his integrity, though you incited me against him to ruin him without any reason."

Several words in that statement are especially significant. The word "incited" has a very strong and sinister meaning in this context. God was telling Satan that he had maliciously influenced God to destroy Job. The word translated as "ruin" literally means "swallow" or "devour." Satan, whom the Bible describes as "the accuser of our brothers, who accuses them before our God day and night" (Revelation 12:10), was trying to arouse God against Job for the purpose of destroying him. God added the words "without any reason," which was expressed in one word in Hebrew, the same word that is translated as "for nothing" in 1:9. God reaffirmed that Job had done nothing whatsoever to deserve suffering those great calamities that robbed him of his children and possessions. It was only to test Job and to prove to Satan that Job was a devout child of God that God permitted Satan to allow such great misfortunes to overtake Job.

In brazen disrespect Satan fired back, "Skin for skin!" From what follows it seems best to understand those words to mean that a person would be willing to give up almost anything else, even his family, if his life could be spared, if he could save his own skin. When Satan stated that Job would curse God to his face if he suffered injury, the devil lived up to his title as "the slanderer." Earlier God had called Job a righteous and devout man. Job had demonstrated true, unselfish fatherly love and concern for his children and would probably have been willing to give his life for any one of them. And yet Satan dared to accuse this man of being selfish and self-centered.

After this second conversation, the LORD permitted Satan to afflict Job, but with the restriction that he must spare Job's life. Again this reminds us that while God may permit the devil to exert his evil influence and power to test people, he sets a limit to what the devil can do. Satan is very powerful, as Martin Luther reminds us in his great hymn "A Mighty Fortress," but he is not at liberty to pursue his mischief whenever and however he pleases. As Christians, we must always be aware of Satan's great power, so great that we are no match for him. We can, however, find our true comfort and strength in knowing that Jesus Christ is even more powerful and has conquered the evil one. Trusting in Jesus, we need not fear the devil.

Job reacts to his personal afflictions

⁷So Satan went out from the presence of the LORD and afflicted Job with painful sores from the soles of his feet to the top of his head. ⁸Then Job took a piece of broken pottery and scraped himself with it as he sat among the ashes.

⁹His wife said to him, "Are you still holding on to your integrity? Curse God and die!"

¹⁰He replied, "You are talking like a foolish woman. Shall we accept good from God, and not trouble?"

In all this, Job did not sin in what he said.

After the second encounter with the Lord, the prince of hell went on his way. The sacred writer tells us that Satan "afflicted Job with painful sores from the soles of his feet to the top of his head." Exactly what that ailment was, we can't say for sure. It appears to have been some severe skin irritation that broke out into ulcers, boils, or blisters yield-ing pus.

Many commentators are of the opinion that Job's ailment was an extreme form of leprosy called elephantiasis. In his detailed two-volume commentary on Job, Albert Barnes expresses that view: "This disease received its name from [the Greek word] *elephas,* an elephant, from the swelling produced by it, causing a resemblance to that animal in the limbs; or because it rendered the skin like that of the ele-phant, scabrous and dark coloured. . . . The disease of Job seems to have been a universal ulcer, producing an eruption over his entire person, and attended with violent pain, and constant restlessness" (*Barnes' Notes on the Old and New Testaments, Job,* Volume 1, page 116). This seems to fit Job's condition as it is described in a number of verses in the book. His reaction was to attempt to give himself relief from the intense pain and itching by scraping himself with a piece of broken pottery as he sat among the ashes.

Those words also strongly imply that Job had left his stately home and had gone to a desolate place where people burned rubbish. The closing verses of this chapter (2:12,13) suggest that in his wretched physical condition Job had isolated himself from other people and had undergone such a radical change in his appearance that people could hardly recognize him.

Now Job's wife is mentioned for the first time. There are only two other references to her in this book. In 19:17, speaking of his loathsome physical condition, Job complains, "My breath is offensive to my wife." In 31:9,10, protesting his innocence of adultery, Job speaks in the form of an oath: "If my heart has been enticed by a woman, or if I have lurked at my neighbor's door, then may my wife grind another man's grain, and may other men sleep with her."

The book of Job says very little about Job's wife; we don't even know her name. The words she spoke to Job were blunt and direct: "Are you still holding on to your integrity? Curse God and die." Some commentators explain those words as having been spoken in deep grief and anxiety. After all, she too had lost children and property, and now she saw her husband, her last earthly support, apparently being taken from her. Most, however, do not excuse her, and refer to statements by some of the early church fathers who were of the opinion that Satan did not deprive Job of his wife because he found her useful to afflict and test Job even further.

In either case, Job's wife was at that time more of a hindrance to Job than a help. In his deep affliction Job needed understanding, encouragement, and support from his wife. Instead, she scolded him and told him to do something very sinful: curse God and die. Do her words reflect a wicked and unbelieving spirit? Or was she so greatly upset over their great misfortunes that she blurted out those words without fully meaning them? We dare not and need not judge her heart. Only God can do that.

We can, however, find fault with her words, whether they were spoken deliberately or impulsively.

Job neither flared up nor took it all silently. He gently rebuked her. He who was suffering so intensely had to be the strong one and show his wife that she was wrong. His reply to her is remarkably gentle under the circumstances: "You are talking like a foolish woman. Shall we accept good from God, and not trouble?" As the footnote in the NIV suggests, "the Hebrew word rendered *foolish* denotes moral deficiency." Her words were serious, not merely silly or stupid. We hope that Job's wife took Job's rebuke to heart and sincerely repented.

In his words to his wife, Job is an admirable example of a good husband, just as in his actions and words in chapter 1 he proved to have been a good father. Above all, he stands as an excellent example of a God-fearing man in accepting trouble as well as good fortune from the Lord, who can both give and take away.

The sacred writer concludes this section with the statement, "In all this, Job did not sin in what he said." What Job said was right and commendable. Once again, Job's trust in the Lord's goodness did not falter, and Satan's second temptation was foiled. But a third test was ahead for Job, and that proved to be more severe than either of the first two.

Job's three friends visit him

¹¹When Job's three friends, Eliphaz the Temanite, Bildad the Shuhite and Zophar the Naamathite, heard about all the troubles that had come upon him, they set out from their homes and met together by agreement to go and sympathize with him and comfort him. ¹²When they saw him from a distance, they could hardly recognize him; they began to weep aloud, and they tore their robes and sprinkled dust on their heads. ¹³Then they sat on the ground with him for seven days and seven nights. No one said a word to him, because they saw how great his suffering was.

We now meet three friends of Job, who introduce the last and most terrible stage of Job's suffering. Each in turn engages in a conversation with Job. The first, Eliphaz, is the speaker in chapters 4, 5, 15, and 22. Bildad also speaks three times—in chapters 8, 18, and 25. The third, Zophar, speaks only twice—in chapters 11 and 20. Job answers them all in turn.

Eliphaz may very well have been the oldest, since he is mentioned first and speaks first. He came from Teman, a place associated with Edom, as was mentioned in the introduction. Bildad is called the "Shuhite." That name could be derived from Shuah, the last-named son of Abraham by his later wife, Keturah, mentioned in Genesis 25:2. It is possible, therefore, that Bildad was a descendant of Abraham. It is difficult to find any clues to Zophar's ancestry or home.

Most likely all three friends lived somewhere in the Middle East since they came together by agreement. All three were no doubt men of distinction and also very likely rather elderly. Eliphaz tells Job, "The gray-haired and the aged are on our side, men even older than your father" (15:10). Later, when addressing the three friends and Job, Elihu says, "I am young in years, and you are old" (32:6).

The fact that the three friends came together and never contradicted one another in their conversations with Job indicates that they were of one mind and in full agreement. It was a three against one situation. And yet, as we will see when they express themselves, each was an individual with his own distinct personality and convictions. We will attempt to describe them and distinguish between them as we consider their arguments.

The three friends had heard about the disasters that had struck Job. The sacred writer informs us that they came for the express purpose of sympathizing with him and comforting him. When they came to him, they could hardly recognize him from a distance. He was not in his usual position of managing and supervising his vast estate. Instead, he was sitting among the ashes and scraping himself with a piece of broken pottery. That must have shocked the three friends. As they came closer, they saw his ghastly sores and his physical disfigurement. Their reaction was to tear their robes and throw dust on their heads. They were so overwhelmed that they didn't speak a word to Job "for seven days and seven nights."

Many questions arise as we study that last verse of this chapter. Why didn't the three friends speak a word? Could it possibly be, as some suggest, that they expected Job to speak first, since he was the host and they were the visitors? Did they actually sit there for seven full days and nights, a total of 168 hours? How could all four have continued in total silence without eating, drinking, or sleeping?

As for their silence, even though they might have expected Job to speak first since he was the host, that would hardly excuse them from speaking words of comfort to their friend. Job was surely justified in telling them later, "Miserable comforters are you all!" (16:2). Did the three friends actually sit for 168 consecutive hours tossing dust and saying nothing? The words "seven days and seven nights" need not be understood in that strict sense. A similar expression is used by our Savior when he refers to Jonah's stay in the belly of the great fish. Jesus says, "For as Jonah was three days and three nights in the belly of a huge fish, so the Son of Man will be three days and three nights in the heart of the earth" (Matthew 12:40). According to Jewish calculation, a part of a period of time could be designated by a full period of time. Jesus was in the tomb from Good Friday evening until early Easter morning. Since that included a part of Friday, all of Saturday, and a part of Sunday, it is referred to by the expression "three days and three nights." Similarly, in this verse the author of Job, using the Hebrew manner of reckoning, could well have used the expression "seven days and seven nights" to refer to the entire time during which the friends sat there in several sessions interrupted by occasional recesses.

To evaluate the friends' behavior, we need only look at the effect it had on Job. His strong language reflects his intense pain and his deep anxiety as well as his impatience with the silence of his friends. The author introduces the long poetic section of the book with the words "After this, Job opened his mouth and cursed the day of his birth" (3:1).

PART TWO

The Discourses of Job and the Three Friends
(3:1–31:40)

A few introductory words about the three rounds of discussion would be in place. Job began with a lament over his intense suffering. Driven by his extreme pain and agony, he blurted out words that under other circumstances he would never even have thought, much less spoken. He wished he had never been born. Then in a merciless manner with increasing intensity, his friends took him to task. All three, each in his own way, sternly rebuked Job and accused him of being a bad person because he was suffering so much. Despite their intentions and efforts, the friends were wrong. They are poor examples of how people should proceed and what they should say to those who need comfort.

The discussion in this greater portion of the book centers around the problem of suffering, particularly the suffering of Job. Why had all these calamities overtaken a man who had been so righteous and prosperous? Job and the three friends were grappling with that important question because none of them knew what only God and Satan knew: that God had permitted Satan to test Job severely to see whether or not it was for personal gain that he feared and loved God. Satan had maintained that if Job were sufficiently tested, he would renounce God. God had maintained that Job would remain faithful in spite of his severe afflictions.

The theme of the discussion of this problem is well expressed by Ludwig Fuerbringer in a booklet entitled *The Book of Job: Its Significance to Ministers and Church-Members*. "This wrestling and struggling to find the real

32

solution of the problem is set forth in the form of a dialogue. . . . The three friends formulate an entirely rational, strictly logical syllogism with a major premise, a minor premise, and an inevitable conclusion. . . . First comes the *major premise:* God is just. . . . This the three friends tell Job in a triple dialogue. Chapters 4–14. Next follows the *minor premise:* The just God must punish the wicked, chapters 15–21, likewise set forth in triplicate. Then comes the *conclusion:* Consequently, Job, since the just God is visiting you in such an exceptional way, it follows that you must also be an exceptionally great sinner. . . . This, too, is driven home in a triple application, save for the fact that Bildad no longer has much to say and Zophar nothing whatever. Logically considered, this deduction is quite correct, and yet it is fundamentally wrong. . . . Therefore also Job does not permit this conclusion to stand, but overthrows it" (pages 46,47).

We will better understand the three friends' wrong argumentation when we consider their speeches. As the three friends express themselves and as Job replies, we will also see that their speeches are not in the form of a strict debate in which a speaker responds point by point to what the previous person has said. Rather, each speaker expressed himself somewhat freely on how he thought and felt about the subject without taking into consideration what the previous speaker had said.

The sacred writer does not explicitly state whether or not there were only four people present during the first part of the prolonged discussion. We do know that a fifth person, Elihu, was present for at least the latter part of the dialogue, for we read in 32:2-5 that he had been listening and then proceeded to give a long speech in which he expressed some disagreement with all four previous speakers.

The third chapter of Job, which opens the long poetic section of the book (chapters 3–41), contains Job's opening statement in which he laments his miserable condition.

The first round of discourses

Job complains, "Why should I live when I suffer so much?"

3 After this, Job opened his mouth and cursed the day of his birth. ²He said:

³ "May the day of my birth perish,
    and the night it was said, 'A boy is born!'
⁴ That day—may it turn to darkness;
    may God above not care about it;
    may no light shine upon it.
⁵ May darkness and deep shadow claim it once more;
    may a cloud settle over it;
    may blackness overwhelm its light.
⁶ That night—may thick darkness seize it;
    may it not be included among the days of the year
    nor be entered in any of the months.
⁷ May that night be barren;
    may no shout of joy be heard in it.
⁸ May those who curse days curse that day,
    those who are ready to rouse Leviathan.
⁹ May its morning stars become dark;
    may it wait for daylight in vain
    and not see the first rays of dawn,
¹⁰ for it did not shut the doors of the womb on me
    to hide trouble from my eyes.

It may seem strange that Job expresses himself so vehemently in this chapter after he had patiently resigned himself to God's will and had spoken the noble words recorded in 1:21 and 2:10. The stark contrast between those previous statements and the words he uttered in this chapter has led many Bible critics to maintain that the Job of this chapter is a different person from the Job of chapters 1 and 2, and that the book is a composite of two different literary works written by at least two different authors. That view, however, not only does violence to the unity of the book but also betrays a misunderstanding of its meaning and theme. In chapters 1 and 2, Satan challenged God to allow him to test Job's faith and loyalty. Now in this chapter, as he was suffering intensely and was getting no sympathy or comfort from his friends, Job also felt the hand of God pressing very heavily upon him. He was no robot but a human being with feelings that reacted to his severe losses and extreme physical pain.

In his nightmare of grief, Job burst forth in a lament. He addressed no one in particular, neither God nor his three friends. He cursed the day of his birth. Although Job uttered strong complaints against God in this speech and others that follow, it is very significant that he never cursed God as Satan had predicted and as Job's wife had suggested.

In remarkable poetic language abounding in striking imagery, Job repeatedly expressed the wish that he had never been born. People generally look to their birthdays with joy and anticipation. In his deep distress, however, Job wished he had no birthday. He viewed his birth as a great disaster. He wished he had never seen the light of day. In verses 4 to 6 the author uses five different words to express the darkness Job wished for. Similarly, in these opening verses three different words that are translated as "curse" are used, each with a specific shade of meaning. In richness of language and power of expression, this chapter is a literary masterpiece. But much more, it is the earnest outpouring of a soul severely tortured and deeply troubled by the fear that God has forsaken him.

Read verses 3 to 10 again and see how Job repeatedly wished that he had never been born. In verse 8 he referred to heathen magicians and sorcerers who claimed to have powers to curse people, things, or events. Some of them claimed to have the power to rouse Leviathan, which in this verse probably refers to a mythical sea monster. Job personified dawn in verse 9. The expression "the first rays of dawn" can literally be translated as "the eyelids of dawn," as though dawn were a person opening her eyes at daybreak. Job expressed the wish that "the doors of the womb" had been closed on him so that he would never have been conceived and born. Such was his intense suffering and anxiety.

> [11] "Why did I not perish at birth,
>   and die as I came from the womb?
> [12] Why were there knees to receive me
>   and breasts that I might be nursed?
> [13] For now I would be lying down in peace;
>   I would be asleep and at rest
> [14] with kings and counselors of the earth,
>   who built for themselves places now lying in ruins,
> [15] with rulers who had gold,
>   who filled their houses with silver.
> [16] Or why was I not hidden in the ground like a stillborn child,
>   like an infant who never saw the light of day?
> [17] There the wicked cease from turmoil,
>   and there the weary are at rest.
> [18] Captives also enjoy their ease;
>   they no longer hear the slave driver's shout.
> [19] The small and the great are there,
>   and the slave is freed from his master.

Job wished he had died at birth. First, he said it would have been better if he had died from the womb. Later, he specifically stated that he wished he had been a stillborn child. He asked, "Why were there knees to receive me and breasts that I might be nursed?" The "knees" refer to the father's knees. In Old Testament times it was customary for a father to place the newborn baby on his knees to show that he accepted the child as his own. Even as a great-grandfather, Joseph received his grandson's children on his knees (Genesis 50:23).

In contrast to the afflictions that tormented him day and night, Job thought of how quiet and peaceful it would be to lie down in the grave. He described death as the great equalizer. Among the dead there is no difference between kings and subjects, masters and slaves, conquerors and captives, rich and poor, old and young. Job even mentioned the wicked and the weary in one verse. All of them have one thing in common: they are dead.

Here we must understand that Job was speaking only of death and the grave in regard to people lying buried far from the activities of life. He was not implying that death is extinction or that there is no difference between the eternal destiny of believers and unbelievers. As we will see, there are other passages in this book in which Job expressed his hope of the resurrection and a life after death. Here, however, he emphasized only one thing: in death there is a physical cessation of the joys and troubles of life. He was so utterly tormented physically, emotionally, socially, and spiritually that he bluntly expressed the wish that he could die and thus be relieved of the suffering he was experiencing.

> [20] "Why is light given to those in misery,
> and life to the bitter of soul,

²¹ **to those who long for death that does not come,**
   who search for it more than for hidden treasure,
²² **who are filled with gladness**
   and rejoice when they reach the grave?
²³ **Why is life given to a man**
   whose way is hidden,
   whom God has hedged in?
²⁴ **For sighing comes to me instead of food;**
   my groans pour out like water.
²⁵ **What I feared has come upon me;**
   what I dreaded has happened to me.
²⁶ **I have no peace, no quietness;**
   I have no rest, but only turmoil."

Job asked some probing questions: Why should people live when they suffer so much? Why can't they die when they long for an end to their miseries? Today also there are people who ask such questions and cry out "Why?" We can think of people who feel the infirmities of old age, people who are bedridden, people who are paralyzed or suffering from incurable diseases, people who have suffered the loss of a dear one, people who in some way or other have had their hopes dashed and ask, "What is there to live for?"

Job wished for death. He felt that God had forsaken him. He asked, "Why is life given to a man whose way is hidden, whom God has hedged in?" (verse 23) Job uses the same expression as Satan used in 1:10, "hedged in," but in a different sense. In 1:10 Satan accused God of putting "a hedge around him" to shield Job from trouble and disaster. Here Job uses it in the sense of confining him so that he was helpless.

Job was suffering so much that he had lost his appetite. Instead of food and drink he had a steady diet of sighing, groans, and tears. He felt his worst fears had been realized, and he concluded this opening speech by expressing his tormented condition in a fourfold manner: "no peace, no quietness; . . . no rest, but only turmoil."

Was Job thinking of suicide as he was speaking these words? It might appear as if he had suicide on his mind, but such a conclusion is not consistent with God's appraisal of Job as a man "blameless and upright, a man who fears God and shuns evil" (1:8). Neither is there any indication of such thoughts as we read his words in this chapter and throughout the book. Job wished for death, but he did not intend to kill himself. Even when complaining to God, he left his life in God's hands.

Job's words might lead one to think that he was an unbeliever who rebelled against God. But we must keep in mind that as he spoke these words, he was suffering under many severe trials and afflictions. The devil had seized him and was mercilessly torturing him. These words and many that follow are the words of a desperate man, but not of an unbelieving man. He used expressions he would never have used under other circumstances.

Job's faith was severely tested, but by God's grace it was not destroyed. God knew in advance that Job would retain his faith even under the most trying circumstances. In his conversations with Satan, God had highly commended Job as one who was blameless and upright (1:8; 2:3). Even while Job was suffering most severely, God did not allow Satan to destroy his faith. He gave Job the grace and strength to retain his faith despite Satan's fiercest attacks.

Job's opening speech introduces the first round of the discussion between him and his three friends. The speaker in the next two chapters is Eliphaz the Temanite.

Eliphaz's first speech

In chapters 4 and 5, we are introduced to the friend Eliphaz the Temanite. He may have been the oldest of the three friends. His age might also account for the fact that he liked to draw on his personal experiences, of which he apparently had many.

Job's former helpfulness to many

4 Then Eliphaz the Temanite replied:

² "If someone ventures a word with you,
   will you be impatient?
   But who can keep from speaking?
³ Think how you have instructed many,
   how you have strengthened feeble hands.
⁴ Your words have supported those who stumbled;
   you have strengthened faltering knees.
⁵ But now trouble comes to you, and you are discouraged;
   it strikes you, and you are dismayed.
⁶ Should not your piety be your confidence
   and your blameless ways your hope?

Eliphaz began his long speech on a gentle note. He appeared almost to apologize for presuming to speak to Job. He reminded him of how in the past Job had been a tower of strength to others. But then Eliphaz changed the tone of his speech and unlovingly reprimanded Job for becoming discouraged and upset after disasters had struck him. He asked him, "Should not your piety be your confidence and your blameless ways your hope?"

With those words Eliphaz questioned the genuineness of Job's faith in God. As Eliphaz saw the situation, if Job truly feared and loved God and led a blameless life, instead of complaining he ought to be able to bear up under his troubles.

Suffering as a consequence of evildoing

⁷ "Consider now: Who, being innocent, has ever perished?
   Where were the upright ever destroyed?

⁸ As I have observed, those who plow evil
   and those who sow trouble reap it.
⁹ At the breath of God they are destroyed;
   at the blast of his anger they perish.
¹⁰ The lions may roar and growl,
   yet the teeth of the great lions are broken.
¹¹ The lion perishes for lack of prey,
   and the cubs of the lioness are scattered.

Here we see the theme of the speeches of all three friends: "Who, being innocent, has ever perished?" If Eliphaz were speaking of the final judgment of God, he would be right. But in referring to the course of events in this world, he is wrong. Many innocent people have perished or suffered great misfortunes. From earliest times until now, people—even God's people—have been cheated, robbed, beaten, killed, and otherwise abused by others. We all know that the good guys don't always win; too often the bad guys do. The book of Job emphatically teaches that suffering is not always a consequence of wrongdoing.

Eliphaz drew on his experience to state that people reap what they sow. Of course, that is often true, but not always. Surely it is not true in this case. Job had God's own commendation (1:8), yet God permitted him to suffer intensely.

Of that Eliphaz was not aware, and his manner of speaking shows it. To support his simplistic argument, Eliphaz resorted to the use of eloquence. He had better qualifications as a lecturer than as a friend. Taking an illustration from nature, he mentioned that even lions can meet with misfortune and die. Eliphaz used five different Hebrew words in his repeated references to the lions in verses 10 and 11. We might wonder whether he intended to refer to Job under the imagery of the lion.

41

God's greatness in contrast to his creatures

¹² "A word was secretly brought to me,
   my ears caught a whisper of it.
¹³ Amid disquieting dreams in the night,
   when deep sleep falls on men,
¹⁴ fear and trembling seized me
   and made all my bones shake.
¹⁵ A spirit glided past my face,
   and the hair on my body stood on end.
¹⁶ It stopped,
   but I could not tell what it was.
   A form stood before my eyes,
   and I heard a hushed voice:
¹⁷ 'Can a mortal be more righteous than God?
   Can a man be more pure than his Maker?
¹⁸ If God places no trust in his servants,
   if he charges his angels with error,
¹⁹ how much more those who live in houses of clay,
   whose foundations are in the dust,
   who are crushed more readily than a moth!
²⁰ Between dawn and dusk they are broken to pieces;
   unnoticed, they perish forever.
²¹ Are not the cords of their tent pulled up,
   so that they die without wisdom?'

Eliphaz's words are poetic. The passage has a mysterious and spooky quality apparently designed to catch and hold Job's attention. It's possible that Eliphaz felt he was not getting through to Job, so he used a different approach. He appealed to a direct revelation that he claimed he saw and heard one night. The message came to him in a whisper as he experienced "disquieting dreams," or visions on the order of nightmares. The language that Eliphaz uses in verses 12 to 16 sounds like a ghost story told on a dark night. While Eliphaz didn't say in so many words that the voice was God's, that implication is clear. Like certain charismatic religious leaders today, Eliphaz told Job that God directly came to him in that vision and told him something that could be helpful to Job.

The message that was supposedly communicated to Eliphaz in that direct and mysterious manner is expressed in the closing verses of this chapter. In verse 17 Eliphaz asks a double question: "Can a mortal be more righteous than God? Can a man be more pure than his Maker?" That double question obviously answers itself in one short word: No! What Eliphaz stated is unquestionably true. Job would never argue with him about that.

The question, however, was really beside the point. Eloquently but pompously, Eliphaz was talking past Job. As he sat there on his ash heap, Job didn't need to be told about the weaknesses and frailties of human beings; he realized that from his own experiences. Job also knew that even the angels, far superior to human beings, are below God in greatness, glory, and power. Moreover, he was aware of the fact that the time would come when he must die; he had even wished for that. What Job needed now was true sympathy, understanding, and comfort. He needed that badly, but so far he had received none of it from Eliphaz's speech.

Troubles that come upon evildoers

5   **"Call if you will, but who will answer you?**
        To which of the holy ones will you turn?
    ² Resentment kills a fool,
        and envy slays the simple.
    ³ I myself have seen a fool taking root,
        but suddenly his house was cursed.
    ⁴ His children are far from safety,
        crushed in court without a defender.

⁵ **The hungry consume his harvest,**
   taking it even from among thorns,
   and the thirsty pant after his wealth.
⁶ **For hardship does not spring from the soil,**
   nor does trouble sprout from the ground.
⁷ **Yet man is born to trouble**
   as surely as sparks fly upward.

Eliphaz's opening statement in this chapter was a cruel challenge to Job. He looked at Job in his misery and concluded from Job's circumstances that no one would answer Job when he called out for help and comfort. Such unsympathetic words must have cut deeply into the heart of Job.

Eliphaz again made the point that it's the evildoer who suffers in this world. He called the evildoer a "fool." That word in this passage means not merely a stupid person but one who rebels against God and therefore lacks true wisdom. While Eliphaz spoke of this "fool" anonymously, it's clear that what he said indirectly pointed to Job. He as much as suggested to Job, "If the shoe fits, wear it."

"Resentment kills a fool, and envy slays the simple." Since Eliphaz was speaking those words to Job, he must have intended them to serve as a warning. Again, he implied that Job was a foolish and simple person.

Eliphaz described the downfall of a fool (verses 3-5). His manner of speaking is pompous and judgmental. While it's true that in many cases the kinds of misfortunes mentioned in these verses have been experienced by the foolish and godless, it's not true in all instances. It was surely not true in the case of Job. By God's own estimate, Job was a blameless and upright man, and yet he suffered all kinds of calamities. Eliphaz was wrong.

In saying that the hungry and thirsty take the fool's possessions, Eliphaz made the point that the fool suffers in a material way. Again, his observation fits some cases but not all.

In verses 6 and 7, Eliphaz concluded that what the godless person suffers is a just reward of his own folly. Once again he missed the point in applying that to Job, whose misfortunes were not the result of his own folly.

The need to turn to God in repentance

> ⁸ "But if it were I, I would appeal to God;
>   I would lay my cause before him.
> ⁹ He performs wonders that cannot be fathomed,
>   miracles that cannot be counted.
> ¹⁰ He bestows rain on the earth;
>   he sends water upon the countryside.
> ¹¹ The lowly he sets on high,
>   and those who mourn are lifted to safety.
> ¹² He thwarts the plans of the crafty,
>   so that their hands achieve no success.
> ¹³ He catches the wise in their craftiness,
>   and the schemes of the wily are swept away.
> ¹⁴ Darkness comes upon them in the daytime;
>   at noon they grope as in the night.
> ¹⁵ He saves the needy from the sword in their mouth;
>   he saves them from the clutches of the powerful.
> ¹⁶ So the poor have hope,
>   and injustice shuts its mouth.

Up to this point Eliphaz's remarks had been rather depressing. He therefore tried to strike a more cheerful note. He continued his prominent references to himself, in effect telling Job, "Now if I were in your place, . . ." What Eliphaz said is indisputably true. Of course Job ought to appeal to God and lay his cause before him. We are left with the feeling that Eliphaz was coldly mouthing pious platitudes without any appreciation or feeling for Job's condition. He was also guilty of oversimplifying and of assuming that what he had said applied to Job. Throughout all of his speeches and those of his friends, one important thing was lacking, and that was love—love for their suffering friend.

Eliphaz praised the greatness of God in greater detail than he had previously done. This section is similar to a number of passages that we will later read in this book (especially chapters 28, 36, 37, and 38). Verses 11 and 12 express thoughts that are almost identical to those found in the prayer of Hannah (1 Samuel 2:8) and the Magnificat of Mary (Luke 2:51,52).

The happiness and prosperity of one who turns to God

¹⁷ "Blessed is the man whom God corrects;
    so do not despise the discipline of the Almighty.
¹⁸ For he wounds, but he also binds up;
    he injures, but his hands also heal.
¹⁹ From six calamities he will rescue you;
    in seven no harm will befall you.
²⁰ In famine he will ransom you from death,
    and in battle from the stroke of the sword.
²¹ You will be protected from the lash of the tongue,
    and need not fear when destruction comes.
²² You will laugh at destruction and famine,
    and need not fear the beasts of the earth.
²³ For you will have a covenant with the stones of the field,
    and the wild animals will be at peace with you.
²⁴ You will know that your tent is secure;
    you will take stock of your property and find
        nothing missing.
²⁵ You will know that your children will be many,
    and your descendants like the grass of the earth.
²⁶ You will come to the grave in full vigor,
    like sheaves gathered in season.
²⁷ "We have examined this, and it is true.
    So hear it and apply it to yourself."

Here is the most beautiful passage in all the speeches of Job's three friends. The opening reminds us of Psalm 1:1 and the Beatitudes of Jesus (Matthew 5:3-11). The word "blessed" can also be translated as "happy." It describes someone whose heart is right with God, who to the best of his ability conducts his life in conformity with God's will, and who lives at peace with God and men. Here Eliphaz correctly stated that a man whom God corrects is truly "blessed," or "happy." Eliphaz was also right when he said, "He wounds, but he also binds up; he injures, but his hands also heal." God's drastic surgery is for the sufferer's highest good, and the heavenly hand that uses the knife also tenderly binds up the wound.

In spite of his pious words, Eliphaz really did not believe that God intended Job's suffering to be a discipline to strengthen his faith. As we will see, he clung to the mistaken notion that Job was suffering as a consequence of some special sins. Eliphaz failed to distinguish between God's punishment of the ungodly and his wholesome chastisement of the godly.

In vivid, concrete language Eliphaz continued his misguided attempt to set Job straight. He used a common literary device employed by ancient writers in that part of the world. It is called *ascending numeration,* where a number that would be complete by itself is increased by one. It is used several times in the Old Testament. Three is raised to four in Proverbs 30:15,18 and Amos 1:3,6,9,11,13. There are other similar examples. In this passage six is raised to seven: "From six calamities he will rescue you; in seven no harm will befall you" (verse 19). It has the effect of further emphasizing what the speaker is saying.

Eliphaz assured Job that all would be well if he would only turn to God and commit his cause to him. God would keep him from calamities, famine, slander, and destruction. He wouldn't need to fear the beasts of the earth. In ancient times wild beasts were very prevalent in that part of the world. Most of them were neither domesticated nor kept in zoos. Roaming around in the open areas, they struck fear into the hearts of people. Eliphaz assured Job that with God's blessing and protection, he need not fear those beasts. Even the stones of the field, which generally are a hindrance to those who till the soil, would cause no problem to Job if he would bow to the will of God.

Getting even closer to Job's present affliction, Eliphaz bluntly assured him that if he would be right with God, his property would be left intact. To add insult to injury, Eliphaz mentioned that Job's children would be many, his descendants numerous, and Job himself would die hale and hearty at a ripe old age. The expression "in full vigor" suggests both maturity and health. One who reaches old age in a state of good health has special reason to thank God.

Try to put yourself in Job's place as he sat on his heap of ashes and heard these words of Eliphaz. Eliphaz spoke of a man who was "blessed," or "happy," and described someone whose situation was the very opposite of Job's. For Job there seemed to be no healing or relief from his excruciating physical pain and mental anguish. He had lost his property. To hear the words of verse 24 ("you will take stock of your property and find nothing missing") was of no comfort whatever to Job after his great loss. But much worse, he had lost his ten children whom he loved very dearly. The words of verse 25 ("you will know that your children will be many") must have torn him apart inside.

On top of all that, Eliphaz told his wretched friend that a good man would live out his life and go to his grave in full vigor at a ripe old age. Is there any possible way Job could identify with such a person? Wouldn't he rather have to conclude that his friend was judging him to be the very opposite, an ungodly man? In later speeches Job's friends would more directly accuse him of being such a person. In fact, in the closing statement in this speech, Eliphaz suggested that very thing when he told Job, "We have examined this, and it is true. So hear it and apply it to yourself." With friends like Eliphaz, who needs enemies?

Job's reply to Eliphaz

Job complains that God has severely afflicted him

6 Then Job replied:

> ² "If only my anguish could be weighed
>   and all my misery be placed on the scales!
> ³ It would surely outweigh the sand of the seas—
>   no wonder my words have been impetuous.
> ⁴ The arrows of the Almighty are in me,
>   my spirit drinks in their poison;
>   God's terrors are marshaled against me.

The words of Eliphaz had stung Job. Instead of giving him comfort, they had only added to his suffering. He used two illustrations to describe his deep affliction.

Ancient scales had two trays balanced from a center pole. Resorting to exaggeration, Job said that if his sufferings were placed on one tray and all the sand of the sea on the other, his sufferings would outweigh them.

In his second illustration Job referred to warfare in which the combatants would shoot poisoned arrows. In his deep affliction Job felt that God had used him as a target for shooting his poisoned arrows, which caused his sickness and pain. He further described God as his enemy who attacked him as a general would marshal his army against a city to capture it.

By his own admission (verse 3), Job's words were impetuous. But although we can't condone Job's strong language in accusing God, we must try to understand that the afflictions which God had permitted Satan to bring upon Job were extremely severe.

> ⁵ **Does a wild donkey bray when it has grass,**
> **or an ox bellow when it has fodder?**
> ⁶ **Is tasteless food eaten without salt,**
> **or is there flavor in the white of an egg?**
> ⁷ **I refuse to touch it;**
> **such food makes me ill.**

Eliphaz had used many striking illustrations to make his point (4:8-11; 5:3-5). Now Job uses two illustrations to show that he had good reasons to complain. Donkeys and oxen need food to be content and survive. If they are hungry, they let their owners know by complaining. Similarly, Job wouldn't complain unless he actually was suffering. He craved understanding and sympathy from his friends but received none; instead, he heard words of scolding. The words of Eliphaz only added to Job's misery.

The reference to "tasteless food" and "the white of an egg," though very striking and concrete, is somewhat difficult. It could refer to his intense sufferings, as do the words in verse 5. It appears more likely to carry the thought further and refer to the words of Eliphaz that made Job react negatively and only added to his suffering. The following verse supports that interpretation: Eliphaz's words were repulsive to Job.

> ⁸ **"Oh, that I might have my request,**
> **that God would grant what I hope for,**
> ⁹ **that God would be willing to crush me,**
> **to let loose his hand and cut me off!**

¹⁰ **Then I would still have this consolation—**
   my joy in unrelenting pain—
   that I had not denied the words of the Holy One.

Harking back to the thoughts he expressed in his opening speech (chapter 3), Job wished he would die. His language is very strong: "that God would be willing to crush me, to let loose his hand and cut me off!" The words "cut me off" mean to cut the thread so a fabric can be removed from the loom; that expression is used to depict death (Job 27:8; Isaiah 38:12). Job wished he could die rather than live. Not only would he then be freed from his many miseries; he would also have the satisfaction that God had heard his prayer for release. Although Job complained to God, he did not deny him or curse him. "The fact that he had not denied the Lord was Job's confidence in the midst of all distress and misery, even if the pain it caused him should be practically unbearable" (P. E. Kretzmann, *Popular Commentary,* Old Testament, Volume 2, page 9).

¹¹ **"What strength do I have, that I should still hope?**
    What prospects, that I should be patient?
¹² **Do I have the strength of stone?**
    Is my flesh bronze?
¹³ **Do I have any power to help myself,**
    now that success has been driven from me?

Job raised five questions, to each of which the answer is decidedly no. He felt his strength had been sapped, and his patience was rapidly running out. He was, after all, made of flesh and bones, not stone or bronze. In his wretched condition, he felt helpless. He no longer had the resources that had enabled him to gain success as a wealthy, respected, and influential man in the community.

Job wishes that his friends would show him sympathy

¹⁴ "A despairing man should have the devotion of his friends,
   even though he forsakes the fear of the Almighty.
¹⁵ But my brothers are as undependable as
         intermittent streams,
   as the streams that overflow
¹⁶ when darkened by thawing ice
   and swollen with melting snow,
¹⁷ but that cease to flow in the dry season,
   and in the heat vanish from their channels.
¹⁸ Caravans turn aside from their routes;
   they go up into the wasteland and perish.
¹⁹ The caravans of Tema look for water,
   the traveling merchants of Sheba look in hope.
²⁰ They are distressed, because they had been confident;
   they arrive there, only to be disappointed.
²¹ Now you too have proved to be of no help;
   you see something dreadful and are afraid.
²² Have I ever said, 'Give something on my behalf,
   pay a ransom for me from your wealth,
²³ deliver me from the hand of the enemy,
   ransom me from the clutches of the ruthless'?

In considerable detail Job pleaded for understanding and sympathy. Loyalty to a friend should be deep and true in spite of what that person might say and do. The words "even though he forsakes the fear of the Almighty" do not imply that Job himself had done so. In fact, even throughout his trials Job feared God. But Job did express his conviction that a troubled person had a right to expect his friends to be loyal and sympathetic.

On the other hand, Job found them to be fair-weather friends. He called them "undependable," literally "treacherous." When he needed them most, they didn't come through. In an extended passage, he compared them to streams that at times overflow and at other times dry up. Job knew what he was talking about, for in that part of the world a sudden rain can fill a dry gulch with rushing waters that will later disappear when the hot sun comes out.

Job further described the fickleness of his friends under the picture of weary desert travelers looking in vain for water for themselves and their animals. Similarly, Job's friends had stood by him in good times, but now when he needed them they gave him no comfort. Rather, the very sight of Job struck fear into their hearts (verse 21). Those words are Job's interpretation of their actions when they first saw him (2:12,13).

Job had not been unreasonable in what he had expected of his three friends. He had asked for no money (verse 22) nor had he requested them to help him out of his trouble (verse 23). Was it too much to expect them to provide a sympathetic listening and offer words of comfort now when he was suffering such great affliction?

> ²⁴ "Teach me, and I will be quiet;
> show me where I have been wrong.
> ²⁵ How painful are honest words!
> But what do your arguments prove?
> ²⁶ Do you mean to correct what I say,
> and treat the words of a despairing man as wind?
> ²⁷ You would even cast lots for the fatherless
> and barter away your friend.
> ²⁸ "But now be so kind as to look at me.
> Would I lie to your face?
> ²⁹ Relent, do not be unjust;
> reconsider, for my integrity is at stake.
> ³⁰ Is there any wickedness on my lips?
> Can my mouth not discern malice?

Job's words show that he was open to his friends' opinions and wanted to discuss his problem with them. He begged them to show him where he was wrong. The first half of verse 25 has been translated various ways. The NIV takes it as an exclamation: "How painful are honest words!" The Hebrew word translated as "painful" also implies frank, honest, straightforward talk. But to be of help to the suffering Job, such talk must result from an understanding of Job's situation, which the friends sorely lacked. Therefore Job added, "But what do your arguments prove?"

By his speech Eliphaz showed that he didn't understand Job's situation. He had ignored what Job said and treated his words as "wind." Irked by Eliphaz's indifference to his suffering, Job overreacted, in turn accusing Eliphaz and his friends of being people who would heartlessly take advantage of defenseless orphans or treat their own friends treacherously.

But again Job pleaded with his friends. Would he act or speak dishonestly? Didn't they know him to be an upright man whose integrity was unquestionable? He asked them to relent, to turn away from unjustly accusing him. Even though his physical appearance might repel them—as he sat in the ashes, disfigured and covered with sores—he insisted he was not guilty of speaking wickedness. He could still distinguish right from wrong.

Job feels that his life on earth is miserable

7 "Does not man have hard service on earth?
   Are not his days like those of a hired man?
   ² Like a slave longing for the evening shadows,
     or a hired man waiting eagerly for his wages,
   ³ so I have been allotted months of futility,
     and nights of misery have been assigned to me.

⁴ **When I lie down I think, 'How long before I get up?'**
The night drags on, and I toss till dawn.
⁵ **My body is clothed with worms and scabs,**
my skin is broken and festering.

Job continued his speech by describing man's life on earth as "hard service." The Hebrew word occurs frequently in the Old Testament. The picture is that of service in the army. In ancient times men were recruited and forced to serve in battle. Therefore, in some passages the word means "army." In a broader sense the word can indicate "warfare" or "enforced service," under which the worker has very little freedom. The same word occurs in Isaiah 40:2, where in the familiar King James Version it is translated "cry unto her, that her warfare is accomplished." The NIV translates that passage "proclaim to her that her hard service has been completed." In the passage before us, that is the meaning of the word.

Job also compares his life to that of a hired man. A hired man worked for another. He had to do his bidding, and had no investment or equity of his own. He was only paid wages. He hoped to receive his wages at the end of a work day, but sometimes he was disappointed.

But worse yet, a slave didn't even earn wages. He was the property of his master and was completely bound to his master's will. Since the slave received no wages, all he had to look forward to after a hard day's work was rest under the shade of a tree or in a shelter.

Job viewed his present life as a prolonged period of misery. He suffered during the day, and at night he found no relief. Only someone who has experienced constant pain and discomfort can possibly relate to Job's statements in verses 4 and 5. Even so, it is questionable whether any other human being except our Savior has suffered more severely than Job.

Verse 5 gives additional information about the nature of Job's physical affliction. "This vivid description gives some insight into the multiple physical complications of Job's illness: fever, sleeplessness, delirium, skin ulcers, and running sores infested with worms" (John E. Hartley, *The Book of Job,* page 145).

> ⁶ "My days are swifter than a weaver's shuttle,
>   and they come to an end without hope.
> ⁷ Remember, O God, that my life is but a breath;
>   my eyes will never see happiness again.
> ⁸ The eye that now sees me will see me no longer;
>   you will look for me, but I will be no more.
> ⁹ As a cloud vanishes and is gone,
>   so he who goes down to the grave does not return.
> ¹⁰ He will never come to his house again;
>   his place will know him no more.

In speaking these words, Job gave expression to the shortness of human life. Compared to eternity, even the longest life is very short. At this time Job was expecting death to arrive soon; indeed, he was wishing it would. He compared his life to a weaver's shuttle. As the web of the weaver's loom would be cut off, so also would Job's life. While he clung to the slender thread of life as his hope, he was convinced that it would soon be cut off. Little did he know that God would grant him an additional 140 years after his restoration (42:16).

In his anxiety Job turned to address God directly (verse 7). He looked for compassion but feared that he would never again be happy. In his pessimistic frame of mind, Job felt he wouldn't see God anymore and that God wouldn't see him. In saying those words Job was in grave danger of falling away from God. His great suffering drove him to say things he would never have said under other circumstances. He viewed his coming death as a sudden event that would snatch him away.

Job's statement in verse 9, "so he who goes down to the grave does not return" (literally, "come up"), is not a denial of Job's belief in the afterlife. Although Job did not have the benefit of the entire Old Testament or of the New Testament, he did express faith in the afterlife, as we will see from later passages, particularly 19:23-27. In this verse, however, he describes death as it appears from the physical viewpoint: people do not return from the grave to this life on earth. They do not come back to their homes and conduct their life as they did before they died.

Job wishes that God would let him alone

¹¹ "Therefore I will not keep silent;
   I will speak out in the anguish of my spirit,
   I will complain in the bitterness of my soul.
¹² Am I the sea, or the monster of the deep,
   that you put me under guard?
¹³ When I think my bed will comfort me
   and my couch will ease my complaint,
¹⁴ even then you frighten me with dreams
   and terrify me with visions,
¹⁵ so that I prefer strangling and death,
   rather than this body of mine.
¹⁶ I despise my life; I would not live forever.
   Let me alone; my days have no meaning.

In the opening verse of this section, Job emphatically stated that he would express himself about his condition. The grammar of the Hebrew makes that clear. The pronoun "I" stands in an emphatic position, and the forms of the three verbs express his strong determination to make his feelings known.

Previously, Job had asked, "Do I have the strength of stone? Is my flesh bronze?" (6:12) Obviously, no. Now he asked, "Am I the sea, or the monster of the deep, that you put me under guard?" Again, no. In his terrible affliction, Job felt that God was constantly watching him as one would watch a dangerous animal.

But even during the night, when he might expect to get relief from his torturous experiences, Job felt that God was scaring him with dreams and visions. Life was such torture that he wished God would strangle him. Again, like Elijah and Jonah, he said he would rather die than live.

In speaking those words, Job was not asking God to abandon him but to stop afflicting him so severely or else to let him die in peace.

In spite of his strong feelings and sharp words, Job still retained his faith in God even though severely tested.

His words "I would not live forever" are the basis of a hymn written by William A. Muhlenberg. Those words have given comfort to many Christians at the time of death—their own impending death or that of loved ones. As you read it, note how the author applies Job's words to a Christian's life and death.

> I would not live alway; I ask not to stay
> Where storm after storm rises dark o'er the way.
> The few lurid mornings that dawn on us here
> Suffice for life's woes, are enough for its cheer.
>
> I would not live alway; thus fettered by sin,
> Temptation without and corruption within;
> E'en rapture of pardon is mingled with fears,
> The cup of thanksgiving with penitent tears.
>
> I would not live alway; no, welcome the tomb;
> Since Jesus hath lain there, I dread not its gloom.

There sweet be my rest till He bids me arise
To hail Him in triumph descending the skies.
(*The Lutheran Hymnal* [TLH] 588:1-3)

[17] "What is man that you make so much of him,
  that you give him so much attention,
[18] that you examine him every morning
  and test him every moment?
[19] Will you never look away from me,
  or let me alone even for an instant?
[20] If I have sinned, what have I done to you,
  O watcher of men?
 Why have you made me your target?
 Have I become a burden to you?
[21] Why do you not pardon my offenses
  and forgive my sins?
 For I will soon lie down in the dust;
  you will search for me, but I will be no more."

Job's words remind us of Psalm 8:4: "What is man that you are mindful of him, the son of man that you care for him?" Those words, however, though penned by David, really refer to Jesus Christ according to his human nature, as we learn from Hebrews 2:6-9, where the sacred writer directly applies them to our Savior.

Job wondered why the great and majestic God should single him out and pick on him. He continued his complaint against God. As in a previous verse, he wished that God would let him alone (7:16).

He protested, "If I have sinned, what have I done to you, O watcher of men?" Job didn't deny that he had sinned. He was well aware of the fact that he was a sinner like all other people. Yet throughout his speeches, he denied that his sins were of such a nature and magnitude that he deserved to suffer so much more than others. Also, he still maintained his faith in God. But his words imply that if he did sin (and he doesn't deny it), what great harm would that do to the majestic God? We can't defend these words of Job, but if we put ourselves in his place, we can understand them.

Job addressed God as "watcher of men." While that sounds disrespectful, we must keep in mind that he was a desperate man who not only suffered intensely but was earnestly trying to find the reason for his suffering. He also referred to himself as a "target" at which God would shoot. Earlier he had used similar language: "The arrows of the Almighty are in me, my spirit drinks their poison" (6:4). In addition, he referred to himself as a "burden" to God. Ironically, he who felt himself carrying a great burden now spoke of himself as God's burden.

Job closed his speech by asking why God does not pardon his offenses and forgive his sins. Some scholars have understood those words in a sarcastic and even blasphemous sense. It seems better to give Job the benefit of the doubt and interpret them in a sincere sense. Job wished for forgiveness from God. Although he was searching for the cause of his great suffering, as a child of God he didn't deny he had sins. His act of offering daily sacrifices for his children (1:5), as previously mentioned, was evidence of that.

Bildad's first speech

God punishes those who do evil

In chapters 4 and 5 Eliphaz had spoken. He liked to reminisce and appeal to his personal experiences. He also spoke of direct revelations that he had received at night. Eliphaz had some of the characteristics of a charismatic.

Bildad, the speaker in this chapter, was different. He kept his own experiences in the background and spoke in a more dogmatic manner. He was a traditionalist who preferred to appeal to the teachings of the fathers. He closely followed what they said and rigidly applied those teachings to Job's situation.

8 **Then Bildad the Shuhite replied:**
> [2] **"How long will you say such things?**
> **Your words are a blustering wind.**
> [3] **Does God pervert justice?**
> **Does the Almighty pervert what is right?**
> [4] **When your children sinned against him,**
> **he gave them over to the penalty of their sin.**

Bildad's words are blunt and unkind. He impatiently scolded Job for talking as he did. He had no sympathy for the poor sufferer. By his opening question, Bildad implied that Job had talked too long and sarcastically called Job's words "a blustering wind." In today's language he called Job a windbag.

He asked a double question: "Does God pervert justice? Does the Almighty pervert what is right?" To accuse God of doing so would surely be blasphemous. Even in his most outspoken moments, Job had not accused God of perverting justice. Yet Bildad's question at least indirectly accused him of that.

To make matters worse, Bildad unlovingly accused Job's children of sinning against God to such an extent that he had punished them with a terrible death. In bringing up that subject, Bildad was extremely cruel. Of all Job's misfortunes, none hurt him more than the sudden death of his ten children. Job had been so deeply concerned about their attitude toward God that when they had their celebrations, he offered sacrifices to God for them (1:5). And now Bildad not only reminded him of their death but even implied that their sinful conduct had led to their deaths! Rigidly, Bildad held to his preconceived belief that misfortune falls exclusively on the wicked.

> ⁵ But if you will look to God
>   and plead with the Almighty,
> ⁶ if you are pure and upright,
>   even now he will rouse himself on your behalf
>   and restore you to your rightful place.
> ⁷ Your beginnings will seem humble,
>   so prosperous will your future be.

In a self-righteous manner, Bildad lectured Job. As though Job had not already turned to God in his desperate condition, Bildad urged him to "look to God." That expression can be more literally translated as "go early to God" or "hurry to God," in other words, "don't waste any time." In itself, what Bildad said is true and sound advice, but the context reveals a self-righteous attitude on his part.

Bildad pompously talked to Job, whom God had highly commended, as if Job were a bad person who needed to straighten out his life. Implying that Job was suffering so much because he had sinned greatly, Bildad urged him to become "pure and upright." He even promised that God would make him more prosperous than he had been before. In fact, his earlier prosperity would seem slight compared to what God would give him.

It is true that God did eventually bless Job with more than he formerly had (42:12). Unknowingly, Bildad predicted that. But he was wrong in claiming that Job's affliction was the result of a special sin. He couldn't see that a godly man might suffer severe afflictions as a test of faith. God himself had stated that in his conversation with Satan, and Elihu would later point it out in one of his speeches (33:19-22).

8 "Ask the former generations
   and find out what their fathers learned,
9 for we were born only yesterday and know nothing,
   and our days on earth are but a shadow.
10 Will they not instruct you and tell you?
   Will they not bring forth words from their understanding?

Bildad had a high regard for the teachings of men who lived before him. His words imply that men of the earlier generations lived longer, for he said, "we were born only yesterday." Those words also suggest that Job and his friends must have lived during the time of the patriarchs. Although their life spans were rather long (Abraham, 175 years; Isaac, 180 years), they were shorter than men of earlier generations. In fact, Noah's son Shem lived 600 years (Genesis 11:10,11). Bildad the traditionalist held the good old days in high regard and considered the venerable fathers far superior to the thinkers of his day. He urged Job to give heed to what they had to teach him—through Bildad himself, of course.

11 Can papyrus grow tall where there is no marsh?
   Can reeds thrive without water?
12 While still growing and uncut,
   they wither more quickly than grass.
13 Such is the destiny of all who forget God;
   so perishes the hope of the godless.
14 What he trusts in is fragile;
   what he relies on is a spider's web.
15 He leans on his web, but it gives way;
   he clings to it, but it does not hold.
16 He is like a well-watered plant in the sunshine,
   spreading its shoots over the garden;
17 it entwines its roots around a pile of rocks
   and looks for a place among the stones.

 ¹⁸ **But when it is torn from its spot,**
    that place disowns it and says, 'I never saw you.'
 ¹⁹ **Surely its life withers away,**
    and from the soil other plants grow.

Bildad insisted that the godless meet misfortune during this life. To make his point, he drew several illustrations from nature. First, he mentioned two plants that abounded in Egypt. No doubt both Bildad and Job were familiar with them. The papyrus plant needs a marsh if it is to grow; reeds need water. Left to themselves, those plants would not survive long; they need moisture. Bildad made the application to the godless, again indirectly including Job among them.

His next illustration is a spider web. Speaking of the ungodly, Bildad said, "What he trusts in is fragile." The Hebrew word translated as "fragile" suggests a thread in a spider web. A delicate spider web can easily be brushed away. According to Bildad, the hope of the godless is just as delicate.

Bildad also compared the wicked man to a plant. There are a number of difficulties in verses 16 to 19, with various translations and interpretations. Some scholars interpret the words to refer to a godly person who prospers during his lifetime. The psalmist gives a similar description of a godly man: "He is like a tree planted by streams of water, which yields its fruit in season and whose leaf does not wither. Whatever he does prospers" (Psalm 1:3). Others refer the words to an ungodly person who for a while flourishes but later comes to a bad end. In this passage the latter interpretation is preferable. Verses 18 and 19 support the view that these verses describe the ungodly rather than the godly. The footnote to verse 19 in the NIV is preferable, and gives a more literal translation: "Surely all the joy it has is that from the soil other plants grow." Such joy is short-lived and has a disastrous end.

Bildad's chief message in his first discourse is clear: the wicked will come to a miserable end. We could agree with him if we considered their fate in the next world. The Bible is abundantly clear in stating that the unbelievers will spend eternity in hell. But Bildad's mistake was in stating that they come to an unfortunate end even in this life. Often that is not true. Many godless people achieve great material success in this life and are also honored at their death.

In a later speech we will see that Job strongly disagreed with Bildad's viewpoint. There are many instances in which the opposite is true: the godly sometimes suffer at the hands of the ungodly (24:1-17). God's children may suffer many hardships in this life, but for believers such suffering is not punishment but loving chastisement.

God blesses those who do good

> ²⁰ "Surely God does not reject a blameless man
>   or strengthen the hands of evildoers.
> ²¹ He will yet fill your mouth with laughter
>   and your lips with shouts of joy.
> ²² Your enemies will be clothed in shame,
>   and the tents of the wicked will be no more."

At some length Bildad had spoken of the misfortunes that would overtake the wicked. He apparently felt he needed to emphasize that to Job. Now more briefly he describes the happiness and prosperity of the godly.

Bildad paints an unrealistic picture of the life of God-fearing people. We might wish they would experience much happiness and success in this life, but in many cases they do not. The Bible warns us that "we must go through many hardships to enter the kingdom of God" (Acts 14:22). It also describes the saints in heaven as such: "These are they who have come out of the great tribulation" (Revelation 7:14). Our Savior has not promised us an easy, carefree life as Christians. Rather, he has told us to be ready to take up our cross and follow him (Matthew 10:38; 16:24).

Many preachers today, including some famous tele-vangelists, preach a "prosperity theology." They make attractive promises to the effect that if you give yourself over to Jesus, all your problems will be solved. Further, if you contribute generously to their television ministry, God will richly bless you. When things don't turn out that way, some will be turned off to religion. Such prosperity theology, with its misleading promises, is no true religion at all, but a caricature.

Job's reply to Bildad

Mortal man is no match for almighty God

9 Then Job replied:
    ² "Indeed, I know that this is true.
        But how can a mortal be righteous before God?
    ³ Though one wished to dispute with him,
        he could not answer him one time out of a thousand.
    ⁴ His wisdom is profound, his power is vast.
        Who has resisted him and come out unscathed?

Job began his reply to Bildad's speech by granting that God is righteous. He does not pervert justice. At this time, however, Job's deep concern was, "How can a mortal be righteous before God?" Job had lost most of his property and all of his children and was suffering such intense pain that he was almost beside himself. His big question was, Why? What had he done to deserve this? Could he possibly have been guilty of such especially great sins as his friends had implied? He was, of course, unaware of the wager that Satan had earlier made with God: that if God would let Satan severely afflict him, Job would curse God (1:11; 2:5).

Job wished he had the opportunity to meet God and discuss his problem with God. In these verses he uses courtroom language. He wanted to present his case before God and plead innocent of whatever charges God held against him.

Job realized that he stood no chance of succeeding in a contest with God. "He could not answer him one time out of a thousand." Later, when God confronted Job, he challenged Job to answer him (38:3; 40:2,7) and Job humbly admitted defeat (40:4,5). Even now Job realized that God is incomparably superior to any human being in wisdom and power. He declared, "His wisdom is profound, his power is vast."

God is so wise and powerful that no one can stand up to him. In the next verses, Job gave many examples of this.

> ⁵ He moves mountains without their knowing it
>   and overturns them in his anger.
> ⁶ He shakes the earth from its place
>   and makes its pillars tremble.
> ⁷ He speaks to the sun and it does not shine;
>   he seals off the light of the stars.
> ⁸ He alone stretches out the heavens
>   and treads on the waves of the sea.
> ⁹ He is the Maker of the Bear and Orion,
>   the Pleiades and the constellations of the south.
> ¹⁰ He performs wonders that cannot be fathomed,
>   miracles that cannot be counted.
> ¹¹ When he passes me, I cannot see him;
>   when he goes by, I cannot perceive him.
> ¹² If he snatches away, who can stop him?
>   Who can say to him, 'What are you doing?'

> ¹³ **God does not restrain his anger;**
> **even the cohorts of Rahab cowered at his feet.**

These words remind us of many poetic passages of the Old Testament, including Psalms 46, 104, and 147 and Isaiah 40:12-31. In these verses Job pictures God's greatness in the universe he created.

God created the mountains. He can also cause great upheavals in them. If he so desires, he can even move them. He asserts his power through such devastating forces in nature as volcanoes, earthquakes, tornadoes, and hurricanes. In some cases such calamities have made permanent changes in the landscape, as when he rained fire from heaven and destroyed Sodom and Gomorrah.

It was God, and not the blind forces of evolution, who created this marvelous universe, which is so vast that even to think about it staggers our imagination. In comparison to some distant stars, the sun is very small, and the earth is but a speck. Yet God placed such great importance on this earth that he chose it for the abode of his highest visible creatures, human beings. It was also on this earth that Jesus lived, suffered, and died for our salvation.

Job stated that God has the power to control the sun and the stars. He has so ordered it that the sun shines during the daytime and the stars appear at night. As we know from experience, God can also cover the sun and the stars with clouds so they are not seen. But God has it in his power to do even more: he could prevent the sun from rising and shining, and he could remove the stars from the sky. He who created this vast universe also has the power to destroy it. The Bible tells us he will do so on judgment day (2 Peter 3:7,10).

Job mentioned four constellations (verse 9), three of which God himself later mentions (38:31-33). The first is called the

Bear. It is also called Arcturus and is generally identified with the Big Dipper, a group of seven stars located in the northern sky that point to the North Star.

The second group is called Orion, a constellation named for a hunter in Greek mythology. It is one of the brightest constellations in the southern sky.

The Pleiades consist of seven large stars named for the seven daughters of Atlas, a figure in Greek mythology who supposedly held the heavens upon his shoulders.

It is difficult to identify the "constellations of the south" precisely. Since the word translated as "constellations" literally means "chambers," some scholars think they were endless spaces in the south where stars could not be seen. Since they are listed with the other three terms, it's more likely that they refer to constellations in the southern sky.

We present-day people are often inclined to underestimate the knowledge of astronomy that people of ancient times possessed. We need to be reminded that those people were well versed in the science. Job reveals that in this speech. Unfortunately, many in ancient times also pursued the false science of astrology, a practice the Bible condemns (Isaiah 47:12-14).

It is very probable that at night Job would gaze into the heavens with wonderment as he examined the stars in those times before smog and other pollution obscured them. He confessed that God's wonders were so great that he couldn't comprehend them.

God has revealed himself in nature, but he himself is invisible. Job would like to see him and meet with him, but Job was at a loss to find him.

In the closing verse of this section, Job again referred to God's great power. He also spoke of God's anger. God's anger is not sinful. It is an expression of his holiness as well as his power. In verse 13 we find the expression "the cohorts of

Rahab." Here "Rahab" refers to enemies of God and the forces of evil, as also in Psalm 89:10. In some passages (Psalm 87:4; Isaiah 30:7) it is applied to Egypt, an enemy of God's people. The word "Rahab" in these passages must not be confused with the name of the prostitute mentioned in Joshua chapter 2. While in English the spelling of the two words is identical, they are two different words in Hebrew.

Job feels helpless in facing God

¹⁴ "How then can I dispute with him?
How can I find words to argue with him?
¹⁵ Though I were innocent, I could not answer him;
I could only plead with my Judge for mercy.
¹⁶ Even if I summoned him and he responded,
I do not believe he would give me a hearing.
¹⁷ He would crush me with a storm
and multiply my wounds for no reason.
¹⁸ He would not let me regain my breath
but would overwhelm me with misery.
¹⁹ If it is a matter of strength, he is mighty!
And if it is a matter of justice, who will summon him?
²⁰ Even if I were innocent, my mouth would condemn me;
if I were blameless, it would pronounce me guilty.
²¹ "Although I am blameless,
I have no concern for myself;
I despise my own life.
²² It is all the same; that is why I say,
'He destroys both the blameless and the wicked.'
²³ When a scourge brings sudden death,
he mocks the despair of the innocent.
²⁴ When a land falls into the hands of the wicked,
he blindfolds its judges.
If it is not he, then who is it?

Job essentially repeats what he had said in verse 3 of this chapter. He continued by admitting that he could only plead for mercy. He realized that he couldn't stand on a one-to-one basis with God. Similarly, David later confessed, "Do not bring your servant into judgment, for no one living is righteous before you" (Psalm 143:2). No one can on his own merits stand before God. That must be the confession of every human being.

Job was in such awe of God that he even feared that God wouldn't give him a hearing. He dreaded God's holiness and almighty power. He even felt that God was taking delight in making him suffer and in multiplying his wounds for no reason. He accused God of acting arbitrarily, for he didn't see why he should suffer so much. This was a severe test of Job's faith in God. He was tempted to think that God was not being just and fair in dealing with him. He also felt incapable of defending himself. In fact, he admitted that his words, though spoken sincerely, would condemn him.

In his suffering, Job defended his uprightness but was almost at the point of despair. Since he, a righteous man, was suffering so much, he even concluded that God destroyed the blameless and the wicked without discrimination (verse 22). Those words are a response to Bildad's smug statement that God would never let harm come to the upright (8:20).

As Job was suffering from the ravages of his disease and from the unsympathetic words of his friends, he fell into the sin of accusing God of treating him unfairly. Earlier he had admitted that God is just (9:3). We can't defend Job's words in verse 24: "When a land falls into the hands of the wicked, he blindfolds its judges. If it is not he, then who is it?"

On the other hand, we must keep in mind that during his affliction Job blurted out words that he would not have spoken under normal circumstances. "Let us not blame Job for his impatience and irreverent language, until we have carefully examined our own hearts in the times of trial like those which he endured. Let us not infer that he was worse than other men, until we are placed in similar circumstances, and are able to manifest better feelings than he did (*Barnes' Notes, Job,* Volume 1, pages 225,226).

> ²⁵ **"My days are swifter than a runner;**
>   **they fly away without a glimpse of joy.**
> ²⁶ **They skim past like boats of papyrus,**
>   **like eagles swooping down on their prey.**
> ²⁷ **If I say, 'I will forget my complaint,**
>   **I will change my expression, and smile,'**
> ²⁸ **I still dread all my sufferings,**
>   **for I know you will not hold me innocent.**
> ²⁹ **Since I am already found guilty,**
>   **why should I struggle in vain?**
> ³⁰ **Even if I washed myself with soap**
>   **and my hands with washing soda,**
> ³¹ **you would plunge me into a slime pit**
>   **so that even my clothes would detest me.**

Again Job referred to the swiftness and shortness of life. In his earlier response to Eliphaz, he had compared the passing of his days to a weaver's shuttle (7:6). Now he compared them to a runner delivering important messages, papyrus boats skimming the waters of the Nile, and eagles swooping down to kill their prey. His words may appear to contradict what he had said when he complained that the hours were dragging on while he was suffering pain day and night (7:2-4). Yet both were true in his case. As slowly as time seemed to pass, Job still felt his life was coming to an end with no prospect of relief. He wasn't able to put on an act and smile as if he had no troubles. His misery was too real for that.

Job felt that God was holding him guilty for some unknown wrong. He graphically described his plight when he said, "Even if I washed myself with soap [or 'snow,' according to the footnote in the NIV], and my hands with washing soda, you would plunge me into a slime pit." No matter how carefully he would wash himself to declare his innocence, he feared that God could still declare him guilty. His words remind us of Pontius Pilate's act of washing his hands (Matthew 27:24). In doing so, Pilate attempted to show he was free from any responsibility for the death of Jesus.

Job wishes for a mediator

³² "He is not a man like me that I might answer him,
     that we might confront each other in court.
³³ If only there were someone to arbitrate between us,
     to lay his hand upon us both,
³⁴ someone to remove God's rod from me,
     so that his terror would frighten me no more.
³⁵ Then I would speak up without fear of him,
     but as it now stands with me, I cannot.

Earlier in this chapter Job had pictured his dispute with God as a courtroom trial. While he hoped for the opportunity for a dialogue with God, he also dreaded it, knowing he would be outmatched (9:3). Now he returned to that theme, but he realized that God is not a man, and so Job could not confront him in court.

Then the thought came to him: "If only there were someone to arbitrate between us." He wished for someone who could take a neutral, impartial position, such as an umpire or a referee in an athletic contest. Such a person might resolve the issue that separated Job and God. Job desperately wanted someone to lay his hand upon both of them. Further, he hoped that such a person could remove God's rod from him and thus reconcile them. Then Job would no longer fear to stand before God.

What comes to mind when you read this? Doesn't this passage point ahead to someone who in the future would do that very thing for Job as well as all human beings? Job had learned about the true God and the true religion. He must also have learned that God would in due time send his Son to be the Savior of this world. The very first book of the Bible tells of the Seed of the woman who would bruise the head of the serpent, Satan (Genesis 3:15). Now Job's words in this passage surely appear to point forward to that one God-man, Jesus Christ, the mediator between God and men.

One writer stated that position very well in an article entitled "The Heart of Job's Theology." "In the Incarnation the divine Christ did appear as man's Umpire, his Middleman, his Mediator. The Referee, Jesus Christ, laid His one hand on God's shoulder and His other hand on man's shoulder and brought them together. He removed the rod of God's just wrath from man by deflecting it and making its deadly strokes fall on Himself. He opened the way for man to approach God and address Him without fear" (Alfred von Rohr Sauer, *Concordia Theological Monthly,* Volume 37, Number 5, page 263).

This passage contains one of several expressions of hope that flashed through Job's mind during his suffering; but in his agony he relapsed into a pessimistic mood and complained to God. The words that follow reflect his disturbed feelings.

Job feels that God has mistreated him

10 "I loathe my very life;
    therefore I will give free rein to my complaint

and speak out in the bitterness of my soul.
² I will say to God: Do not condemn me,
  but tell me what charges you have against me.
³ Does it please you to oppress me,
  to spurn the work of your hands,
  while you smile on the schemes of the wicked?
⁴ Do you have eyes of flesh?
  Do you see as a mortal sees?
⁵ Are your days like those of a mortal
  or your years like those of a man,
⁶ that you must search out my faults
  and probe after my sin—
⁷ though you know that I am not guilty
  and that no one can rescue me from your hand?

Job again lamented his condition. He couldn't understand why God was afflicting him. Was it because he was guilty of some special sin? Or was God punishing him without any good reason? He was unaware of the fact that God had two good reasons to send those great afflictions. First, God permitted Satan to afflict him to prove Job would remain faithful to God even under such severe suffering. Also, God used those troubles to test and strengthen Job's faith. Unless we keep those two facts in mind, we miss the chief point of the book. It teaches us much more than mere patience in suffering. In fact, Job was frequently impatient rather than patient.

It is also important to remember that although Job complained much, he never directly asked God to cure him from his disease and physical pain. His chief concern was to get an answer to the questions "Why am I suffering so much?" and "How can I declare my innocence before God?"

Although Job realized that he was not sinless, he was convinced that he was still a pious and faithful child of God. He therefore asked God several questions. Why should God pick on him and afflict him so severely while apparently letting the wicked get by with plotting and carrying out evil? Does God, who is a spirit, actually have eyes of flesh? Does he judge imperfectly as human beings do? Will the time come when God will die, as human beings do? Does he therefore have to be sure he can get even with Job before he (God) dies? Is it possible that God is, after all, only human? In this emotional outburst Job spoke to God as though he were speaking to another human being. In the verses that follow, Job pleads to God and describes himself in some detail as the work of God's hands.

Job appeals to God, who created him

8 "Your hands shaped me and made me.
   Will you now turn and destroy me?
9 Remember that you molded me like clay.
   Will you now turn me to dust again?
10 Did you not pour me out like milk
   and curdle me like cheese,
11 clothe me with skin and flesh
   and knit me together with bones and sinews?
12 You gave me life and showed me kindness,
   and in your providence watched over my spirit.

In its touching sentiment and poetic beauty, this is one of the most striking passages in this book. Job pleaded with God not to destroy him and return his body to dust. He reminded the Lord of the delicate manner in which God had created and formed him. He used several words to describe the creative process. First, he stated, "Your hands shaped me." That verb pictures God as a sculptor who intricately carved Job into human form. Continuing his vivid description, Job described God as the one who "made" him and who "molded" him like clay. Again, he pictured God as a master craftsman.

Then, going back to his very origin as an embryo in the womb of his mother, Job strikingly described God's act of creating him. From the very beginning, he grew and developed as cheese is formed from milk. God's great care and concern for the individual are further described: "You gave me life and showed me kindness, and in your providence watched over my spirit."

As we read these words, we are reminded of another passage in the Old Testament that in similar detail describes the great miracle of human conception and birth. In Psalm 139:13-16 David gratefully exclaims,

> For you created my inmost being;
>   you knit me together in my mother's womb.
> I praise you because I am fearfully and
>   wonderfully made;
>   your works are wonderful,
>   I know that full well.
> My frame was not hidden from you
>   when I was made in the secret place.
> When I was woven together in the depths
>   of the earth,
>   your eyes saw my unformed body.
> All the days ordained for me
>   were written in your book
>   before one of them came to be.

In the line "your eyes saw my unformed body," the word "unformed" does not imply something defective or wrong. It refers to an early stage in the development of the embryo.

Both of these passages (Job 10:8-12; Psalm 139:13-16) strikingly portray the marvelous miracle that God performs in the conception and birth of a human being. Equally remarkable is the fact that each human being is a distinct individual with his or her own characteristics and personality. The same parents may produce several children, and yet in most cases, the children will be different from one another in looks, manners, and personality. That is surely a remarkable mystery.

From these passages we can also be reminded that the conception and birth of a human being are not merely the result of sexual relations between a man and a woman. Above all, God is present and active. Throughout the Bible that is emphasized. When old Jacob saw the sons of Joseph and asked, "Who are these?" Joseph didn't tell him they were the sons his wife had given him, but he replied, "They are the sons God has given me here" (Genesis 48:8,9).

These passages from Job and Psalms also clearly point out that an embryo is not merely a part of a woman's body, something that may be kept or removed like tonsils, an appendix, or a gall bladder. There are those who maintain that a woman has full rights to her body and may therefore have an abortion if she so desires. Those people ignore the fact that the embryo is a real human being with an immortal soul. The Bible clearly teaches that fact, and pictures of an embryo during its early stages prove that it is a tiny human being. One who takes the Bible seriously is compelled to regard human life in all its stages as sacred and to condemn abortion as murder.

From Job's words we are also reminded to thank God for having created us, for having given us body and soul, eyes, ears and all our members, our mind and all our abilities, and for preserving them, as Martin Luther beautifully explains in the First Article of the Apostles' Creed.

Job feels frustrated

¹³ "But this is what you concealed in your heart,
    and I know that this was in your mind:
¹⁴ If I sinned, you would be watching me
    and would not let my offense go unpunished.
¹⁵ If I am guilty—woe to me!
    Even if I am innocent, I cannot lift my head,
  for I am full of shame
    and drowned in my affliction.
¹⁶ If I hold my head high, you stalk me like a lion
    and again display your awesome power against me.
¹⁷ You bring new witnesses against me
    and increase your anger toward me;
    your forces come against me wave upon wave.

After his beautiful description of his conception and birth, Job fell back into his complaint. He was guilty of accusing God of maliciously hurting him. No one, including Job, can read God's heart and mind. When God later spoke to Job (chapters 38–41), he reminded Job of that. God is too majestic and wonderful for any mortal to comprehend. It was therefore impertinent of Job to declare that God had created him only to destroy him.

Job accused God of watching him—no longer in the sense of lovingly caring for him, but spying on him, trying to catch him. Whether he was guilty or innocent, he felt he had no way out; he just couldn't win. He complained, "I am full of shame and drowned in my affliction." In the text the NIV has "drowned in." The Hebrew word can be better translated as "aware of," as the footnote indicates. Job was constantly aware of his affliction.

Job's words "you stalk me like a lion" have been understood in two different ways. The question might be, Who is compared to a lion—Job or God? Some scholars are of the opinion that Job's words picture a scene in which men hunt lions, as ancient Assyrian kings enjoyed doing. Then the lion would represent Job. It is more consistent with the description of lions in the Bible to understand the lion as being the aggressor. The lion would hunt its prey and attack it. Thus Job described God in this passage. Like a lion, God was stalking Job.

Job also accused God of bringing new witnesses against him. Who were those witnesses? Were they people? That doesn't seem likely in Job's case, since we know of only three witnesses at the time he spoke these words: Eliphaz, Bildad, and Zophar. Rather, the witnesses referred to in verse 17 were his additional sufferings, which were of numerous kinds: physical, mental, emotional, and spiritual. Like his friends, Job failed to see suffering as an experience through which God would test and strengthen his faith. But unlike his friends, he refused to admit that his extreme suffering was the result of any special sins.

Job saw God as his enemy who angrily and relentlessly attacked him. He pictured God as sending military forces against him to overwhelm him. Again, although Job's words cannot be justified, they are the words of a desperate man, not a godless, unbelieving man.

Job wishes that he might die

18 "Why then did you bring me out of the womb?
    I wish I had died before any eye saw me.
19 If only I had never come into being,
    or had been carried straight from the womb to the grave!
20 Are not my few days almost over?
    Turn away from me so I can have a moment's joy
21 before I go to the place of no return,
    to the land of gloom and deep shadow,

**²² to the land of deepest night,
  of deep shadow and disorder,
  where even the light is like darkness."**

Again we hear Job expressing the wish that he had died before experiencing life here on earth. In his misery he had forgotten the many happy and prosperous years he had enjoyed with his large family and many acquaintances and friends. Now he sat in his misery with three unsympathetic men. Now he could only wish that God would end his misery. He repeated thoughts that he had expressed at greater length in chapters 3 and 7. He begged God to turn away from him. He wished for a moment's joy before leaving this earth.

In bleak terms Job described the grave and the state of the dead as "the place of no return." From the viewpoint of life in this world, that is true. With only a few exceptions mentioned in the Bible, people have not returned from death to life in this world. To describe the darkness of death, Job heaped up words: "gloom," "deep shadow," "deepest night," "disorder," and "darkness." As one reads verses 21 and 22, the effect is overwhelming.

In his pessimistic mood Job expected to die soon, unaware of the fact that he would live many more years. He viewed the end of his life as a dark and forbidding experience. But from his words we must not conclude that Job believed death was the final end. Here and there in his speeches we find glimpses of a hope of life after death (14:14,15; 16:19-21; 19:25-27). Although Job did not have the full revelation of the death and resurrection of Jesus that the New Testament gives us, from some of his words we can conclude that Job had the confidence that he would be raised to life after death. That is the promise the Bible gives to all believers, and Job was a true believer according to God's own testimony (1:8; 2:3; 42:7-9).

Zophar's first speech

Zophar condemns Job's words as idle talk

In this chapter we are introduced to Zophar, the third of Job's friends. From his words we soon learn that Zophar was unsympathetic and tactless. In a blunt and outspoken manner, he took Job to task.

11 **Then Zophar the Naamathite replied:**

² **"Are all these words to go unanswered?**
Is this talker to be vindicated?
³ **Will your idle talk reduce men to silence?**
Will no one rebuke you when you mock?
⁴**You say to God, 'My beliefs are flawless**
and I am pure in your sight.'
⁵**Oh, how I wish that God would speak,**
that he would open his lips against you
⁶**and disclose to you the secrets of wisdom,**
for true wisdom has two sides.
Know this: God has even forgotten some of your sin.

His pompous manner and sharp words show that Zophar had no feeling for Job's pain and anxiety. To him, Job's strong outbursts were not the sincere expression of grief over deep distress. Zophar heard them only as the babble and complaint of a person who deserved to be scolded. He began by asking four questions that obviously answer themselves. He felt he had to respond to Job's complaints. He called Job's statements "idle talk" and accused Job of mocking God. That was an unjust accusation. Job had complained and even challenged God, but he had not mocked or blasphemed God.

Zophar accused Job of claiming "My beliefs are flawless and I am pure in your sight." That was a false accusation. When Job had stated "I am blameless" (9:21), he was claiming to be innocent of any special sin that warranted such severe punishment. He did not claim that he was flawless.

Zophar expressed the wish that God would speak, a wish that Job himself shared, for he had hoped for a dialogue with God. Zophar stated that God would then reveal to Job the secret of his wisdom. Zophar described God's wisdom as having "two sides." Various interpretations have been offered for that expression. The best explanation appears to be that "God knows both sides of every matter, the manifest as well as the hidden, and that it is the hidden side that he would reveal if he were to speak to Job's challenge" (Marvin H. Pope, *The Anchor Bible,* Volume 15, pages 84,85).

Zophar added, "Know this: God has even forgotten some of your sin." Zophar's words may at first sound charitable, but they strongly imply that Job had sinned so greatly that no punishment would be great enough to cover his sin. He was also asserting that Job's suffering was a form of punishment rather than a wholesome test of his faith, as Eliphaz had suggested (5:17).

Zophar praises God's majesty

7 **"Can you fathom the mysteries of God?**
  Can you probe the limits of the Almighty?
8 **They are higher than the heavens—what can you do?**
    They are deeper than the depths of the grave—what can
        you know?
9 **Their measure is longer than the earth**
    and wider than the sea.
10 **"If he comes along and confines you in prison**
    and convenes a court, who can oppose him?

¹¹ **Surely he recognizes deceitful men;**
     and when he sees evil, does he not take note?
¹² **But a witless man can no more become wise**
     than a wild donkey's colt can be born a man.

In striking and beautiful poetry Zophar spoke of the great wonders and mysteries of God. He barraged Job with question after question. What Zophar said about God no one could dispute. Job himself had spoken similarly (9:4-13), and so had Eliphaz (5:9-16). In later chapters we also will read of the great mysteries of God. Zophar effectively used dimensions such as "higher," "deeper," "longer," and "wider" to picture God's mysteries. His words remind us of Paul's language in the concluding verses of a doctrinal section in the epistle to the Romans:

> Oh, the depth of the riches of the wisdom and
>   knowledge of God!
> How unsearchable his judgments,
>   and his paths beyond tracing out!
> "Who has known the mind of the Lord?
>   Or who has been his counselor?"
> "Who has ever given to God,
>   that God should repay him?"
> For from him and through him and to him are all
>   things.
> To him be the glory forever! Amen. (11:33-36)

Turning from the great mystery of God to his power (verse 10), Zophar showed Job how useless it would be to try to resist God. Not only can God imprison one who goes against him, he can also summon that person to court. Job had hoped for such an appearance so that he could present his complaint before God. Now Zophar implied that God would force Job to appear before him. Did Zophar also imply that the court would consist of himself and his friends?

In his words in verses 11 and 12, Zophar indirectly accused Job of being deceitful, evil, and witless. Those were cruel words, and they must have deeply hurt Job. Perhaps quoting a proverb, Zophar implied that Job was dull. He called him "witless," or "empty headed," lacking brains and judgment. For such a person to become wise would be as unlikely as a donkey's colt being born a human being.

The solution for Job: turn to God

¹³ "Yet if you devote your heart to him
   and stretch out your hands to him,
¹⁴ if you put away the sin that is in your hand
   and allow no evil to dwell in your tent,
¹⁵ then you will lift up your face without shame;
   you will stand firm and without fear.
¹⁶ You will surely forget your trouble,
   recalling it only as waters gone by.
¹⁷ Life will be brighter than noonday,
   and darkness will become like morning.
¹⁸ You will be secure, because there is hope;
   you will look about you and take your rest in safety.
¹⁹ You will lie down, with no one to make you afraid,
   and many will court your favor.
²⁰ But the eyes of the wicked will fail,
   and escape will elude them;
   their hope will become a dying gasp."

After his sharp words, Zophar appealed to Job to change his ways, as Eliphaz had done earlier (5:8). He told Job to make the first move: "If you devote your heart to him [God]." The pronoun *you* is emphatically stated in the Hebrew. Zophar told Job it was up to *him.*

His manner of speaking reminds us of the "decision theology" that is prominent in the preaching of certain religious evangelists today. They may preach eloquently about the sins of people; they may movingly proclaim our Savior's suffering and death. But then they will add words to this effect: "You must make a decision for Christ. Come to the altar and commit your life to him." Instead of presenting faith as the empty hand that receives forgiveness and salvation, they present it as making a decision to accept Jesus Christ and to invite him into their hearts. In the same way, Zophar called upon Job to take the necessary steps to reconcile himself to God.

Zophar also made beautiful but unrealistic promises that if Job turned to God, everything would be fine. He would no longer experience shame and fear (verse 15) or trouble (verse 16). Life would be bright and sunny (verse 17), he would be secure (verse 18), and he could peacefully lie down to rest (verse 19). People would again court his favor and seek his advice as in the past (29:7-13).

Today there are also television preachers who make such glowing promises. As we mentioned in our comments on 8:20-22, such prosperity theology is false and misleading. Some preachers use it as a gimmick to induce their listeners to contribute generously to their radio or TV ministry. "Send in a generous contribution," they say, "and God will take care of you." But where in the Bible does God promise that? He surely doesn't promise his true believers a life free from troubles in the manner that Zophar described the life of the godly. Neither does he condemn as ungodly those who suffer troubles and sorrows. Indeed, the Bible tells us, "My son, do not despise the LORD's discipline and do not resent his rebuke, because the LORD disciplines those he loves, as a father the son he delights in" (Proverbs 3:11,12; also quoted in Hebrews 12:5,6).

In the concluding verse Zophar made another statement that is questionable for two reasons. First, he categorically stated that the wicked will fail, have no escape, and come to a hopeless end. That is not true. Often they are successful in this life. He further implied that Job was one of the wicked unless he turned to God. He therefore presumed to judge Job to be a wicked person. In so doing, Zophar sided with Satan against God, who commended Job.

Job's reply to Zophar

Job disagrees with the arguments of his friends

12 Then Job replied:

² "Doubtless you are the people,
and wisdom will die with you!
³ But I have a mind as well as you;
I am not inferior to you.
Who does not know all these things?
⁴ "I have become a laughingstock to my friends,
though I called upon God and he answered—
a mere laughingstock, though righteous and blameless!
⁵ Men at ease have contempt for misfortune
as the fate of those whose feet are slipping.
⁶ The tents of marauders are undisturbed,
and those who provoke God are secure—
those who carry their god in their hands.

Job had listened to each of his three friends as they took him to task. While some of what they said was true, they were wrong in concluding that Job's suffering was punishment for special sins he had committed. They were also wrong in maintaining that if he turned away from his sinful course, he could again experience health and prosperity. His own experience was, in fact, the very opposite, as he had earlier reminded them. Yet they disregarded his complaints and felt little if any sympathy for him. Instead of comforting him, they only added to his misery.

Their speeches aroused Job to react with sarcastic words: "Doubtless you are the people, and wisdom will die with you!" Obviously, they knew it all. The world would be much poorer with their passing!

But Job wouldn't concede that his friends were right in their arguments or that they had a corner on wisdom. He claimed to be their equal in intelligence and wisdom. In fact, many of the things his friends had said were trite and stale and didn't convince Job but only irritated him. He felt that what he had to say had more substance.

The friends had repeatedly maintained that the godly prosper whereas the ungodly suffer misfortune. Zophar had emphatically stated that in his speech immediately preceding this chapter. Job could by no means agree. In fact, to him the very opposite appeared to be true. He who had been a God-fearing and blameless man was now suffering intensely. He who had been a highly respected man had now become a laughingstock to his friends and an object of contempt to those who saw him. On the other hand, the ungodly appeared to prosper and enjoy a life of contentment.

At a later time, the psalmist Asaph made a similar observation. When he was experiencing troubles, he complained,

> But as for me, my feet had almost slipped;
>   I had nearly lost my foothold.
> For I envied the arrogant
>   when I saw the prosperity of the wicked.
> They have no struggles;
>   their bodies are healthy and strong.
> They are free from the burdens common to man;
>   they are not plagued by human ills.

This is what the wicked are like—
always carefree, they increase in wealth.
(Psalm 73:2-5,12)

When Asaph considered the final destiny of the wicked, he realized that in the end ungodliness does not pay (Psalm 73:17). Job also came to that realization, as we know from words he spoke later (27:7-10). At this time, however, it is obvious that Job's irritation at his friends' unkind accusations made him react by overstating his case. Would you or I react differently?

The closing line of verse 6 is difficult. It has been translated various ways, as we can learn from a comparison of English versions. We might improve the NIV translation by changing the words "their god" to "God." It would then read "those who carry God in their hands." Having no respect for God, the wicked would presume to control and manipulate him as if he were a magical object.

> ⁷ "But ask the animals, and they will teach you,
>   or the birds of the air, and they will tell you;
> ⁸ or speak to the earth, and it will teach you,
>   or let the fish of the sea inform you.
> ⁹ Which of all these does not know
>   that the hand of the LORD has done this?
> ¹⁰ In his hand is the life of every creature
>   and the breath of all mankind.
> ¹¹ Does not the ear test words
>   as the tongue tastes food?
> ¹² Is not wisdom found among the aged?
>   Does not long life bring understanding?

These verses serve as a transition between verses 1 to 6 and 13 to 25. In speaking these words, Job protested that his friends had a distorted picture of the reason for his suffering. He stated that even the lowly creatures understood what his friends either failed to understand or chose to ignore. The animals, the birds, and the fish, who were placed under the rule of man at creation (Genesis 1:26) recognized what Job's friends refused to admit: it was the hand of the almighty God that had brought Job's affliction on him. In saying that, Job no doubt stretched the truth somewhat. We might ask, Do animals, birds, and fish really know such things? Perhaps their instinct leads them to recognize certain things in nature, but we would at least question whether they would have such comprehension of God's power and rule.

Yet Job was right in protesting that he was not guilty of any especially great sins that directly brought on his suffering. He did not know that God had permitted Satan to afflict him so severely. Satan was the one who had instigated his suffering. He tried to destroy Job. And while God permitted Satan to afflict him, God did so to test and strengthen Job's faith so that in the end he would be richly blessed. But little did Job know it at this time.

Verses 11 and 12 express important truths, but it is difficult to fit them into this context. Perhaps it is best to understand them as Job's reply to his friends to the effect that he was not willing to accept their statements. He had listened to what they said, and he begged to differ. He too had lived and experienced many things. He too had wisdom and understanding. But as he continued his discourse, Job reminded his friends that there is one who, unlike human beings, has unlimited wisdom and power—God.

God has power over all

¹³ **"To God belong wisdom and power;
counsel and understanding are his.**

¹⁴ What he tears down cannot be rebuilt;
   the man he imprisons cannot be released.
¹⁵ If he holds back the waters, there is drought;
   if he lets them loose, they devastate the land.
¹⁶ To him belong strength and victory;
   both deceived and deceiver are his.
¹⁷ He leads counselors away stripped
   and makes fools of judges.
¹⁸ He takes off the shackles put on by kings
   and ties a loincloth around their waist.
¹⁹ He leads priests away stripped
   and overthrows men long established.
²⁰ He silences the lips of trusted advisers
   and takes away the discernment of elders.
²¹ He pours contempt on nobles
   and disarms the mighty.
²² He reveals the deep things of darkness
   and brings deep shadows into the light.
²³ He makes nations great, and destroys them;
   he enlarges nations, and disperses them.
²⁴ He deprives the leaders of the earth of their reason;
   he sends them wandering through a trackless waste.
²⁵ They grope in darkness with no light;
   he makes them stagger like drunkards.

In these words Job praises the wisdom and power of God while still protesting his own innocence of the charges his friends had leveled against him. His language is forceful and repeatedly emphasizes the truth that God is far above the men in highest places: counselors, judges, kings, priests, advisers, elders, nobles, and all the high and mighty in this world. All of those dignitaries are puny in the sight of God.

In his speech recorded in the previous chapter, Zophar had briefly referred to the wisdom of God (verses 6-11), but he had spoken those words to rebuke Job. Earlier Job had praised God's infinite wisdom and power at some length (9:1-24). Now in his response to Zophar, Job again describes God in considerable detail as the one who is so incomparably powerful that no one can stand up to him. It is this God who also allowed Job to suffer.

Job reacted to Zophar's short and bitter rebuke (chapter 11) with a long speech recorded in three chapters (12–14). After his calm and objective account of the wisdom and power of God (12:13-25), Job's words in the two chapters that follow are intensely personal and tinged with bitterness.

The advice of Job's friends is worse than useless

13 "My eyes have seen all this,
my ears have heard and understood it.
² What you know, I also know;
I am not inferior to you.
³ But I desire to speak to the Almighty
and to argue my case with God.
⁴ You, however, smear me with lies;
you are worthless physicians, all of you!
⁵ If only you would be altogether silent!
For you, that would be wisdom.

In their vain attempt to comfort Job, his three friends have succeeded only in making him feel worse. Their approach has been legalistic, the law approach, instead of evangelical, the gospel approach. Their argument has been from effect to cause. They have as much as told him, "Job, since you're suffering so much, you must have sinned greatly."

They had little awareness of his problem and even less true sympathy for him. Their words only made Job feel worse and had the effect of irritating him and arousing him to strike back at them. Using the language of medicine, Job accused them of smearing him with lies and of being quack doctors whose diagnosis was wrong and whose prescription was worse than useless. As counselors they did more harm than good. The best thing they could do from now on would be to keep silent. But they would not be silenced, as we know from reading chapters 15, 18, 20, 22, and 25.

Job pleads with his friends to listen to him

> [6] **Hear now my argument;**
> **listen to the plea of my lips.**
> [7] **Will you speak wickedly on God's behalf?**
> **Will you speak deceitfully for him?**
> [8] **Will you show him partiality?**
> **Will you argue the case for God?**
> [9] **Would it turn out well if he examined you?**
> **Could you deceive him as you might deceive men?**
> [10] **He would surely rebuke you**
> **if you secretly showed partiality.**
> [11] **Would not his splendor terrify you?**
> **Would not the dread of him fall on you?**
> [12] **Your maxims are proverbs of ashes;**
> **your defenses are defenses of clay.**

Job begged his friends to listen to him. He asked them if they intended to show God partiality. The expression "show partiality" means to try to gain favor from someone by bribery or some other improper motivation.

Job asked if they were trying to curry God's favor by downgrading him, and if they were attempting to act as God's lawyers. He warned them that God wouldn't stand for that. He would severely punish them for their uncharitable conduct toward Job. They had a very weak case against him. Their arguments, when tested and challenged, would crumble like pots of clay.

As we will learn from the closing chapter of this book, God was greatly displeased with their conduct and words.

> ¹³ "Keep silent and let me speak;
>   then let come to me what may.
> ¹⁴ Why do I put myself in jeopardy
>   and take my life in my hands?
> ¹⁵ Though he slay me, yet will I hope in him;
>   I will surely defend my ways to his face.
> ¹⁶ Indeed, this will turn out for my deliverance,
>   for no godless man would dare come before him!
> ¹⁷ Listen carefully to my words;
>   let your ears take in what I say.
> ¹⁸ Now that I have prepared my case,
>   I know I will be vindicated.
> ¹⁹ Can anyone bring charges against me?
>   If so, I will be silent and die.

Again Job pleaded with his friends to let him speak. He had to get things off his chest. He also anxiously hoped to speak to God. Verse 14 in the NIV reads, "Why do I put myself in jeopardy and take my life in my hands?" In the original Hebrew the first line is more concrete: "Why should I take my flesh in my teeth?" Some English versions also translate it that way. That expression has been understood in a number of ways. From the words that follow, it appears best to understand it as an expression of Job's fierce determination to risk his very life and limbs in appearing before God to plead his case.

Verse 15 is a remarkable expression of Job's faith in God. Regardless of what might happen to Job, he would still hope and trust in God. Smitten with disease and wracked with pain, Job felt he was already close to being killed. Yet his desire to lay his case before God was so intense that he would risk everything in the hope of being judged innocent of the charges brought against him by his friends. Job felt convinced that God would justify him. As we will see in later passages, particularly 19:25-27, Job looked beyond this life to the eternal life to come. His primary concern was not his physical suffering but his relationship with his God. We can all learn a valuable lesson from Job in that regard.

The great reformer Martin Luther was also a man who experienced many trials and afflictions as he served the Lord and his fellow human beings. When he spoke out against the false teachings and practices in the church, he was excommunicated and declared an outlaw. Humanly speaking, Luther could have held a high position in the Roman Catholic Church if he had gone along with its teachings and practices, but his conscience would not permit him to do so. As he stood alone before the authorities of state and church at the Diet of Worms, he declared that he could not with a clear conscience recant what he had spoken and taught, and added the words "God help me."

Like Job, Luther desperately clung to his faith in his Lord and Savior. Luther's faith was that of a little child—simple and sincere, even though he was a man of profound intellect and learning. In one passage of his vast volume of writings, Luther makes reference to this verse from Job (verse 15). He states, "To accept it as true and certain that God provides for us and loves us as His children calls for faith, which alone is the master who looks aright at God's Word and works and teaches us thoroughly to understand them. Now the Word clearly testifies that God chastens those whom He loves and scourges every son whom He receives (Hebrews 12:6), as Scripture everywhere proclaims. . . . Faith holds to words such as these, directs its course accordingly, allows God to manage and provide, and says with Job: . . . Though God were to slay me, yet I will hope in Him and rely on His grace."

As believers in Jesus Christ, let us pray for God to give us such a simple and strong faith and enable us to have the confidence to confess with Paul, "Who will bring any charge against those whom God has chosen? It is God who justifies. Who is he that condemns? Christ Jesus, who died—more than that, who was raised to life—is at the right hand of God and is also interceding for us" (Romans 8:33,34).

Job pleads with God to be merciful to him

> ²⁰ "Only grant me these two things, O God,
>   and then I will not hide from you:
> ²¹ Withdraw your hand far from me,
>   and stop frightening me with your terrors.
> ²² Then summon me and I will answer,
>   or let me speak, and you reply.
> ²³ How many wrongs and sins have I committed?
>   Show me my offense and my sin.
> ²⁴ Why do you hide your face
>   and consider me your enemy?
> ²⁵ Will you torment a windblown leaf?
>   Will you chase after dry chaff?
> ²⁶ For you write down bitter things against me
>   and make me inherit the sins of my youth.
> ²⁷ You fasten my feet in shackles;
>   you keep close watch on all my paths
>   by putting marks on the soles of my feet.
> ²⁸ "So man wastes away like something rotten,
>   like a garment eaten by moths.

In the NIV the opening line of verse 20 reads "Only grant me these two things." It can be more literally translated as "Only don't do two things to me." There were two things Job asked God not to do to him. He begged him not to over-power him by laying a heavy hand on him or to frighten him with his overwhelming majesty. If God would grant him that wish, Job would dare to come before him.

In the closing verses of this chapter, Job asked God to make clear to him what wrongs he had committed. He was not denying that he had sinned, but he wanted to know what specific sins had brought about his great afflictions. He was not convinced that he was guilty of the many sins of which his friends had accused him.

Job also felt that God was taking advantage of him and tormenting him. He compared himself to a wind-blown leaf and dry chaff, and he felt as if he were something rotten, like a garment eaten by moths. In his predicament Job compared himself to a prisoner whose feet are placed in stocks so he can't move and to a slave whose feet are branded so that his footsteps are marked and leave an imprint in the ground wherever he goes.

Man's life is short and full of sorrow

14 "Man born of woman
is of few days and full of trouble.
2 He springs up like a flower and withers away;
like a fleeting shadow, he does not endure.
3 Do you fix your eye on such a one?
Will you bring him before you for judgment?
4 Who can bring what is pure from the impure?
No one!
5 Man's days are determined;
you have decreed the number of his months
and have set limits he cannot exceed.
6 So look away from him and let him alone,
till he has put in his time like a hired man.

In these verses Job makes several remarkable statements. To the reader of today they may sound too pessimistic, but are they? Let's put ourselves in Job's place. He had lost his property and children, and now he was suffering indescribable pain, intense anxiety, and deep loneliness. He received no help from his unfeeling friends. Their visit rather increased his distress. In addition, he was tempted to feel that even God had forsaken him.

Having his own condition particularly in mind, Job realized that human life is short and full of trouble. At its longest, life is short, for it has an end. Compared to eternity, even a long life is nothing. As we all know, life has many troubles and sorrows. Comparing his present condition to his previous prosperity, Job saw himself as a flower that blossoms for a short time only to wither away.

Realizing his own wretched condition, he made one of his profoundest statements by asking, "Who can bring what is pure from the impure? No one!" That is certainly true. Job realized he was a sinner and didn't deny it. Ever since the fall of our first parents in the Garden of Eden, sin has contaminated every human being except our Lord Jesus Christ. As a result of sin we experience troubles, sorrows, and illnesses, and finally death. Job was keenly aware of that and confessed it.

In his affliction Job felt God was watching him, keeping an eye on him to punish him. He also referred to the fact that God knows in advance how long each person will live, having determined his days and set a limit on his months. In his own case Job felt his life was one of affliction and misery, so he wished that God would soon give him relief from his affliction. That could mean either death, something Job had earlier wished for (6:8,9), or an end to his suffering during his lifetime. In Job's case it turned out to be a restoration to a happy earthly life with even greater blessings than he had previously experienced (42:10).

Does man have hope for the afterlife?

> 7 "At least there is hope for a tree:
>   If it is cut down, it will sprout again,
>   and its new shoots will not fail.
> 8 Its roots may grow old in the ground
>   and its stump die in the soil,
> 9 yet at the scent of water it will bud
>   and put forth shoots like a plant.
> 10 But man dies and is laid low;
>   he breathes his last and is no more.
> 11 As water disappears from the sea
>   or a riverbed becomes parched and dry,
> 12 so man lies down and does not rise;
>   till the heavens are no more, men will not awake
>   or be roused from their sleep.

After having complained of the brevity and sorrows of life, Job drew a comparison between mankind and a tree. Verses 7 to 9 strikingly express a truth about a tree: if it is cut down, it will sprout again. I was convinced of the truth of that statement a few years ago. I had planted a tiny poplar tree in our front yard. It didn't thrive and almost died. Then I cut it down even with the grass. It soon gave evidence of new life. It grew rapidly and, at the time of this writing, it is the largest tree on our property and will provide shade for our house in the future. It is a constant reminder of Job's words, "If it is cut down, it will sprout again." With God's blessing, proper amounts of rain and sunshine will make even a seemingly dead tree grow and thrive. Job knew that.

Thinking of man, Job wished he could say the same thing. Human experience, however, led him to declare, "But man dies and is laid low; he breathes his last and is no more." Then, after having compared man to a dry riverbed, he concluded, "So man lies down and does not rise; till the heavens are no more, men will not awake or be roused from their sleep."

On this profound matter of the resurrection to a life hereafter, Job was torn between two possibilities: either there is an afterlife, or there is not an afterlife. Here we see him waver and doubt that there is a resurrection. Only two verses later (verse 14) it appears as if Job had hope of a resurrection, and in a later passage (19:25-27), he boldly professed such hope. This is no contradiction. Job was only human, with his ups and downs. In his affliction Job at times was tempted to doubt, but at other times he desperately clung to the hope that he would be raised from the dead to live forever.

It is significant that in verse 12 Job uses three terms that suggest resurrection from the dead: "rise," "awake," "be roused." As we will see, in verse 14 there is another word ("renewal") that also appears to refer to the resurrection.

> [13] "If only you would hide me in the grave
>   and conceal me till your anger has passed!
> If only you would set me a time
>   and then remember me!
> [14] If a man dies, will he live again?
>   All the days of my hard service
>   I will wait for my renewal to come.
> [15] You will call and I will answer you;
>   you will long for the creature your hands have made.
> [16] Surely then you will count my steps
>   but not keep track of my sin.
> [17] My offenses will be sealed up in a bag;
>   you will cover over my sin.

In contrast to the verses that precede, these verses express a wish and a hope. Job had felt the heavy hand of God resting on him. He greatly feared the anger of God. He wished God would hide him in the grave. Then he uttered the hope that after his death God would remember him. The word "remember" here has a strong, loving connotation. In the account of the great flood, we read that "God remembered Noah" (Genesis 8:1). That does not imply that God had ever forgotten him, but it tells us that God was deeply concerned about Noah and all who were with him in the ark. It was Job's wish that God would similarly show Job his loving concern.

Job then asked a penetrating question, a question that concerns the eternal welfare of every human being: "If a man dies, will he live again?" Earlier Job had given the answer no (14:10-12). His reason and experience had prompted that answer. It didn't seem possible that a person could be raised from the dead, and he hadn't seen anyone who had been raised. The last part of verse 14, however, strongly suggests the answer yes. Here Job's faith came to the fore and shone as a bright light in the darkness of his pessimism.

Despite all outward considerations, Job clung to his conviction that God was his Savior and Redeemer, a conviction that he was later to express even more boldly (19:25-27). One key word in this passage (verse 14) is the word "renewal": "I will wait for my renewal to come." The Hebrew word is of the same root as the word translated as "sprout again" in verse 7. There it refers to the new growth of a tree that has been cut down. What a striking picture that is of the resurrection! It points forward to Saint Paul's description of our resurrection on the Last Day: "The trumpet will sound, the dead will be raised imperishable, and we will be changed. For the perishable must clothe itself with the imperishable, and the mortal with immortality" (1 Corinthians 15:52,53). Job also expressed the hope that he could then stand in the presence of God as one whom God had pronounced innocent. The God who had created Job loved Job as the work of his hands.

Job continued, "Surely then you will count my steps." Elsewhere he used that expression in an unfavorable sense: that God would closely watch and spy on a person and hold his sins against him (see 31:4; 34:21). Here the expression is used in a favorable sense, as we know from the words that immediately follow, "but not keep track of my sin." If the words meant that God would spy on Job, we would surely expect him to keep track of Job's sins.

Verse 17 gives further evidence that God would count Job's steps in a loving manner, as a dear Father deeply concerned about him. Job adds, "My offenses will be sealed up in a bag; you will cover over my sin." What a beautiful expression of God's forensic act of justification! God would not hold Job's sins against him. In this moment of faith Job had the firm confidence that God would declare him righteous. God would be *for* Job instead of *against* him. At this moment when his spirit was lifted up, Job expressed the hope that God would deliver him and declare him innocent not only of the charge his friends had directed against him but of all his sins.

His optimism, however, was soon to turn to pessimism.

Job returns to his feeling of futility

> [18] "But as a mountain erodes and crumbles
>   and as a rock is moved from its place,
> [19] as water wears away stones
>   and torrents wash away the soil,
>   so you destroy man's hope.
> [20] You overpower him once for all, and he is gone;
>   you change his countenance and send him away.

²¹ **If his sons are honored, he does not know it;**
   if they are brought low, he does not see it.
²² **He feels but the pain of his own body**
   and mourns only for himself."

Unfortunately, Job's optimistic hope was short-lived. Again his thoughts turned to his wretched condition. He saw himself as a person disfigured almost beyond recognition by the ravages of disease. He felt powerless as he sat in the ashes and scraped his tortured body with pieces of broken pottery. For the moment he forgot the hope he had so nobly confessed in the previous verses. God's awesome power reminded him that he was at God's mercy.

Job stated that as mountains, stones, and soil will wear out and wash away, so will man's hope. To Job the future again looked dismal. He had come down from cloud nine and again found himself floundering in the valley of pessimism. His reason and experience again led him to doubt an existence after death. Using the illustration of a person who has died and was survived by his children, Job theorized, "If his sons are honored, he does not know it; if they are brought low, he does not see it." In a sense that is true, for in death a person is ignorant of that which takes place on earth and is not aware of the good or bad fortune of his children or others who are still alive. Nevertheless, there will be a reunion with loved ones after death; such a reunion Job doesn't mention in these pessimistic words.

When Job spoke these words he no doubt felt the loss of his own children very keenly, and that added to his feeling of frustration. His loneliness is reflected in his closing words: "He feels but the pain of his own body and mourns only for himself." Job's final speech in this first round of discourses ends on a pessimistic note.

The second round of discourses

After Job's initial complaint in chapter 3, each of the three friends made one speech. Eliphaz spoke at greatest length, then Bildad, and finally Zophar, who spoke most briefly. After each speech Job replied. His speeches were longer and more detailed than those of his friends. In the seven chapters that follow, the three friends again speak, and in turn Job answers them. Again Eliphaz begins this cycle of speeches.

Eliphaz's second speech

Eliphaz describes Job's words as empty

15 Then Eliphaz the Temanite replied:
² "Would a wise man answer with empty notions
   or fill his belly with the hot east wind?
³ Would he argue with useless words,
   with speeches that have no value?
⁴ But you even undermine piety
   and hinder devotion to God.
⁵ Your sin prompts your mouth;
   you adopt the tongue of the crafty.
⁶ Your own mouth condemns you, not mine;
   your own lips testify against you.

In his first speech (chapters 4,5) Eliphaz had spoken in a tactful and almost apologetic manner. He had addressed Job as one who had been both instructive and helpful to others and had gently chided Job for complaining when trouble struck him. He had emphasized the fact that God is greater than mortal man. Implying that Job was guilty of some special sins, he had urged Job to turn to God in repentance.

Then, according to Eliphaz, Job would experience happiness and success.

In his second speech Eliphaz abandoned his earlier tactful approach and pointedly accused Job of reckless and foolish speaking and of ungodliness. He said, "You even undermine piety and hinder devotion to God." Those words contradict God's own appraisal of Job in the opening chapter of the book: "He is blameless and upright, a man who fears God and shuns evil" (1:8). God also commended him in the closing chapter (42:7-9) and blessed him even more than at first (42:12,13). In his accusations Eliphaz was unjust and unkind.

> **7 "Are you the first man ever born?**
> **Were you brought forth before the hills?**
> **8 Do you listen in on God's council?**
> **Do you limit wisdom to yourself?**
> **9 What do you know that we do not know?**
> **What insights do you have that we do not have?**
> **10 The gray-haired and the aged are on our side,**
> **men even older than your father.**
> **11 Are God's consolations not enough for you,**
> **words spoken gently to you?**
> **12 Why has your heart carried you away,**
> **and why do your eyes flash,**
> **13 so that you vent your rage against God**
> **and pour out such words from your mouth?**

In a sarcastic manner, Eliphaz bombarded Job with six questions, all of which suggest a negative answer. First he asked if Job was older than anyone else, born before the hills were created. Obviously, he was not. Nor did Job listen in on God's council to advise the Almighty. He certainly wasn't wise enough to do that. Previously, Job had maintained that he was equal to his friends intellectually (13:2). Now Eliphaz turned that remark back on Job by asking, "What do you know that we do not know? What insights do you have that we do not have?"

Eliphaz's questions in verses 7 and 8 may appear to be similar to some questions that the Lord asks in chapter 38. However, there are at least two basic differences. First, Eliphaz was a human being with strong prejudices, whereas the Lord is the almighty God who has perfect wisdom and knowledge. Further, Eliphaz's speech only irritated Job, whereas God's speech caused Job to bow before God in repentance and gratitude.

Surprisingly, Eliphaz added, "The gray-haired and aged are on our side, men even older than your father." Does that mean that they were extremely old and Job was very young? Not necessarily. Nor does it imply that Job's father was alive at that time. More likely he had died. Eliphaz's words could very well mean that there were people at that time who had reached a greater age than Job's father when he died. Eliphaz seemed to equate wisdom with age, which is not true in every case. There are times when old people speak and act foolishly. From Eliphaz's words we might conclude that at least some of the three friends were older than Job, perhaps Eliphaz himself, since of the three he was the first speaker.

In this speech Eliphaz chided Job for failing to take his admonitions to heart. It appears that his vanity had been hurt.

> ¹⁴ **"What is man, that he could be pure,**
> **or one born of woman, that he could be righteous?**
> ¹⁵ **If God places no trust in his holy ones,**
> **if even the heavens are not pure in his eyes,**
> ¹⁶ **how much less man, who is vile and corrupt,**
> **who drinks up evil like water!**

In this section we cannot disagree with the words of Eliphaz. His words in verse 14 are similar to Job's words in chapter 14: "Man born of woman is of few days and full of trouble" (verse 1) and "Who can bring what is pure from the impure? No one!" (verse 4). Eliphaz and Job agreed that man is mortal, frail, sinful and, in Eliphaz's words, "vile and corrupt." God is also incomparably higher and greater than angels. Although God's angels are noble and sinless, they are creatures of God and therefore are limited and far beneath him in dignity and power. Eliphaz could therefore truthfully say, "God places no trust in his holy ones," the angels. How much less does he place trust in sinful, mortal men!

The fate of the wicked is sad

¹⁷ "Listen to me and I will explain to you;
   let me tell you what I have seen,
¹⁸ what wise men have declared,
   hiding nothing received from their fathers
¹⁹ (to whom alone the land was given
   when no alien passed among them):
²⁰ All his days the wicked man suffers torment,
   the ruthless through all the years stored up for him.
²¹ Terrifying sounds fill his ears;
   when all seems well, marauders attack him.
²² He despairs of escaping the darkness;
   he is marked for the sword.
²³ He wanders about—food for vultures;
   he knows the day of darkness is at hand.
²⁴ Distress and anguish fill him with terror;
   they overwhelm him, like a king poised to attack,
²⁵ because he shakes his fist at God
   and vaunts himself against the Almighty,
²⁶ defiantly charging against him
   with a thick, strong shield.

²⁷ **"Though his face is covered with fat**
     and his waist bulges with flesh,
²⁸ **he will inhabit ruined towns**
     and houses where no one lives,
     houses crumbling to rubble.
²⁹ **He will no longer be rich and his wealth will not endure,**
     nor will his possessions spread over the land.
³⁰ **He will not escape the darkness;**
     a flame will wither his shoots,
     and the breath of God's mouth will carry him away.
³¹ **Let him not deceive himself by trusting what is worthless,**
     for he will get nothing in return.
³² **Before his time he will be paid in full,**
     and his branches will not flourish.
³³ **He will be like a vine stripped of its unripe grapes,**
     like an olive tree shedding its blossoms.
³⁴ **For the company of the godless will be barren,**
     and fire will consume the tents of those who love bribes.
³⁵ **They conceive trouble and give birth to evil;**
     their womb fashions deceit."

In a condescending and patronizing manner, Eliphaz proceeded to lecture Job on how to change his ways to improve his present condition. Eliphaz was convinced that those who suffered were the wicked. That theme runs through the last half of this chapter. Earlier all three friends—Eliphaz (5:12-14), Bildad (8:12-19), and Zophar (11:20)—had more briefly depicted to Job the bad fortunes of the wicked.

In this chapter "Mr. Personal Experience" gave a rambling and tedious account of all the troubles and disasters that overtake the wicked. Darkness and dreadful noises will haunt him, marauders will attack him, and anguish will frighten him. He will go without food. In the first line of verse 23, the text of the NIV reads, "He wanders about—food for vultures."

In the footnote it reads as "looking for food." The footnote reading more accurately translates the Hebrew, "food—where is it?" In the text the translators followed the reading of an ancient Greek translation of the Old Testament called the Septuagint, which has the word for "vultures." It is normally a better policy to give preference to the Hebrew text, and the reading "looking for food" fits the context better.

In the closing verses of his speech, particularly verses 27 to 35, Eliphaz heaped up illustration after illustration in his attempt to convince Job of the downfall of the ungodly. He who accused Job of being a windbag (15:2) was himself verbose in this speech.

His chief mistake, however, was his assertion that God will always punish the ungodly *in this life*. That is simply not true. As you and I know today, evil and godless people often prosper and gain wealth and prestige. But in the hereafter, the ungodly will be punished eternally—unless they repent before they die. But Eliphaz didn't say that. Besides, he implied that Job was suffering so much because Job was guilty of such sins as the ungodly commit.

Job's reply to Eliphaz

Job calls his friends "miserable comforters"

16 Then Job replied:

2 "I have heard many things like these;
   miserable comforters are you all!
3 Will your long-winded speeches never end?
   What ails you that you keep on arguing?
4 I also could speak like you,
   if you were in my place;
   I could make fine speeches against you
   and shake my head at you.

⁵ **But my mouth would encourage you;**
  comfort from my lips would bring you relief.

Eliphaz's speech had the effect of irritating Job. He had recited a long list of examples of various disasters that overtake the wicked. Job had heard similar statements before. He said in effect, "You're not telling me anything new." He called his friends "miserable comforters." Earlier he had described them as "worthless physicians" (13:4), quacks who had no qualifications for healing people. Instead of administering salve, they were rubbing salt into Job's wounds.

For the first seven days of their visit, the friends had said nothing (2:13), and so they let Job's misery build up within him. Once they began to talk, they lectured him in a manner that was pompous and uncharitable. Instead of consoling him, they argued with him. They kept telling him, "Job, you're suffering so much because you have committed many sins."

Job said that if they were in his place and he in theirs, he would encourage and comfort them instead of making them feel worse. One basic difference between the theology of Job and that of his friends was that Job had a knowledge and appreciation of the gospel whereas theirs was strictly a law-based theology. While Job complained to God about his suffering, as we also learn from the next section in this chapter that he did realize that God permits affliction to come to his children for their spiritual good. Later, Elihu also emphasized that (33:19-30), a fact that sets his speeches apart from those of the three friends.

Job complains against God about his wretched condition

⁶ **"Yet if I speak, my pain is not relieved;**
  and if I refrain, it does not go away.

⁷ Surely, O God, you have worn me out;
   you have devastated my entire household.
⁸ You have bound me—and it has become a witness;
   my gauntness rises up and testifies against me.
⁹ God assails me and tears me in his anger
   and gnashes his teeth at me;
   my opponent fastens on me his piercing eyes.
¹⁰ Men open their mouths to jeer at me;
   they strike my cheek in scorn
   and unite together against me.
¹¹ God has turned me over to evil men
   and thrown me into the clutches of the wicked.
¹² All was well with me, but he shattered me;
   he seized me by the neck and crushed me.
   He has made me his target;
¹³   his archers surround me.
   Without pity, he pierces my kidneys
   and spills my gall on the ground.
¹⁴ Again and again he bursts upon me;
   he rushes at me like a warrior.

Job could find no relief either in speech or in silence. He turned to address God in strong language similar to that which he had used earlier (6:4). He stated that God had worn him out and devastated his household. He saw himself as emaciated and gaunt (verse 8). He felt that God and men were in league against him. In vivid language Job accused God of shattering and crushing him and making him a target for shooting arrows. It was not right of Job to say those things, but we must remember that he was severely tested. Job was not a robot; he was a human being.

Verse 10 is especially concrete and vivid. Job complains, "Men open their mouths to jeer at me; they strike my cheek in scorn and unite together against me." This verse uses language strikingly similar to that of Psalm 22, which is a vivid prophetic picture of the suffering and crucifixion of our Savior Jesus Christ. In that psalm we read, "All who see me mock me; they hurl insults, shaking their heads" (verse 7) and "Dogs have surrounded me; a band of evil men has encircled me, they have pierced my hands and my feet" (verse 16).

In the Old Testament there is no better example of human suffering than that of Job. There are a number of striking parallels between Job's suffering and Christ's. Although Job was a sinner, his suffering was not directly related to any particular sins of his own. Likewise, the sinless Jesus Christ suffered not for any sins of his own, for he had none, but for the sins of the world. In both cases Satan was responsible for their suffering. Satan challenged God to allow him to test Job to the limit, and that led to Job's ordeal. Because Satan had successfully tempted our first parents to sin in the Garden of Eden, Jesus Christ came to suffer and die for our sins. It was also the will of God that Jesus endure great suffering. God permitted Satan to afflict Job severely with great losses and intense suffering. He did so for two reasons: to prove to Satan that Job would not renounce God, and to test and strengthen Job's faith.

It was God's love, not his anger, that allowed Job to suffer. It was that same love that led God to give his Son to suffer and die on the cross for our salvation. Shouldn't we be eternally grateful for that?

> ¹⁵ "I have sewed sackcloth over my skin
>   and buried my brow in the dust.
> ¹⁶ My face is red with weeping,
>   deep shadows ring my eyes;
> ¹⁷ yet my hands have been free of violence
>   and my prayer is pure.

These verses give us Job's reaction to his great afflictions. As a sign of grief and humility, he sewed rough sackcloth over the scabby skin that covered his gaunt and misshapen body. He buried his brow in the dust. The literal meaning of the word translated as "brow" is "horn." In the Old Testament, the word *horn* is sometimes used to express what is strong and proud. In his present humiliation, Job felt his strength and pride were crushed.

His intense pain drove him to much weeping. Yet in spite of his suffering, Job knew he was innocent of any violence, and he could pray with a clear conscience and a pure heart. Job's greatest crisis was the crisis of faith, not of suffering. Though severely attacked, his faith stood the test.

Job appeals to his witness in heaven

¹⁸ "O earth, do not cover my blood;
  may my cry never be laid to rest!
¹⁹ Even now my witness is in heaven;
  my advocate is on high.
²⁰ My intercessor is my friend
  as my eyes pour out tears to God;
²¹ on behalf of a man he pleads with God
  as a man pleads for his friend.
²² "Only a few years will pass
  before I go on the journey of no return.

These words are some of the most profound and eloquent in the entire book of Job. Job felt he was soon to die, but he pleaded that his blood would remain unburied in order that it might cry to heaven for justice. He wished that someone would hear his case and declare him justified. Then in a flash of confident faith, Job declared, "Even now my witness is in heaven, my advocate is on high." He had the assurance that there would be one who would attest to his innocence so that he could be justified. Job had longed for such a mediator

(9:33). He expressed the confidence that there was such a witness.

The better translation of the first line of verse 20 is "My friends treat me with scorn," as it appears in a number of other translations. That translation also fits better with the rest of the verse, "as my eyes pour out tears to God."

Now who is that witness, that advocate who pleaded Job's case with God as a man pleads for his friend? Notice that Job distinguishes this witness from God. Yet, as one who is in heaven, he cannot be a mere human being. Therefore, that witness can be none other than the Son of God, who became true man when he was born in Bethlehem many centuries after the time of Job. From eternity he is God, yet is distinct from God the Father.

Of Jesus Christ Paul confessed, "There is one God and one mediator between God and men, the man Jesus Christ" (1 Timothy 2:5). Similarly John stated, "If anybody does sin, we have one who speaks to the Father in our defense—Jesus Christ, the Righteous One" (1 John 2:1). In the last passage the King James Version has the word "advocate." These words assure us that, in spite of his suffering and feelings of depression, Job retained his faith in his God and Savior. He had not yielded to Satan's temptation to renounce God.

In the closing verse of this chapter Job again expressed a pessimistic thought. He felt there would be no turning back. What did he mean? In one sense what he said was true. He would not return from death to live again here on earth. Did he deny a resurrection to the next world? We prefer to think he did not. Three chapters later he eloquently professed his faith in the resurrection (19:25-27). His faith, however, frequently wavered.

This last verse headed him into another "down" mood, as we will see from the next chapter.

Job is disappointed over his troubles and his unsympathetic friends

17 My spirit is broken,
　　my days are cut short,
　　the grave awaits me.
² Surely mockers surround me;
　　my eyes must dwell on their hostility.

In the preceding verse, Job had pessimistically stated, "Only a few years will pass before I go on the journey of no return" (16:22). Now he described his spirit as "broken" and his days as "cut short," literally snuffed out, as a fire might be extinguished. He had only the grave to look forward to. He referred to his friends as "mockers" who could only bear "hostility" against him. The charges they had brought against him were very serious. If the charges were false, his friends could be punished severely for falsely accusing him, according to the law of God as recorded by Moses in Deuteronomy 19:16-19.

³ "Give me, O God, the pledge you demand.
　　Who else will put up security for me?
⁴ You have closed their minds to understanding;
　　therefore you will not let them triumph.
⁵ If a man denounces his friends for reward,
　　the eyes of his children will fail.

Job obviously addresses God, even though the word "God" is not found in the Hebrew text. Since his friends were of no help, Job turned to God and begged God to give him a pledge that he was innocent of the charges leveled against him. These words indicate that Job still had faith in God and that God (the Son) would be the witness he spoke of in the previous chapter (16:19).

In verse 4 Job describes his friends as shortsighted and narrow-minded. Job added that they acted like traitors against him, and their children would have to bear the consequences of their parents' uncharitable actions.

> ⁶ "God has made me a byword to everyone,
>   a man in whose face people spit.
> ⁷ My eyes have grown dim with grief;
>   my whole frame is but a shadow.
> ⁸ Upright men are appalled at this;
>   the innocent are aroused against the ungodly.
> ⁹ Nevertheless, the righteous will hold to their ways,
>   and those with clean hands will grow stronger.

Returning to the subject of his own wretched physical appearance, Job blamed God for making him a "byword." People had come to associate the name *Job* with the most humiliating suffering. When they saw him, they shouted and spit in his face. He called his body a mere "shadow"—his limbs were skinny and weak and his whole appearance was gaunt. What a contrast to his earlier noble appearance when he was respected as the greatest man in the community!

There is an abrupt change in Job's words in verses 8 and 9. He suddenly turned from a description of his three unfeeling friends to a description of true friends who are righteous and loyal. Such friends would defend the innocent and condemn the guilty. He then confidently expressed the hope that in the end the godly will prosper. No doubt Job had himself in mind when he said that.

> ¹⁰ "But come on, all of you, try again!
>   I will not find a wise man among you.
> ¹¹ My days have passed, my plans are shattered,
>   and so are the desires of my heart.

¹² These men turn night into day;
    in the face of darkness they say, 'Light is near.'
¹³ If the only home I hope for is the grave,
    if I spread out my bed in darkness,
¹⁴ if I say to corruption, 'You are my father,'
    and to the worm, 'My mother' or 'My sister,'
¹⁵ where then is my hope?
    Who can see any hope for me?
¹⁶ Will it go down to the gates of death?
    Will we descend together into the dust?"

Job saw little hope of progress in the discussion with his three friends because their minds were closed. He bluntly told them, "I will not find a wise man among you." He returned to his complaint over his trouble, but in his perturbed state he again turned to his complaint about his friends. "These men turn night into day; in the face of darkness they say, 'Light is near.'" In his *Popular Commentary,* P. E. Kretzmann explains those words as follows: "According to the consolations of his friends, his present trouble was just like the darkest hour which just precedes the dawn, if he would but admit the guilt which they ascribed to him" (Old Testament, Volume 2, page 25).

In vivid language Job spoke of what he felt lay in store for him: the final destruction of his diseased body in death. Having lost his children and having been practically forsaken by his wife, Job had no family to look forward to except corruption and worms. His speech concludes with four rapid questions expressing his hopelessness. This was another of Job's frequent "down" moods.

In his next speech (chapter 19), Job was even more severely depressed before he burst forth in his most eloquent profession of faith. But meanwhile Bildad had some harsh words to speak, as we will learn from the next chapter.

Bildad's second speech

Bildad rebukes Job

18 Then Eliphaz the Temanite replied:
² "When will you end these speeches?
    Be sensible, and then we can talk.
³ Why are we regarded as cattle
    and considered stupid in your sight?
⁴ You who tear yourself to pieces in your anger,
    is the earth to be abandoned for your sake?
    Or must the rocks be moved from their place?

True to the character of his first speech (chapter 8), Bildad minced no words in his second reply to Job. Earlier he had chided Job with the sarcastic remark, "How long will you say such things? Your words are a blustering wind" (8:2). Bildad's second speech sounds similar: "When will you end these speeches? Be sensible, and then we can talk."

Bildad appears to have been as sensitive of his own feelings as he was insensitive of the feelings of others. He may have recalled Job's earlier words, "Ask the animals, and they will teach you" (12:7). At any rate, he asked Job, "Why are we regarded as cattle and considered stupid in your sight?"

We can all use Bildad as a warning example for when we visit someone who is sick or depressed. How unfortunate it is to turn a visiting session into a lecture or a heated argument! Bildad surely appears to have been more interested in arguing with Job than in trying to understand and help him. Having run out of ideas, he even resorted to sarcasm when he accused Job of frenzied anger and of arrogantly regarding himself as the center of the universe (verse 4).

The fate of the wicked is sad

⁵ "The lamp of the wicked is snuffed out;
    the flame of his fire stops burning.
⁶ The light in his tent becomes dark;
    the lamp beside him goes out.
⁷ The vigor of his step is weakened;
    his own schemes throw him down.
⁸ His feet thrust him into a net
    and he wanders into its mesh.
⁹ A trap seizes him by the heel;
    a snare holds him fast.
¹⁰ A noose is hidden for him on the ground;
    a trap lies in his path.

After having spoken harsh words addressed to Job personally, Bildad continues with an extended description of the wicked. As Eliphaz had previously done (15:20-35), he gave example after example of the troubles that overtake the wicked man. Without directly identifying that person with Job, he strongly implied that it was Job he was speaking of.

The expressions "lamp," "flame," "fire," and "light" indicate that all is well with a person and that he is safe and secure in the night as well as in the day. Throughout the Bible the expression "light" has a favorable connotation. On the other hand, "darkness" represents confusion, stumbling, loss, evil, and death. Such, said Bildad, is the destiny of the wicked.

In verses 8 to 10, Bildad used another picture: that of falling into a trap. In ancient times many different kinds of hunting devices were used to catch animals and birds. Bildad piled up term after term to designate those traps. The NIV uses five words: "net," "mesh," "trap" (twice), "snare," and "noose." Two different Hebrew words are translated as "trap" in the NIV, so Bildad really described six different kinds of traps. According to Bildad, the wicked would get caught one way or another, and his words hint that Job was such a man.

> ¹¹ Terrors startle him on every side
>   and dog his every step.
> ¹² Calamity is hungry for him;
>   disaster is ready for him when he falls.
> ¹³ It eats away parts of his skin;
>   death's firstborn devours his limbs.
> ¹⁴ He is torn from the security of his tent
>   and marched off to the king of terrors.
> ¹⁵ Fire resides in his tent;
>   burning sulfur is scattered over his dwelling.

Continuing in his lecture on the troubles besetting the wicked, Bildad described Job as a victim of terrors, calamity, and disaster. The "terrors" could be animals or people or simply inward fears. Such terrors would "dog his every step" so that Job could find no rest. Bildad pictured calamity as someone who is starved and eager to devour the wicked. Disaster was at the side of the wicked, ready to grab him when he fell.

Bildad further stated that such calamity "eats away parts of his skin." By the expression "death's firstborn" Bildad probably referred to disease, which "devours his limbs" so they could hardly be recognized.

Verses 14 and 15 give further stark details about the plight of the ungodly. He is driven from his home after having lost his dwelling and property. In verse 15 the text reads, "Fire resides in his tent." The footnote in the NIV gives a better translation: "Nothing he had remains in his tent." In other words, he has lost everything.

As Job heard those words he must have realized that they were directed against him. As he sat in his lonely place in the rubbish, he knew that many of those same disasters had struck him. How those cruel words must have stung! And how much better it would have been if Bildad hadn't opened his mouth! But he had even more to say.

> ¹⁶ **His roots dry up below**
> **and his branches wither above.**
> ¹⁷ **The memory of him perishes from the earth;**
> **he has no name in the land.**
> ¹⁸ **He is driven from light into darkness**
> **and is banished from the world.**
> ¹⁹ **He has no offspring or descendants among his people,**
> **no survivor where once he lived.**
> ²⁰ **Men of the west are appalled at his fate;**
> **men of the east are seized with horror.**
> ²¹ **Surely such is the dwelling of an evil man;**
> **such is the place of one who knows not God."**

Earlier, Job had compared a man to a tree and had concluded that there was more hope for a tree than for a human being (14:7-12). Now, in considerable detail Bildad compared the wicked man to a tree with dried roots and withered branches. Such a person would have no descendants, and his name would disappear from the earth.

In contrast to many in our society today, people in Old Testament times regarded it as a great blessing to have many children (see Psalms 127,128). God had blessed Job and his wife with ten children (1:2). On the other hand, people felt deprived and unhappy if they were childless. Such was the case with Sarah (Genesis 16:1-5), Manoah's wife (Judges 13:2), and Hannah (1 Samuel 2:6-11).

Now, however, Job had lost his ten children. As he heard the cruel words of Bildad, he must have felt every cutting syllable that his so-called friend had spoken. The fact that

121

Bildad did not address him as "Job" or "you" in these verses could not conceal the obvious reference to him.

When he heard these words, Job must have been irritated for two reasons. First, Bildad listed catastrophes that clearly pointed to Job's own experiences. Job had lost his children and cattle and had been struck with a loathsome and painful disease that drove him to his solitary place among the rubbish. He had been made to feel that his wife, other human beings, and even God had forsaken him.

But even worse, Job must have cringed as he heard Bildad keep repeating the false arguments that he and his two friends had used in their speeches. In spite of Job's objections, they kept insisting that Job's afflictions were the direct result of special sins he had committed. They kept maintaining that he suffered so much because he was such an especially bad sinner. Their theology was strictly a law theology without any gospel element, a theology of works and not a theology of grace. They refused to acknowledge that God would permit a godly person to suffer affliction.

On the other hand, in spite of his complaints, Job realized that godly people also experience troubles. In his desperate state, he still clung to a theology of grace. He was later brought to a clearer realization of the role that suffering may play in the life of the believer. But meanwhile Job had something to say in response to his friends. In his speech that follows, we will find a remarkable expression of Job's faith in his Redeemer.

Job's reply to Bildad

Job bitterly complains that he feels forsaken

19 Then Job replied:
² **"How long will you torment me
and crush me with words?**

³ Ten times now you have reproached me;
  shamelessly you attack me.
⁴ If it is true that I have gone astray,
  my error remains my concern alone.
⁵ If indeed you would exalt yourselves above me
  and use my humiliation against me,
⁶ then know that God has wronged me
  and drawn his net around me.

Job's friends had shown that they had no true feeling for Job's suffering. They were incapable of putting themselves in Job's place. Their viewpoint was strictly detached and academic. No wonder then that Job replied as he did: "How long will you torment me and crush me with words?" His friends' feeble attempts at comforting him actually had the effect of tormenting and crushing him. He felt they were continually scolding him for his sins. That led him to say, "Ten times now you have reproached me," a round number expressing their repeated attacks.

Job then resorted to sarcasm when he continued, "If it is true that I have gone astray, my error remains my concern alone." From those words it appears that he was neither confessing nor denying he had done wrong but was telling them it was none of their business. If he had done wrong, it was God he had to deal with. Job also resented their manner of making themselves look good at his expense.

In his desperation Job again turned to blaming God for his troubles and viewing God as taking delight in afflicting him. Job did not know that it was Satan who was tormenting him and desperately trying to get him to renounce his faith in God. Fortunately, Satan did not succeed, but he did drive Job to the point of making some strong accusations against God, accusations he later deeply regretted. Listen to him speak about God.

⁷ "Though I cry, 'I've been wronged!' I get no response;
    though I call for help, there is no justice.
⁸ He has blocked my way so I cannot pass;
    he has shrouded my paths in darkness.
⁹ He has stripped me of my honor
    and removed the crown from my head.
¹⁰ He tears me down on every side till I am gone;
    he uproots my hope like a tree.
¹¹ His anger burns against me;
    he counts me among his enemies.
¹² His troops advance in force;
    they build a siege ramp against me
    and encamp around my tent.

These words of Job are striking in their imagery and expressive of the turmoil raging within his soul. They are words of a suffering and desperate man. Using one illustration after another, Job pictures God treating him as an enemy and refusing to listen to his pleas for justice. He felt that God had built up a wall to prevent him from coming to God. Like a strong warrior, God had ruthlessly attacked him and taken from him his honor and power. He who had ruled over a magnificent estate was now sitting in disgrace among the rubbish, stricken by disease and tormented by pain. Job's great hopes of noble descendants had been dashed when the storm killed his children. He felt he had nothing left to live for. He hoped his days on earth would soon end.

He was convinced that God regarded him as his enemy and was attacking him as an army besieges its enemy in war. He also felt himself forsaken by his friends, neighbors, and even his own wife, as we learn from the verses that follow.

¹³ "He has alienated my brothers from me;
    my acquaintances are completely estranged from me.

¹⁴ My kinsmen have gone away;
　　my friends have forgotten me.
¹⁵ My guests and my maidservants count me a stranger;
　　they look upon me as an alien.
¹⁶ I summon my servant, but he does not answer,
　　though I beg him with my own mouth.
¹⁷ My breath is offensive to my wife;
　　I am loathsome to my own brothers.
¹⁸ Even the little boys scorn me;
　　when I appear, they ridicule me.
¹⁹ All my intimate friends detest me;
　　those I love have turned against me.
²⁰ I am nothing but skin and bones;
　　I have escaped with only the skin of my teeth.

Job continued to blame God for his troubles. In this section Job described in graphic detail the abrupt changes for the worse in his social life. Job felt that God had afflicted him so that he had become utterly repulsive to all who looked at him. His friends and relatives avoided him. House guests to whom he had shown generous hospitality now regarded him as a stranger. Servants who had formerly promptly carried out his orders now ignored him when he called them. The offensive odors given off by his diseased body drove people away. The stench from his breath made him repulsive to his wife. He who had been honored and respected as a great man was now ridiculed even by little children. Except for the men sitting with him, he was alone. And they only added to his misery with their tactless words. This section closes with a striking expression that has often been quoted: "I have escaped with only the skin of my teeth."

Can we try to put ourselves in Job's place? How would we respond in such a situation? Would our words be kinder and gentler than Job's? Would we be less inclined to complain to our fellow human beings or to God? If we were forsaken by relatives and acquaintances as Job was, if we were made to feel we were forsaken even by God, would we stand up better than Job? Hardly, we fear.

At this point Job appears to have hit an all-time low. He was in the dumps. He felt desperate. We might safely say that of all the characters in the Bible, none was more forsaken than Job—except one, Jesus Christ. As our Savior hung on the cross, he uttered those plaintive words, "My God, my God, why have you forsaken me?" (Matthew 27:46; Mark 15:34; see Psalm 22:1). During the moments he hung on the cross, our Savior was indeed forsaken by his heavenly Father, and unlike even Job, he suffered the pangs of hell for all of us—including Job, you, and me. He did so in order that you and I might for all eternity be spared that dreadful experience of being forsaken by God.

It was this Savior who was Job's only hope in his despair. Of him Job made a most remarkable confession later in this chapter. But meanwhile he issued an urgent plea to his three friends.

> ²¹"Have pity on me, my friends, have pity,
>   for the hand of God has struck me.
> ²² Why do you pursue me as God does?
>   Will you never get enough of my flesh?

Job pleaded with his friends to have pity on him. In his misery and pain, he felt that the hand of God had struck him. He yearned for some comfort and support from those who owed it to him. He feared that such would not be the case, judging from their previous performance, so he asked a double question: "Why do you pursue me as God does? Will you never get enough of my flesh?" It appeared as if his friends took almost sadistic delight in attacking him. There seemed to be no end to their malicious accusations.

With those words Job hit rock bottom, but he was soon to rise to the mountaintop with words that give expression to his greatest hope, words that have been a source of comfort to countless Christians over the centuries that have passed since Job spoke them.

Job expresses his faith in his Redeemer and his hope of his own resurrection

²³ "Oh, that my words were recorded,
    that they were written on a scroll,
²⁴ that they were inscribed with an iron tool on lead,
    or engraved in rock forever!
²⁵ I know that my Redeemer lives,
    and that in the end he will stand upon the earth.
²⁶ And after my skin has been destroyed,
    yet in my flesh I will see God;
²⁷ I myself will see him
    with my own eyes—I, and not another.
    How my heart yearns within me!

Job had repeatedly protested that he was innocent of the charges his friends had made against him. Unknowingly, his friends had served Satan's purposes in attacking Job, for Satan had accused Job of selfish motives in serving God. Satan had maintained that if God would stretch out his hand and strike Job, Job would curse him to his face (1:11). Satan had boldly accused Job of not being a true child of God.

Job's three friends played right into Satan's hands by concluding that since Job suffered so much, he must have been guilty of some very special sins and so could hardly be a child of God. While he did not deny that he was a sinner, Job was convinced that his friends had accused him unjustly. He desperately sought to defend himself. Since he was apparently making no headway in convincing his friends, he wished that his words might be recorded so that his defense of his righteousness might be preserved for future generations.

Since the ordinary writing materials of that day would be subject to the destructive forces of nature and the ravages of time, he expressed the wish that his words could be engraved on a rock forever with an iron stylus.

Job's wish indeed came true. His words were probably not engraved with a stylus on a rock, but they have been preserved for future generations. In this book that we are reading we have Job's words, as well as the words of the other speakers. In his wonderful way God inspired the author of the book of Job to write this book, a book in which profound instruction is clothed in beautifully poetic language. That is surely true of every verse in this book, but it is true in a special sense of the words that immediately follow the expression of Job's wish, verses 25 to 27.

The words "I know that my Redeemer lives" are a profound and confident expression of faith in the coming Savior. Job had learned of the true God, Yahweh (Jehovah), and lived in a close relationship with him, as we know from chapters 1 and 2. In his conversation with Satan, God highly commended Job and called him his servant and a man who was blameless and upright (1:8; 2:3).

As a man who lived on such close terms with God, Job must also have known of the Savior to come and of the prophecies about his death and resurrection. It must have been his faith in his God and Savior that kept him from collapsing under his severe sufferings and trials. As Job looked ahead in faith to his Savior, he could for the moment forget his present troubles and in faith see what lay ahead for him after his life on earth had ended. These words express the firm hope of Job's own bodily resurrection after his death and that hope has been shared by true believers ever since.

It is on the basis of these words that the poet Samuel Medley wrote the beloved Easter hymn "I Know that My Redeemer Lives" (*Christian Worship* [CW] 152). In the 32 lines of those 8 stanzas, the word "lives" occurs in every line except 2. Job confessed, "I know that my Redeemer lives."

And because his Redeemer would again arise from the dead and live, Job was confident that he too would be raised from the dead and see his Redeemer face-to-face. The last word in verse 25, "earth," can more literally be translated as "dust." In this verse it refers to the grave, from which Job expects his Redeemer to raise him to life.

From these verses we can conclude that Job believed that he would be raised from the dead. There are also other passages in the Old Testament that strongly suggest the teaching of the resurrection from the dead. The expression "he was gathered to his people" occurs several times in the Old Testament. It is used with reference to the death of Abraham (Genesis 25:8), Ishmael (Genesis 25:17), Isaac (Genesis 35:29), Jacob (Genesis 49:29,33), Aaron (Numbers 20:24,26; 27:13), and Moses (Deuteronomy 32:50). It is also used with reference to the death of a few others in the Old Testament. That expression suggests more than merely the burial of the person's body in a grave near his relatives. It implies that those people were still in existence in the other world. When they died they were not annihilated, but their souls lived on, to be reunited with their bodies at the resurrection. Our Savior himself declares that Abraham, Isaac, and Jacob are in heaven. He says, "I say to you that many will come from the east and the west, and will take their places at the feast with Abraham, Isaac and Jacob in the kingdom of heaven" (Matthew 8:11).

When the Lord appeared to Moses in the burning bush, he identified himself by saying, "I am the God of your father, the God of Abraham, the God of Isaac and the God of Jacob" (Exodus 3:6). Jesus quoted that passage as proof of the resurrection when he engaged in a dispute with the Sadducees, who denied that teaching. He demolished their arguments against the resurrection when he said, "About the resurrection of the dead—have you not read what God said to you, 'I am the God of Abraham, the God of Isaac, and the God of Jacob'? He is not the God of the dead but of the living" (Matthew 22:31,32).

There are passages in the Old Testament that also indicate that King David believed that he would be raised from the dead. He gives expression to such faith in some of his psalms. Addressing the Lord, he closes one psalm with the beautiful words, "And I—in righteousness I will see your face; when I awake, I will be satisfied with seeing your likeness" (Psalm 17:15). In those words David is not merely speaking of awaking from natural sleep the next morning; he is speaking of awaking from the sleep of death, after which he will see God, just as Job confesses that he will see God in the words of this chapter of his book.

That David believed in the resurrection is also evident from his words after the death of his son. God had sent his prophet Nathan to impress David with the seriousness of his adultery with Bathsheba. Nathan told David that the child of their adulterous union would die. After the prophet left, the child became seriously ill. Deeply repentant, David fasted and pleaded with God to spare the infant's life. A week later the child died. When he learned of his son's death, David made a remarkable statement. He said, "I will go to him, but he will not return to me" (2 Samuel 12:23). Those words surely express the hope of a reunion with the child after death.

In the last chapter of his book, Daniel prophesies the resurrection with words that are unmistakably clear: "Multitudes who sleep in the dust of the earth will awake: some to everlasting life, others to shame and everlasting contempt" (Daniel 12:2). There can be no question that those words clearly state that all the dead—believers and unbelievers—will be raised from the dead on the Last Day. Jesus makes that abundantly clear when he tells the Jews, "Do not be amazed at this, for a time is coming when all who are in their graves will hear his voice and come out—those who have done good will rise to live, and those who have done evil will rise to be condemned" (John 5:28,29).

As believers in Old Testament times, Abraham, Isaac, Jacob, Moses, David, and Daniel could in spirit join Job in confessing, "I know that my Redeemer lives." Those words can also be the confession of every believer, including you and me, as surely as we trust in Jesus for our salvation. These words of Job clearly profess his faith in the Redeemer who on the Last Day will raise him from the dead.

And yet many Bible scholars today maintain that this passage does not refer to the resurrection. They claim that Job is merely speaking of appearing in the presence of God, who will defend him against the charges leveled against him. Instead of translating the Hebrew word *Go'el* as "Redeemer," some translate it as "Vindicator," one who defends someone against unjust charges and declares him innocent. Although it is true that Jesus will defend Job against the attacks of Satan as well as the three friends, "Vindicator" is an inadequate translation of the Hebrew word. The word *Go'el* also includes the idea of "kinsman," "relative," and in the Book of Ruth it is thus rendered in some translations when it speaks of Boaz. A prominent aspect of the word *Go'el* is that of claiming back something or someone from another's authority and servitude. Therefore, the word *redeem* is the best one to express the idea of the Hebrew word in verse 25.

The expression "Redeemer" is indeed appropriate for our Savior, in whom Job confesses his faith in these verses. Jesus Christ is our Kinsman. True God from eternity, he was born as a real human being. He became our Kinsman, our Brother, our Immanuel, God with us. He assumed our flesh and blood, lived a perfect life, was crucified, died, was buried, and rose again. With Job we can truly confess, "I know that my Redeemer lives."

In his book *Faith on Trial,* Roland Cap Ehlke states, "Someday God himself will come and redeem Job, that is, save him or defend him. Not only will God redeem Job from false accusations, but from death itself" (page 33). Such is also our hope as Christians.

In the original Hebrew this passage, particularly verse 26, is one of the most difficult passages in the Old Testament. It has proved to be very challenging to translators throughout the centuries in its vocabulary and grammar. In particular, the verb in the first line of verse 26 has been a challenge to translators and interpreters. There are two possible meanings for the verb in the Hebrew text. Such is the case also with certain English verbs—for example, the verb *cleave*, which may mean either "split" or "cling."

The NIV, from which the text is given for this book, translates the verb in the first line of verse 26 as "has been destroyed." Most English versions translate it similarly. The King James Version adds the word *worms:* "Worms destroy this body." As the italics in the KJV indicate, that word is not in the Hebrew text. The translation "has been destroyed," as in the NIV, is surely a possible translation.

Although most versions translate the verb with the meaning of "destroy," it can be translated differently. In his German

Bible Martin Luther translates that word with the German expression "*umgeben werden,*" which means "be surrounded." William F. Beck also translates it in that manner in his American Translation. That translation has support from two early translations of the Old Testament: the Greek translation known as the Septuagint, a few centuries before Christ, and the Latin translation known as the Vulgate, about A.D. 400.

The authors of one of our Lutheran confessions, *The Formula of Concord,* also understood that verb to mean "surround" rather than "destroy." In his *Popular Commentary of the Bible,* Old Testament, Volume 2, P. E. Kretzmann interprets that word to mean "surround" rather than "destroy." Speaking of Job, Dr. Kretzmann states, "He is sure that there will be a glorious resurrection of the body on the Last Day, that the very skin which clothed him during his mortal life here on earth will again cover the flesh which has become subject to decay and corruption. . . . The body which, in the corruption of death, was stripped of its skin will once more be clothed with that covering, and then, from out of that same body, Job would see God" (pages 27,28).

The author of this volume of The People's Bible also prefers the translation "surround." While it is certainly true that our bodies will decay and our skin will be destroyed in death, it is equally true that each of us will be raised up with the same body and one's own skin, but in a glorified condition. It appears to this writer that the entire verse speaks of the resurrection.

In this remarkable confession of faith in his Redeemer, Job looked forward to seeing God. He declared, "In my flesh I will see God." How could Job see God during this life? Didn't God tell Moses, "No one may see me and live" (Exodus 33:20)? In his sinful flesh while he was here on earth, Job could not bear to see God. Were he to do so, he would be annihilated.

When he spoke the words of these verses, he was referring to the afterlife, when in heaven he would see God. That is clear from his concluding words in this beautiful passage: "I myself will see him [God] with my own eyes—I, and not another. How my heart yearns within me!" The word translated as "heart" literally means "kidneys." In the Old Testament the internal organs were regarded as the seat of the deepest emotions. Job yearned to be with God in heaven. Isn't that also true in the case of some elderly Christians who have suffered trials and afflictions during their lifetimes? We have heard such people say, "How I wish I could die and go to heaven!"

The message of these verses from the book of Job has been beautifully expressed by an unknown author in two stanzas of the hymn "Jesus Christ, My Sure Defense." Whether we read or sing those stanzas, we can share with Job in the confident assurance of the resurrection of our own body.

> Glorified, I shall anew
> With this flesh then be enshrouded;
> In this body I shall view
> God, my Lord, with eyes unclouded;
> In this flesh I then shall see
> Jesus Christ eternally.
>
> Then these eyes my Lord shall know,
> My Redeemer and my Brother;
> In His love my soul shall glow—
> I myself, and not another!
> Then the weakness I feel here
> Shall forever disappear.
>
> (TLH 206:5,6)

[28] **"If you say, 'How we will hound him,**
since the root of the trouble lies in him,'

²⁹ **you should fear the sword yourselves;**
    for wrath will bring punishment by the sword,
    and then you will know that there is judgment."

After his eloquent and noble confession of faith in his
Redeemer, Job rather abruptly returns to the matter he had
been discussing with his friends. He had been, so to speak,
transported for a moment into heaven. Now he was back on
earth, still suffering from his severe physical ailments and
the unkind treatment of his friends.

He warned his friends against continuing to accuse him
unjustly. The concluding verse in this chapter issues his
warning: "You should fear the sword yourselves, for wrath
will bring punishment by the sword, and then you will
know that there is judgment." His words proved to be
prophetic, for we read in the concluding chapter of this
book, "After the LORD had said these things to Job, he said
to Eliphaz the Temanite, 'I am angry with you and your
two friends, because you have not spoken of me what is
right, as my servant Job has. So now take seven bulls and
seven rams and go to my servant Job and sacrifice a burnt
offering for yourselves. My servant Job will pray for you,
and I will accept his prayer and not deal with you according to your folly. You have not spoken of me what is right,
as my servant Job has" (42:7,8).

Zophar's second speech

Zophar reacts to Job's speech

20 Then Zophar the Naamathite replied:

² **"My troubled thoughts prompt me to answer**
    because I am greatly disturbed.
³ **I hear a rebuke that dishonors me,**
    and my understanding inspires me to reply.

A considerable amount of time must have passed since Zophar had last spoken. Chapter 11 records his first speech, a rather brief speech of 20 verses. In his blunt manner, Zophar had been sharply critical of Job. His sharp words caused a strong reaction from Job (12:2,3). Job's response to Zophar was his longest up to that time, comprising a total of 75 verses in 3 chapters.

That long response as well as Job's next two speeches (chapters 16,17,19) must have struck a tender nerve in Zophar and disturbed him greatly. He appears to have been anxiously waiting to get back at Job for the humiliation he felt he had suffered. Now that he finally had his opportunity, he first gave expression to his displeasure over Job's remarks. Then, in the verses that follow, he continued on the theme that he and his two friends had been pursuing.

The end of the wicked is disastrous

4 "Surely you know how it has been from of old,
      ever since man was placed on the earth,
5 that the mirth of the wicked is brief,
      the joy of the godless lasts but a moment.
6 Though his pride reaches to the heavens
      and his head touches the clouds,
7 he will perish forever, like his own dung;
      those who have seen him will say, 'Where is he?'
8 Like a dream he flies away, no more to be found,
      banished like a vision of the night.
9 The eye that saw him will not see him again;
      his place will look on him no more.
10 His children must make amends to the poor;
      his own hands must give back his wealth.
11 The youthful vigor that fills his bones
      will lie with him in the dust.

Zophar's words reflect a condescending attitude toward Job. The words "surely you know" suggest that Job really had no case at all. The argument was closed. By his words Zophar implied, "Come on, Job, admit that you're wrong and I'm right. You can't be so ignorant as to deny that what I'm saying is true."

Then Zophar essentially repeated the theme that Eliphaz (4:7–5:14; 15:20-35) and Bildad (8:12-22; 18:5-21) had previously pursued in their argument with Job. Like all of the previous speeches, this speech by Zophar abounds in poetic expressions. While the speeches of the three friends basically have the same theme, each of them differs from the others in details. What the three friends said is rather superficial and oversimplified, but the language they used is strikingly beautiful. The reader might wonder how Job and his friends could speak in such exquisitely poetic language while they were discussing such profound subjects as good and evil, prosperity and adversity. One thing is clear: the author who recorded their words was a superb master of literary expression. No one who has read and studied the book can deny that.

In these verses Zophar first appealed to ancient tradition. He said that from earliest times the good fortune of the wicked person has changed to bad. The wicked's joy would be brief and momentary and his honor would be turned to dishonor. His success would be as fleeting as images in a dream, and he himself would disappear so that he would no longer be recognized. According to verse 10, the wicked would be reduced to poverty, so that his children would be indebted even to the poor. Because the wicked father had cheated others out of their money and impoverished them, his own children would impoverish themselves by having to pay back that debt. In the end, the ungodly person himself will die and be buried. Zophar's words suggest that the wicked person's death will be a dishonorable one.

It seems as if Zophar was at least indirectly pointing his finger at Job and implying that he was such a wicked person. He implied that Job had acquired his wealth at the expense of others and was now brought low through the calamities that had befallen him.

We might ask, Is this always true of the wicked? Does an ungodly person always come to a disastrous end in this life? Haven't there been many instances in which the opposite is true—that the wicked appear to succeed throughout this life? Not so, according to Zophar, as we learn from his next words.

Troubles afflict the wicked in this life

¹² "Though evil is sweet in his mouth
   and he hides it under his tongue,
¹³ though he cannot bear to let it go
   and keeps it in his mouth,
¹⁴ yet his food will turn sour in his stomach;
   it will become the venom of serpents within him.
¹⁵ He will spit out the riches he swallowed;
   God will make his stomach vomit them up.
¹⁶ He will suck the poison of serpents;
   the fangs of an adder will kill him.
¹⁷ He will not enjoy the streams,
   the rivers flowing with honey and cream.
¹⁸ What he toiled for he must give back uneaten;
   he will not enjoy the profit from his trading.
¹⁹ For he has oppressed the poor and left them destitute;
   he has seized houses he did not build.
²⁰ "Surely he will have no respite from his craving;
   he cannot save himself by his treasure.
²¹ Nothing is left for him to devour;
   his prosperity will not endure.
²² In the midst of his plenty, distress will overtake him;
   the full force of misery will come upon him.

Zophar pictures the evil that a wicked person commits as delightful food that he enjoys. After he has eaten it, however, he suffers severe indigestion which leads to vomiting. The food turns to poison in his stomach. According to Zophar the evildoer's greed is fatal. "He will suck the poison of serpents; the fangs of an adder will kill him."

Zophar's language in these verses is unusually picturesque. The point he was making was that the very activity the wicked man enjoys carries within it the seeds of his own destruction. In his greed the evildoer will not live to enjoy that which he contrived to gain for himself. In fact, he will have to restore the wealth he accumulated, and he himself will end up being impoverished.

Verse 17 describes prosperity under the picture of "rivers flowing with honey and cream," or as the last word might better be translated, "curds." In the pre-refrigeration days of old, the milk was preserved in a form similar to cottage cheese or yogurt. Milk and honey were symbols of prosperity, as we know from the expression "land of milk and honey." But the evildoer would have no such prosperity, according to Zophar. Instead, he would find himself in the miserable condition of having a constant craving that could not be satisfied. He would experience distress where he had previously enjoyed plenty. Again, was Zophar pointing a finger at Job?

> [23] When he has filled his belly,
>   God will vent his burning anger against him
>   and rain down his blows upon him.
> [24] Though he flees from an iron weapon,
>   a bronze-tipped arrow pierces him.
> [25] He pulls it out of his back,
>   the gleaming point out of his liver.
> Terrors will come over him;

²⁶ **total darkness lies in wait for his treasures.**
A fire unfanned will consume him
and devour what is left in his tent.
²⁷ **The heavens will expose his guilt;**
the earth will rise up against him.
²⁸ **A flood will carry off his house,**
rushing waters on the day of God's wrath.
²⁹ **Such is the fate God allots the wicked,**
the heritage appointed for them by God."

In these verses the picture of the evildoer's plight changes from that of food poisoning to that of violent destruction. Earlier Job had spoken of God as attacking him (19:7-12). Now Zophar pictured God as violently attacking a wicked man. "The evildoer will discover the truth in the adage that while God's anger kindles slowly, it burns exceedingly hot. When God's anger burns hotly, he *will rain* on his foe an arsenal of munition from his heavenly storehouse" (John E. Hartley, *The Book of Job,* page 307).

Zophar's reference to the "bronze-tipped arrow" appears to recall Job's earlier remarks that God shot his poisoned arrows into Job (6:4; 16:13). By indirectly identifying Job with the ungodly man he was describing, Zophar seems to have rejected Job's earlier appeal to God as his witness in heaven (16:19) and his recent confession of faith in his Redeemer (19:25-27). Job's profound words in the previous chapter apparently rolled off Zophar like water off a duck's back.

Zophar concluded his last speech in a manner similar to Bildad's conclusion of his previous speech (18:21). Zophar could see only one thing in this discussion: God will destroy the wicked even in this world. That is utterly untrue, as experience has indicated time and again throughout history.

Job's reply to Zophar

Job pleads with his friends to listen

21 Then Job replied:

² "Listen carefully to my words;
 let this be the consolation you give me.
³ Bear with me while I speak,
 and after I have spoken, mock on.

⁴ "Is my complaint directed to man?
 Why should I not be impatient?
⁵ Look at me and be astonished;
 clap your hand over your mouth.
⁶ When I think about this, I am terrified;
 trembling seizes my body.

Zophar had lectured Job on the troubles of the ungodly. Without directly labeling Job as such an ungodly person, Zophar had strongly implied that Job was. Like his two friends, Zophar had shown no sympathy to Job.

Having concluded that his friends could offer him no consolation by their words, Job pleaded with them to be quiet long enough to listen to what he had to say. They could at least offer him comfort by remaining silent.

Job began by addressing all three of his friends. In the Hebrew, the verb forms in verse 2 and the first half of verse 3 are in the plural, as though he was saying, "All three of you listen; all three of you bear with me." But then Job apparently turned to Zophar, the last speaker, and addressed him in the words "mock on." The form of that verb is in the singular. No doubt Job referred to the harsh words Zophar had just spoken.

Verses 4 to 6 are introductory to Job's speech in this chapter. His disturbed state of mind is reflected in his language. A very literal translation of verse 4 would read, "And I—to man is my complaint?" In better English we could translate it, "As for me, is my complaint to man?" His question "Is my complaint directed to man?" implies that Job was complaining to God rather than to his friends, as he had also previously complained to God (6:1-9). Perhaps there were two reasons why his complaint was directed to God rather than men. First, he felt that God had sent this affliction upon him. Second, he still had hope that God would help him and eventually deliver him from his troubles. His friends offered no such hope.

In another appeal to his unsympathetic friends, Job begged them to look at his emaciated and disease-wracked body in the hope that it might lead them to express at least a little sympathy for him. He also urged them to put their hands over their mouths and refrain from speaking, since their words only added to his irritation.

Job confessed that his physical troubles terrified him. No doubt he dreaded the prospect of suffering even greater pain and discomfort. He also must have been tempted to believe that God was not just but that he blessed the ungodly with success whereas he made the righteous Job suffer pain and humiliation. The words that follow relate what Job had observed about the prosperity of the wicked.

The wicked seem to prosper in this life

⁷ Why do the wicked live on,
  growing old and increasing in power?
⁸ They see their children established around them,
  their offspring before their eyes.
⁹ Their homes are safe and free from fear;
  the rod of God is not upon them.
¹⁰ Their bulls never fail to breed;
  their cows calve and do not miscarry.

¹¹ **They send forth their children as a flock;**
    their little ones dance about.
¹² **They sing to the music of tambourine and harp;**
    they make merry to the sound of the flute.
¹³ **They spend their years in prosperity**
    and go down to the grave in peace.
¹⁴ **Yet they say to God, 'Leave us alone!**
    We have no desire to know your ways.
¹⁵ **Who is the Almighty, that we should serve him?**
    What would we gain by praying to him?'
¹⁶ **But their prosperity is not in their own hands,**
    so I stand aloof from the counsel of the wicked.

In an exaggerated manner, Job's friends had pictured the misfortunes of the wicked in this life. They had stated that the ungodly suffer troubles and disasters whereas the righteous are successful and happy. Reacting to their false and one-sided statements, Job pictured the wicked as successful in whatever they undertake. In his anxious attempts to correct their false statements, Job was also guilty of overstatement and oversimplification. But since he was comparing the apparent success of the wicked with his own wretched situation, it's understandable that he spoke as he did.

"Why do the wicked live on, growing old and increasing in power?" The word translated as "power" also suggests "wealth." Through their resources in property and money, those ungodly people gained great influence and power. Such influence and power Job himself had formerly enjoyed, but suddenly disaster after disaster had struck him and driven him from his large estate to the ash heap where he was now sitting.

Job's three friends had falsely stated that an individual's suffering is commensurate with his sin: the more one suffers, the more he must have sinned. They had also maintained that the more godly a person is, the more he will prosper in this life. Job sharply disagreed with that simplistic theory. In verses 7 to 9 he took issue with specific statements that each of his three friends had made. Zophar had recently stated that the wicked die prematurely (20:11). Job maintained that the wicked live on, grow old, and increase in power (verse 7). Bildad had said that the wicked die childless (18:19). Job declared that they have many children and that their children become prosperous (verse 8). Eliphaz had asserted that if Job would turn to God in repentance, his "tent" (home) would be safe (5:24). Job said the homes of the wicked were safe and at peace (verse 9).

It seemed to Job as if everything the ungodly did was crowned with success. Their livestock reproduced without fail. Since fertile herds were regarded as a blessing from God, Job must have been tempted to conclude that God loved the wicked more than he loved Job, who had lost his livestock. In contrast to him, the wicked enjoyed large flocks of healthy livestock. The wealth of their flocks and herds seemed to guarantee security to their households. Their little children enjoyed dancing and singing and were apparently carefree. As they grew older, they experienced prosperity.

In two psalms (127:3,4; 128:3,4) the Bible describes children as a great blessing of God. To Job that was a perplexing problem. Why should God bless the wicked with many children and permit the God-fearing Job to be deprived of his seven sons and three daughters? Didn't it seem as if God showed favoritism to the ungodly? Hadn't God apparently heaped blessing after blessing upon those people whose conduct and life didn't merit those blessings? It certainly seemed as if they had it made!

It also disturbed Job to observe that in spite of their material prosperity, the wicked did not acknowledge God as the

Giver of all good things. On the contrary, they defied God and wanted nothing to do with him. Job described their attitude well in verses 14 and 15: "Yet they say to God, 'Leave us alone! We have no desire to know your ways. Who is the Almighty, that we should serve him? What would we gain by praying to him?'" Those words are certainly descriptive of the attitude of many today who are blessed in material things and yet renounce God.

Yet in spite of what Job said about the prosperity of the wicked in this life, he did believe that their success was only temporary. At least it would not last beyond this life. By his words "But their prosperity is not in their own hands" he probably meant that they did not have final control over their prosperity and their destiny. That was in God's hands, not their own. Therefore, regardless of how much he had to suffer, Job wanted nothing to do with the lifestyle of the wicked. As a child of God, Job was aware of the fact that the final destiny of a godly person is a truly happy and blessed one, but that "the way of the ungodly shall perish" (Psalm 1:6, KJV). Although at times Job questioned whether it was worthwhile to be a believer, this statement expresses his belief that it is truly worthwhile.

In his deep suffering and his irritation over the words of his friends, however, Job returned to his theme of the prosperity of the ungodly, as the verses that follow indicate.

> [17] "Yet how often is the lamp of the wicked snuffed out?
> How often does calamity come upon them,
> the fate God allots in his anger?
> [18] How often are they like straw before the wind,
> like chaff swept away by a gale?
> [19] It is said, 'God stores up a man's punishment for his sons.'
> Let him repay the man himself, so that he will know it!

²⁰ Let his own eyes see his destruction;
    let him drink of the wrath of the Almighty.
²¹ For what does he care about the family he leaves behind
    when his allotted months come to an end?

²² "Can anyone teach knowledge to God,
    since he judges even the highest?
²³ One man dies in full vigor,
    completely secure and at ease,
²⁴ his body well nourished,
    his bones rich with marrow.
²⁵ Another man dies in bitterness of soul,
    never having enjoyed anything good.
²⁶ Side by side they lie in the dust,
    and worms cover them both.

Although he had stated that he himself would not adopt the lifestyle of the wicked (verse 16), Job reaffirmed his opinion that those people prosper during their lifetime. Job's opening statement in this section is a rebuttal of Bildad's assertion that "the lamp of the wicked is snuffed out" (18:5). Changing the word picture, he continued by asking how often the ungodly are swept away like straw and chaff in the wind. His questions are worded in such a manner as to expect the answer, "Rarely, if ever."

The verses that follow (verses 19-21) are rather difficult. In the NIV the words "It is said" are given in half-brackets, indicating that they are not in the Hebrew text. The addition of those three words suggests that Job quoted the position of his friends and not his own. Job did not agree with Eliphaz (5:4) and Zophar (20:10) that God stores up a man's punishment for his sons. Job's friends used the argument of delayed retribution, that the children of the wicked would suffer punishment for the sins of their father.

In his anxiety Job appears to have overreacted, but he was closer to the truth than were his friends. He felt that it would be a matter of little concern to the wicked man if his children suffered disaster after his death. To Job it seemed that such an ungodly person would hardly place his children's interest above his own. In Job's opinion the wicked would be judged on the basis of his own rejection of God and his own evil doings, and so would his sons. That judgment, however, would not necessarily occur during this lifetime.

Job confessed that we cannot understand God, much less presume to instruct him. God, who judges the highest, including even the angels, surely knows how to deal with us mere mortals. Yet it is often difficult for us to understand and accept his dealings with us. It seems as if some people experience success in whatever they do and live in luxury. In Job's words, "One man dies in full vigor, completely secure and at ease, his body well nourished, his bones rich with marrow." Others meet the opposite fate, as we learn from the words of Job that follow: "Another man dies in bitterness of soul, never having enjoyed anything good." The pitiful condition of the world's many poor and homeless comes to mind.

Regardless of whether or not they prosper during their lifetime, all people must expect to die. In Job's words, "Side by side they lie in the dust, and worms cover them both." After death all are subject to the process of disintegration, and the grave knows no difference and shows no preference. Job's words are sobering indeed.

According to Job, it simply does not follow that the godly always prosper and the ungodly always meet affliction in this life. Job had repeatedly pointed out that the opposite is often true. His concluding words in this chapter again state his position.

> ²⁷ **"I know full well what you are thinking,**
> **the schemes by which you would wrong me.**

²⁸ **You say, 'Where now is the great man's house,**
   the tents where wicked men lived?'
²⁹ **Have you never questioned those who travel?**
   Have you paid no regard to their accounts—
³⁰ **that the evil man is spared from the day of calamity,**
   that he is delivered from the day of wrath?
³¹ **Who denounces his conduct to his face?**
   Who repays him for what he has done?
³² **He is carried to the grave,**
   and watch is kept over his tomb.
³³ **The soil in the valley is sweet to him;**
   all men follow after him,
   and a countless throng goes before him.

³⁴ **"So how can you console me with your nonsense?**
   Nothing is left of your answers but falsehood!"

Job realized that his friends were judging him to be
wicked because he was suffering the fate they claimed
only the wicked suffer. Their question "Where now is
the great man's house, the tents where wicked men
lived?" was clearly pointed at him. Their logic: the
wicked suffer; Job suffers; therefore, Job is wicked. That
hurt him deeply.

Again Job reminded his friends that there are many
instances of ungodly people who are "spared from the day
of calamity." People do not rebuke them or requite them
for their evil deeds. In his commentary on Job, Norman
C. Habel states, "Since tyrants have great power, they are
not 'requited' by any earthly court or authority (v. 31b).
Subjects prefer to flatter despots rather than denounce
them. Even in death the rich tyrant is accompanied by
a grand procession of fawning followers" (page 330). We
see many examples of that today. Preachers pronounce
glowing eulogies over the caskets of influential men who
during their lifetime did not hesitate to take advantage
of others.

Job's closing words in this speech express his strong dissatisfaction with the vain attempts of his friends to console him. He called their words "nonsense" and "falsehood." What they said was worthless, untrue, and unkind. We would all do well to examine ourselves and pray for God to enable us to be more helpful and sympathetic when we are in a position to help others who experience afflictions.

The third round of discourses

Each of Job's three friends had expressed himself twice, and Job had answered each in turn. While the speeches of the three friends differed considerably in detail, all carried essentially the same message: the righteous are successful, but the wicked are unsuccessful during their lifetime. Job repeatedly protested that such was not the case. In fact, he said, the opposite was often true.

Perhaps all four were beginning to realize that they had reached an impasse, and that they were only talking past each other. But the friends gave it one more try. As we will see from the chapters that follow, Eliphaz spoke at some length (30 verses), Bildad had very little to say (6 verses), and Zophar said nothing at all the third time around. The friends were apparently running out of ammunition. On the other hand, Job spoke at considerable length in this concluding round of discourses. But first it was Eliphaz's turn, so he took up the cudgels and did battle for his position.

Eliphaz's third speech

Job's wickedness is the cause of his disasters

22 Then Eliphaz the Temanite replied:
² "Can a man be of benefit to God?
Can even a wise man benefit him?

³ What pleasure would it give the Almighty if you
were righteous?
What would he gain if your ways were blameless?
⁴ "Is it for your piety that he rebukes you
and brings charges against you?
⁵ Is not your wickedness great?
Are not your sins endless?
⁶ You demanded security from your brothers
for no reason;
you stripped men of their clothing,
leaving them naked.
⁷ You gave no water to the weary
and you withheld food from the hungry,
⁸ though you were a powerful man, owning land—
an honored man, living on it.
⁹ And you sent widows away empty-handed
and broke the strength of the fatherless.
¹⁰ That is why snares are all around you,
why sudden peril terrifies you,
¹¹ why it is so dark you cannot see,
and why a flood of water covers you.

In its bluntness the tone of this final speech of Eliphaz differs considerably from his tactful first speech
(chapters 4,5). In his three speeches we can detect a
growing spirit of sharpness and impatience. Whereas at
first Eliphaz had spoken in rather vague generalities, in
his second speech he became more personal (15:3-13),
and in this final speech he directly attacked Job.

Beginning with several rhetorical questions, Eliphaz
asked Job if God needs human beings in order to exist and
be successful. The obvious answer is no. God is totally self-
sufficient. We poor mortals cannot do anything to help or
harm him. We cannot do anything that would put him under

bligation to us. Job would have agreed with Eliphaz's four questions in verses 2 and 3, and so must we.

In the questions that follow, however, Eliphaz became more personal. He had heard Job repeatedly protest his innocence of the charges his friends had leveled against him. While Job surely admitted that he was a sinner, he was unwilling to admit that his sins were so flagrant that they warranted the special afflictions he was enduring. Of course, neither Job nor his friends were aware of the fact that God had permitted Satan to afflict Job so severely to test the genuineness of his faith. While we cannot defend Job's sharp complaints against God, we can understand his feelings in his deep suffering. Moreover, his misery was only increased by the sharp and unkind words of his unfeeling friends.

Becoming more specific as he spoke, Eliphaz asked Job three questions that accused and condemned him. The first question (verse 4) obviously expects the answer no. No one is rebuked for his piety. Therefore, the implication was that Job was not pious but was ungodly, for he was suffering so much. Then Eliphaz asked two questions that imply the answer yes: "Is not your wickedness great? Are not your sins endless?" With those words Eliphaz outdid even Bildad and Zophar in accusing Job of extreme wickedness.

Eliphaz continued his false line of reasoning, an argument from effect to cause. Judging from Job's present miserable condition, Eliphaz trumped up false charges against him. He figured that Job must have been guilty of many faults and crimes since Job was now suffering so intensely. Eliphaz enumerated one social wrong after another. In the original Hebrew, the four verbs in verses 6 and 7 ("demanded," "stripped," "gave," "withheld") are all in the tense called the imperfect. The use of that tense indicates that those were repeated occurrences in the past. Eliphaz not only accused

Job of treating his fellow human beings shabbily, but of doing so regularly. If Job could have interrupted him at the time he spoke those words, he would probably have vehemently denied those charges. Not only do Job's own words in a later speech contradict that false accusation (29:12-17), but even Eliphaz's earlier words commend Job for his good deeds (4:3,4).

Now, however, Eliphaz accused Job of mistreating and cheating his fellow men, the weary and hungry, the widows and fatherless, even though he himself was well-to-do. Eliphaz arbitrarily maintained that Job's afflictions came upon him for those reasons. The expressions "snares," "peril," "dark," and "flood of water" are descriptive of the condition of a person who has experienced distress. Then to lend a religious tone to his accusing words, Eliphaz gave a brief but stirring account of the greatness of God.

God is majestic and great

> ¹² "Is not God in the heights of heaven?
> And see how lofty are the highest stars!
> ¹³ Yet you say, 'What does God know?
> Does he judge through such darkness?
> ¹⁴ Thick clouds veil him, so he does not see us
> as he goes about in the vaulted heavens.'
> ¹⁵ Will you keep to the old path
> that evil men have trod?
> ¹⁶ They were carried off before their time,
> their foundations washed away by a flood.
> ¹⁷ They said to God, 'Leave us alone!
> What can the Almighty do to us?'
> ¹⁸ Yet it was he who filled their houses with good things,
> so I stand aloof from the counsel of the wicked.
>
> ¹⁹ "The righteous see their ruin and rejoice;
> the innocent mock them, saying,

²⁰ **'Surely our foes are destroyed,
and fire devours their wealth.'**

Previously Job (9:4-13) and Zophar (11:7-9) had spoken of the majestic greatness of God. Now Eliphaz appealed to God's greatness in attempting to expose fallacies in Job's arguments and to help Job see his errors.

There could be no argument between the two men regarding the majestic greatness of God. Eliphaz had apparently misconstrued some earlier statements of Job. Job had spoken of God's majestic greatness, but Eliphaz interpreted his remarks to mean that God was ignorant of the affairs of human beings. Eliphaz pictured Job as a deist, one who believes in an impersonal god who does not care about what goes on in this world. As we know from many of his statements, that is untrue. To Job, God was a very personal God to whom he spoke, prayed, offered sacrifices, and rendered worship. During his suffering Job frankly brought his complaints to God. Job was surely no deist.

As a friend, Eliphaz ought to have known that Job was a godly man who faithfully practiced his religion. But Eliphaz ignored Job's godly life and former position of honor and prestige, and accused him of ungodly conduct. He asked Job, "Will you keep to the old path that evil men have trod?" Then, by way of warning, he referred to the disastrous end of some of those evil men: "They were carried off before their time, their foundations washed away by a flood." It's possible that Eliphaz was referring to the great flood described in the book of Genesis. The tradition of a universal flood was preserved among many ancient nations. The word translated as "flood" in this verse is not the same as used in the Genesis account; the word used by Eliphaz may also be translated as "river," as in many translations. Whether or not he had those people in mind, Eliphaz was uncharitably comparing Job to people like those who perished in the great flood and in the destruction of Sodom and Gomorrah.

In this speech Eliphaz repeated two statements Job had made in his previous speech. Job had represented the ungodly as addressing God in the words "Leave us alone" (21:14). Then, speaking for himself, Job added, "I stand aloof from the counsel of the wicked" (21:16). Without acknowledging that he had borrowed the two statements from Job, Eliphaz repeated them and maliciously implied that Job was included among the wicked who would have nothing to do with God. Eliphaz's comments about the ruin of the wicked (verse 19) and the "fire" that "devours their wealth" again suggest that the misfortunes of Job were the result of some special sins he had committed. What Eliphaz said did not apply to Job.

The remaining verses of Eliphaz's speech contain an appeal to Job to repent of those sins which Eliphaz had unjustly accused him.

The only solution: return to God

²¹ "Submit to God and be at peace with him;
    in this way prosperity will come to you.
²² Accept instruction from his mouth
    and lay up his words in your heart.
²³ If you return to the Almighty, you will be restored:
    If you remove wickedness far from your tent
²⁴ and assign your nuggets to the dust,
    your gold of Ophir to the rocks in the ravines,
²⁵ then the Almighty will be your gold,
    the choicest silver for you.
²⁶ Surely then you will find delight in the Almighty
    and will lift up your face to God.
²⁷ You will pray to him, and he will hear you,
    and you will fulfill your vows.
²⁸ What you decide on will be done,
    and light will shine on your ways.

²⁹ **When men are brought low and you say, 'Lift them up!'**
then he will save the downcast.
³⁰ **He will deliver even one who is not innocent,**
who will be delivered through the cleanness of
your hands."

Eliphaz now changed the tone of his speech. He
pleaded with Job. He began by saying, "Submit to God."
The Hebrew word translated as "submit" suggests that Job
place himself in God's service and make himself useful to
God. Eliphaz's words subtly imply that Job had not
served God, even though God himself had commended
Job as his servant (1:8). Eliphaz also urged Job to receive
instruction from God willingly instead of complaining of
his suffering.

Eliphaz was right in urging Job to turn to God. Job
needed to do so, just as Eliphaz, you, I, and all people
need to repent. Like all of us, Job also needed to turn to
God in prayer. There is much truth in Eliphaz's words in
the opening verses of this section. And yet his words
have a hollow ring. They reveal a lack of true sympathy
for his friend. Worse yet, some of his words subtly suggest that Job may have gained his wealth from unjust
practices (verses 23,24).

In a later speech (31:24-28) Job would strongly deny that
he was a slave to riches or that he gained them by unjust
means. Job was convinced that he had gained his great
wealth through proper means. He had not cheated or
defrauded people, and yet he lost his property. He must
have asked himself repeatedly, "Why did I lose it?"

No doubt intending to help Job, Eliphaz rather irritated
him when he repeatedly mentioned that God would bless him
by giving him gold if he repented. Implying that Job had lost
his wealth through his ungodliness, Eliphaz tried to assure
him that by turning to God he would receive gold and silver.

In verses 24 and 25, gold is mentioned three times and silver once. These verses might suggest that Eliphaz's name, which means "my God is gold," was indeed appropriate. It seems as if he liked to talk about it. However, it would be more charitable to interpret his name to mean "God is his treasure" than to mean his treasure is his god.

In his closing words Eliphaz tried to assure Job of the great blessings he would bring upon himself and others if he would turn to the Lord. God would hear his prayers and fulfill his decisions. Job would experience many blessings, as he had previously experienced them. He would pray for God to help the lowly, and God would do so.

Eliphaz closed his speech by assuring Job that he could even influence God to deliver one who is guilty. Did Eliphaz overshoot the mark when he said that? Some commentators think he did. They are of the opinion that the guilty will remain guilty despite the efforts of a righteous man and that the guilty will not be delivered. We can properly understand Eliphaz's words to express the truth that a godly person can effectively pray for the forgiveness of a guilty person and that God will forgive that person. We have an example of that in the closing chapter of this book. Because Job's three friends had unjustly accused Job, God was angry with them. He told Eliphaz that they had not spoken properly of God as his servant Job had. He ordered Eliphaz and his friends to sacrifice seven bulls and seven rams. He said his servant Job would pray for them. He accepted their offerings and Job's prayer and forgave them (42:7-9).

Ironically, Eliphaz's statement in verse 30 was fulfilled in that incident, and he himself was one of the guilty whom God delivered through Job's prayer. Although outwardly Eliphaz was a respectable person, the words in his final speech reveal an unkind attitude toward his suffering friend.

Did he and his friends appreciate Job's kindness and forgiving attitude that he showed when he prayed for them? Did they learn from that incident to be more forgiving themselves? Can you and I learn from this to be less judgmental and more charitable? Let's hope so.

Job's reply to Eliphaz

In this speech (chapters 23,24) Job's words are not directly addressed either to Eliphaz, who had previously spoken, or to God. Rather, his words indicate that Job was speaking to himself, wishing he could somehow approach God with his complaint. His complaint involves not only himself in his great suffering but also other people who were victims of injustice.

Job longs to meet God

23 Then Job replied:
² "Even today my complaint is bitter;
　　his hand is heavy in spite of my groaning.
³ If only I knew where to find him;
　　if only I could go to his dwelling!
⁴ I would state my case before him
　　and fill my mouth with arguments.
⁵ I would find out what he would answer me,
　　and consider what he would say.
⁶ Would he oppose me with great power?
　　No, he would not press charges against me.
⁷ There an upright man could present his case before him,
　　and I would be delivered forever from my judge.

Job's speech begins with the words, "Even today my complaint is bitter." Do the words "even today" imply that another day had passed since Job had previously spoken? Had perhaps several days passed? During how long a period of time did the discussion between Job and his friends take place? Did their discussion go on uninterrupted, or did it resume after one day or several days of recess? Could the length of the discussion up to this time (chapters 3–22) as well as the fact that Job did not directly answer Eliphaz's speech (chapter 22) lead us to conclude that some time had passed between this speech and the previous one? Maybe so, but we can't say for sure. The book of Job does not specifically inform us whether or not they continued their discussion without interruption.

In this speech Job did not directly address God, but he did express the strong wish to appear before God and declare his innocence. Since he could get nowhere with his friends in defending himself, Job longed for the opportunity to appear before God. Instead of merely talking about God, as his friends did, Job desired to talk to God.

Earlier, Job had expressed a great fear of appearing before God. He had said, "How can a mortal be righteous before God? Though one wished to dispute with him, he could not answer him one time out of a thousand" (9:2,3). Although Job would again express such fear in this speech (verses 15,16), Job now showed more boldness. He was ready to go before God and state his case. He would await God's response and be satisfied, whatever God's verdict would be. Job confidently answered his own question: "Would he oppose me with great power? No, he would not press charges against me." The last part of that verse can also be translated as "No, surely he would pay attention to me." Those two translations are closer in meaning than they might appear to be. If God would pay attention to Job, he would not press charges against him. Job was convinced he was innocent of the charges his friends had directed against him. He was also confident he would be vindicated and delivered from his affliction.

We know from the concluding verses of this book that God did declare Job innocent of those charges and that he blessed Job even more richly than he had previously. But before that, God taught Job some necessary lessons in humility, as we learn from chapters 38 to 41. Job also needed to learn that God is so majestic that we mortals dare not try to comprehend his greatness or question his dealings with us.

God is hidden, yet Job is confident

8 "But if I go to the east, he is not there;
   if I go to the west, I do not find him.
9 When he is at work in the north, I do not see him;
   when he turns to the south, I catch no glimpse of him.
10 But he knows the way that I take;
   when he has tested me, I will come forth as gold.
11 My feet have closely followed his steps;
   I have kept to his way without turning aside.
12 I have not departed from the commands of his lips;
   I have treasured the words of his mouth more than my
      daily bread.

Job was determined to come face-to-face with God and confront him, but he was at a loss to know where he could find God. Although he tried to go every direction, it seemed as if God eluded him. The NIV and most other modern translations name the directions: east, west, north, and south. In the King James Version, verses 8 and 9 are translated thus: "Behold, I go forward, but he is not there; and backward, but I cannot perceive him: On the left hand, where he doth work, but I cannot behold him: he hideth himself on the right hand, that I cannot see him." As different as those two translations may appear to be, they are essentially the same. Both are correct. The Hebrews faced east in determining their directions. To them east, the direction of the rising sun, was forward. West was behind them, and the word translated as "west" in the NIV literally means "after" or "behind." As the Hebrews faced east, the direction south was to their right, and north was to their left. Their names for the four directions are more concrete than ours (east, west, north, south).

Job was looking in every direction in his attempt to find God, but he couldn't see God in the same manner he could see his three friends. And yet he was convinced that God existed. Job was no atheist; he believed in God and worshiped him (1:20). In fact, he knew that God was everywhere, even though he was invisible.

Job was yearning for the assurance of God's presence so that he could present his case before God. Job was convinced that he was a true child of God. He was confident that he was innocent of the false charges of his friends. Although he did not know why he was afflicted so severely, he did realize he was being tested. He said, "When he has tested me, I will come forth as gold." As we know from the remaining chapters of this book, Job was to be tested even more before God restored him and blessed him with greater wealth than before.

In his own defense, Job spoke of his life as a child of God. He sincerely tried to conform his actions and words to God's will and commands. Although he was not sinless, Job was a man whom God had highly commended as "blameless and upright, a man who fears God and shuns evil" (1:8).

Job stands in great awe of God

> [13] "But he stands alone, and who can oppose him?
>   He does whatever he pleases.
> [14] He carries out his decree against me,
>   and many such plans he still has in store.

¹⁵ **That is why I am terrified before him;**
when I think of all this, I fear him.
¹⁶ **God has made my heart faint;**
the Almighty has terrified me.
¹⁷ **Yet I am not silenced by the darkness,**
by the thick darkness that covers my face.

Job realized that the God whom he was seeking was far different from any human being. "He [God] stands alone." That same confession is made in Deuteronomy 6:4: "Hear, O Israel: The Lord our God, the Lord is one." Twice in that short verse the expression "Lord" is written in four capital letters, which expresses his name, commonly given as Jehovah but more precisely written Yahweh. In that verse Moses describes the Lord as one. The word "one" emphasizes the fact that he is unique, one of a kind. There is only one God, but as we know from other passages in the Bible, this one God exists in three persons: Father, Son, and Holy Spirit. We are commanded to baptize in the name of the Father, the Son, and the Holy Spirit (Matthew 28:19). The word for "alone" in verse 13 of this chapter in Job is the same as the word translated as "one" in Deuteronomy 6:4. Like Moses and the other Israelites, Job confessed that God is one—one of a kind, unique.

Job also rightly stated that God "does whatever he pleases." God does not need to answer to anyone else. Job appears to have been guilty of accusing God of being arbitrary when he added, "He carries out his decree against me, and many such plans he still has in store." Because Job suffered so much, he was tempted to believe that God acted without any good reason, that he had it in for Job and sadistically delighted in seeing him suffer. Earlier, Job had expressed that mistaken idea. He had said, "The arrows of the Almighty are in me, my spirit drinks in their poison; God's terrors are marshaled against me" (6:4). Later in that same speech, he addressed God, "If I have sinned, what have I done to you, O watcher of men? Why have you made me your target? Have I become a burden to you?" (7:20).

If at this time Job was accusing God of arbitrarily picking on him, he was wrong. In his love God permitted Job to suffer afflictions to prove to Satan that Job was a child of God and to test and strengthen Job's faith in God.

In his deep affliction, Job's chief concern was not his great losses and his severe physical suffering, but his relationship with God. He still clung to God in faith even though at times he stood in terror of him, as we learn from the closing verses in this chapter (verses 15-17). As he continued his discourse in the chapter that follows, Job expressed his concern for others who found themselves in misery. As we read those verses and also think of the many cases of injustice and violence in today's society, we can only conclude that the nature of mankind has not changed during the thousands of years that have come and gone since the time of Job.

The poor and oppressed suffer many injustices

24 "Why does the Almighty not set times for judgment?
Why must those who know him look in vain for such days?
² Men move boundary stones;
they pasture flocks they have stolen.
³ They drive away the orphan's donkey
and take the widow's ox in pledge.
⁴ They thrust the needy from the path
and force all the poor of the land into hiding.
⁵ Like wild donkeys in the desert,
the poor go about their labor of foraging food;
the wasteland provides food for their children.
⁶ They gather fodder in the fields
and glean in the vineyards of the wicked.

⁷ **Lacking clothes, they spend the night naked;**
    they have nothing to cover themselves in the cold.
⁸ **They are drenched by mountain rains**
    and hug the rocks for lack of shelter.
⁹ **The fatherless child is snatched from the breast;**
    the infant of the poor is seized for a debt.
¹⁰ **Lacking clothes, they go about naked;**
    they carry the sheaves, but still go hungry.
¹¹ **They crush olives among the terraces;**
    they tread the winepresses, yet suffer thirst.
¹² **The groans of the dying rise from the city,**
    and the souls of the wounded cry out for help.
    But God charges no one with wrongdoing.

As we know from their speeches, Job's friends had repeatedly stated that God rewards the upright and punishes the evildoers. Job strongly disagreed. Indeed, his experience had taught him that quite the opposite was often true. He had frequently mentioned his own experiences as an example of a pious and upright person who had suffered great misfortunes and losses.

Now he turned to the sad plight of others who were steeped in poverty and victimized by selfish and unscrupulous people. His words sound like an inventory of crimes. It appears as if Job is asking God, "What are you doing about all this crime? Are you just closing your eyes to it? When will you straighten things out?" We usually think of Job as the great example of patience, but when he spoke these words, he appeared to be rather impatient. He expected God to step in and correct this injustice immediately. He wanted to set a timetable for God. While his friends appeared to have been blind to the injustices in society, Job was very much aware of what was going on. In that respect Job was right. But he was wrong in accusing God of allowing such injustices to continue. God would in his own time and in his own way bring about justice. In fact, it is presumptuous of any human being to sit in judgment over God. His thoughts and ways are infinitely higher and greater than ours.

In the opening verses of this chapter, Job reminded his friends of many instances of injustice. Unscrupulous people took advantage of the poor and helpless and violated their human rights. They resorted to cheating by moving stones that marked their land boundaries. Since property is a sacred possession of individuals, God strictly forbids moving such landmarks (Deuteronomy 27:17). There were greedy and heartless people who deprived the poor of their flocks. Among the victims of such people in ancient times were the widows and the orphans. In those days people did not have social security, pensions, life insurance policies, and other investments as is the case today. The husband was usually the sole breadwinner, and if he died and left a family, the widow and children were often in dire straits. If they owed money, the children might even be taken into slavery, as we learn from the account about the widow whom Elisha visited (2 Kings 4:1-7). Job deplored the unkind act of taking an orphan's donkey or a widow's ox to pay off a debt. In those days donkeys and oxen were essential for the people's livelihood just as tractors and machinery are essential for farmers today. Worse yet, there were people in Job's day who would take young children as payment of a debt.

While Job was describing the selfish motives and ruthless actions of the wicked, he was also pointing out the plight of the victims. No longer able to make ends meet, they were driven from their homes to live the life of poverty-stricken vagrants. They searched for food, gathered it, and gleaned in the vineyards of the wicked. The word translated as "glean" in verse 6 suggests that those people came after the owner had already harvested the field, and took what little was left.

Since the owner had selfishly harvested as much as he could, the poor people would have only slim pickings for their efforts.

The miserable condition of those people is vividly described in these verses. They are pictured as lacking clothes and suffering the effects of cold nights. When it rained, they would seek shelter in the rocks. They were hungry and thirsty and were desperately seeking some way to satisfy their need for food and drink. They would die in their wretched condition, their cries for help apparently unheeded.

We can surely relate to these words of Job. On television and in the newspapers, we are constantly reminded of the many people who are homeless. Particularly in the large cities, there are many street people who do not have a place to sleep. While no doubt there are many drifters who prefer to sleep in public shelters, in subway stations, under bridges, or even out in the streets, there are also those who just can't afford to rent a room. While there are alcoholics and drug addicts among the homeless, there are also victims of circumstances over which they had no control. While there are people who don't want a job or can't keep one, there are also the unemployed who lack the skills or the health or the opportunity to hold a job. To such our heart must go out.

Can we, as Christians, be untouched by their condition? Shouldn't we try to do more as individuals and as a society to make it possible for such people to get back on their feet and become more productive citizens? That such conditions exist today also in our own prosperous country is not to our credit as individuals or as a nation. Sadly, the conditions Job describes are applicable to the United States of America today. And that is equally true of the more violent types of behavior that he describes in the verses that follow.

Evildoers commit many crimes

¹³ "There are those who rebel against the light,
who do not know its ways
or stay in its paths.
¹⁴ When daylight is gone, the murderer rises up
and kills the poor and needy;
in the night he steals forth like a thief.
¹⁵ The eye of the adulterer watches for dusk;
he thinks, 'No eye will see me,'
and he keeps his face concealed.
¹⁶ In the dark, men break into houses,
but by day they shut themselves in;
they want nothing to do with the light.
¹⁷ For all of them, deep darkness is their morning;
they make friends with the terrors of darkness.

The previous verses (1-12) describe the injustices that cruel and heartless people commit against their less fortunate fellow human beings. These verses (13-17) paint a stark picture of flagrant crimes such as murder, adultery, and burglary. In every verse of this section, mention is made of night and darkness. In Job's day, as in ours, criminals preferred to make their attacks during the darkness of night so that people couldn't see them. Job described them as "those who rebel against the light, who do not know its ways or stay in its paths." Jesus spoke similarly when he said, "This is the verdict: Light has come into the world, but men loved darkness instead of light because their deeds were evil. Everyone who does evil hates the light, and will not come into the light for fear that his deeds will be exposed" (John 3:19,20).

Job mentioned three kinds of criminals who preferred to do their dastardly deeds at night: the murderer, the adulterer, and the burglar. It is significant that those crimes are gross violations of the Fifth, Sixth, and Seventh Commandments.

In the closing verse of this section, we read, "For all of them, deep darkness is their morning." The darkness of night is prime time for such criminals. They prefer to remain under cover during broad daylight, but at night they do their work at the expense of their victims. On an even greater scale than in the days of Job, criminals today resort to violence of all manner. They commit most of their violent acts at night. Drunken brawls not infrequently lead to murder. Sexual orgies also sometimes end in violence. Lust leads to rape, and victims of rape are often silent on account of the embarrassment and psychological stress that result if they bring a charge. The rapid rise in cases of burglary today has made people lock their houses and install burglar alarms.

There have always been crimes committed in darkness—at the time of Job, at the time of Jesus, and today. People have not changed. Sin is a part of human nature, and it can manifest itself to a frightening degree. That appears to be particularly true today. With the aid of modern technology, people are capable of committing even worse crimes than before. Automatic guns in the hands of robbers in banks, burglars in homes, and hijackers on airplanes leave innocent victims at their mercy. Automobiles driven by drunken drivers take a terrible toll on highways. A strong craving for drugs leads addicts to rob and senselessly kill people who happen to be convenient victims. Job's verses in this section are truly descriptive of our time.

In the verses that follow, Job reminds us that there will eventually be a day of accounting for evildoers.

Evildoers will finally come to a bitter end

¹⁸ "Yet they are foam on the surface of the water;
their portion of the land is cursed,
so that no one goes to the vineyards.

¹⁹ As heat and drought snatch away the melted snow,
   so the grave snatches away those who have sinned.
²⁰ The womb forgets them,
   the worm feasts on them;
  evil men are no longer remembered
   but are broken like a tree.
²¹ They prey on the barren and childless woman,
   and to the widow show no kindness.
²² But God drags away the mighty by his power;
   though they become established, they have no assurance
      of life.
²³ He may let them rest in a feeling of security,
   but his eyes are on their ways.
²⁴ For a little while they are exalted, and then they are gone;
   they are brought low and gathered up like all others;
   they are cut off like heads of grain.
²⁵ "If this is not so, who can prove me false
   and reduce my words to nothing?"

Many critical commentators feel that Job could not have spoken these words. In their opinion, these words contradict the words he had just spoken (verses 1-17). They feel that these are rather the words of one of Job's three friends. As we will see, they also deny that Job is the speaker in 26:5-14 and 27:13-23 because the words appear to express the viewpoint of the friends rather than that of Job. They also base their claim on the fact that Bildad's third speech is very short (25:1-6), that Zophar did not give a third speech, and that Job's closing speech is very long (chapters 26–31).

But if Bildad or Zophar would have been the speaker in verses 18-25 of this chapter or in either of the other two passages mentioned above, their names would have been listed at the beginning of their speeches as in the case of all the previous passages in which they spoke. This writer believes that Bildad had little more to say and that Zophar had no further response to Job's statements. On the other hand, Job, who had been viciously attacked by the three, felt the need of making lengthy remarks in his own defense.

And yet these words do appear to contradict what Job had previously said. Various attempts have been made at harmonizing them with Job's earlier statements. Some commentators maintain that Job is here quoting the views of his friends for the sake of refuting them. Others contend that Job is quoting their views sarcastically in order to ridicule them. It seems more likely that in this section and the two later sections, Job is looking beyond the prosperity of the ungodly in this life to their final destiny.

God does not punish the wicked immediately. In many instances he does not do so in this life. Job appears to have arrived at the same conclusion as David in Psalm 37 and Asaph in Psalm 73. Job's words in verse 24 are similar to David's in Psalm 37:35,36: "I have seen a wicked and ruthless man flourishing like a green tree in its native soil, but he soon passed away and was no more; though I looked for him, he could not be found." Although Job complained of the apparent prosperity of the wicked, when he considered their final destiny, he realized that their end would be destruction. Likewise the psalmist Asaph, speaking of the evildoers whom he was tempted to envy, concluded, "Then I understood their final destiny" (Psalm 73:17). And what was their destiny? Addressing God, Asaph declared, "Those who are far from you will perish; you destroy all who are unfaithful to you" (Psalm 73:27).

In verses 18 to 25 of this chapter, Job again mentions the cruel and vicious deeds of the wicked as they do violence to helpless women (verse 21). For a while they prosper and feel secure (verse 24). But their prosperity will not last forever. In very picturesque language, they are described as "foam on the surface of the water" and as "melted snow." They will die and become a feast for worms; they are also compared to a broken tree. Although they may feel secure in their lifestyle, God will call them to account. The last line of verse 23 ("but his eyes are on their ways") is best understood to mean that God is watching evildoers and will not let their deeds go unpunished.

In his closing words Job challenged his friends to disagree with him. As we will learn from his brief response, Bildad avoided directly answering Job's challenge. In fact, he spoke in general terms about a very uncontroversial subject: the majestic greatness of God.

Bildad's third speech

God's greatness is contrasted with man's smallness

25 Then Bildad the Shuhite replied:

² "Dominion and awe belong to God;
  he establishes order in the heights of heaven.
³ Can his forces be numbered?
  Upon whom does his light not rise?
⁴ How then can a man be righteous before God?
  How can one born of woman be pure?
⁵ If even the moon is not bright
  and the stars are not pure in his eyes,
⁶ how much less man, who is but a maggot—
  a son of man, who is only a worm!"

This final speech by Bildad is very short—only five verses. As the reader will notice, there is no third speech by Zophar. On the other hand, six chapters are attributed to Job (26–31). This is a departure from the previous pattern in which Job would speak alternately with his three friends, although usually at greater length. Consequently, many scholars have reassigned the speeches to lengthen Bildad's third speech and to give a third speech to Zophar. They generally give two reasons for such reassignment. First, they feel that the length of the speeches as given in the Bible text is too uneven. Second, they contend that some of the statements of Job do not agree with his own previous statements but rather with the statements of his friends.

Following that principle, they do not hesitate to rearrange the verses and even certain chapters. We can see such rearrangement in the volume on Job by Marvin H. Pope in *The Anchor Bible.* Although that commentary has many fine qualities, such rearrangement of the text is unwarranted. Job could very well have spoken those words. And since the three friends were making no progress in convincing Job that he was guilty of especially great sins, it is not strange that Bildad had very little to say in his last speech and that Zophar had nothing to add. On the other hand, since he had been accused of serious sins, Job felt compelled to defend himself at length.

In his closing speech Bildad contrasted the holy, majestic God with sinful, lowly man. God holds dominion over everyone and everything. Not even the highest angels in heaven can challenge his rule. God is in complete control there. In Bildad's words, "He establishes order in the heights of heaven." The word translated as "order" is the Hebrew word *shalom,* literally, "peace." It expresses complete well-being and order, with everything in its proper place. With such peace and order there can be no rebellion or disturbance. And if there are no powers that can oppose God in heaven, certainly there can be none on earth. God is in complete control even though it may sometimes seem as if he is not. Job certainly had to agree with that statement.

As in many other passages in the Old Testament, God is pictured as a triumphant warrior. David describes him as such in Psalm 24:8: "The LORD strong and mighty, the LORD mighty in battle." God also bestows upon mankind the gift of light. Bildad asks, "Upon whom does his light not rise?" What a wonderful gift light is! God's first recorded speech in the Bible is "Let there be light" (Genesis 1:3). Without light it would be impossible for us to survive.

In verses 4 to 6 the abject lowliness of a human being is starkly contrasted with the glorious majesty of God. In verses 4 and 6 Bildad uses two expressions in each verse to indicate man's lowliness. In the first line of each verse the word "man" is used. In the original that word emphasizes man's weak, frail, and mortal nature.

In the second line of verse 4 the expression "one born of woman" occurs. A similar expression is found in the second line of verse 6: "a son of man." Those expressions also suggest that a human being is subject to death. The word "woman" is used of the first mother, Eve, in Genesis chapters 2 and 3. Not until Genesis 4:1 is she called by her name "Eve." In the expression "a son of man," the word "man" is *adam* in Hebrew, the same word that is consistently used for the first human being, Adam. Although Adam and Eve were created sinless, they yielded to the devil's temptation and thus brought sin into the world. As a consequence of their fall into sin, they died.

To emphasize the extreme lowliness of man, Bildad concluded by referring to a human being as "but a maggot" and "only a worm," expressions suggesting the most loathsome and disgusting of earthly creatures.

Most of Bildad's final speech is of a general nature, expounding on the majesty of God and the lowliness of man. In verse 4, however, he does make an indirect reference to Job.

He asks Job, "How then can a man be righteous before God? How can one born of woman be pure?" In his concluding comments on this verse, P. E. Kretzmann states, "Bildad emphasized the general sinfulness of man, his statements implying the admonition that Job should now confess with proper humility. It is so much easier to reprove others than to take a proper inventory of one's own weaknesses and sins" (page 35).

Bildad and his two friends detected the sins and shortcomings of Job more quickly than their own. Isn't that sometimes true also of you and me? Don't we perhaps need to apply to ourselves a statement of Jesus in his Sermon on the Mount? In strong language our Savior addresses all who emphasize the faults of others while ignoring their own: "Why do you look at the speck of sawdust in your brother's eye and pay no attention to the plank in your own eye? How can you say to your brother, 'Let me take the speck out of your eye,' when all the time there is a plank in your own eye? You hypocrite, first take the plank out of your own eye, and then you will see clearly to remove the speck from your brother's eye" (Matthew 7:3-5). Those words really hit home, don't they? We would do well to keep that passage in mind whenever we are tempted to exaggerate the faults of others and minimize our own.

Job's reply to Bildad and Job's concluding remarks

In his last speech Bildad had very little to say. That has led several modern scholars to rearrange the verses in these chapters in order to give Bildad a longer final speech. Some have taken verses 5 to 14 of Job's speech in chapter 26 and added them to the six verses of chapter 25, since they feel those words are more in harmony with the speech of Bildad (25:1-6) than with the opening verses of the speech of Job (26:1-4). We must, however, object to such arbitrary rearrangement of the sacred text. If Bildad spoke the words of verses 5 to 14, they would either directly follow the verses in chapter 25, or they would be introduced by the expression "Then Bildad the Shuhite replied," as in his previous speeches (8:1; 18:1; 25:1). Throughout the book that system is used consistently.

Bildad's last speech is short because he had little to say. He had apparently given up trying to convince Job of his guilt. Instead, he gave a brief discourse on the greatness of God and the lowliness of man. It would be difficult for anyone to differ with him on that subject. We are convinced that Job is the speaker throughout chapter 26. If we resort to tacking 26:5-14 on to the end of chapter 25, we lose the effect of Bildad's closing words: "How much less man, who is but a maggot—a son of man, who is only a worm" (25:6). In our comments on verses 5 to 14 of chapter 26, we will note that those words are very appropriately ascribed to Job.

Job responds to Bildad

26 Then Job replied:
² "How you have helped the powerless!
How you have saved the arm that is feeble!
³ What advice you have offered to one without wisdom!
And what great insight you have displayed!
⁴ Who has helped you utter these words?
And whose spirit spoke from your mouth?

Job had grown weary of the repeated efforts of his friends to "straighten him out." Time and again they had stated that Job's sufferings were the result of especially great sins on his part. In his earlier speeches, Bildad had sharply rebuked Job (8:2; 18:2) and had classified him among the wicked people. Nor was Bildad's last speech (chapter 25) of any help to

Job in solving the problem of his great suffering and God's apparent inattentiveness to his plight.

Irritated by Bildad's words, Job replied, "How you have helped the powerless! How you have saved the arm that is feeble! What advice you have offered to one without wisdom! And what great insight you have displayed!" Those words are best understood as exclamations (as in the NIV) and not as questions (as in the KJV). They are a sarcastic outpouring of Job's feelings.

Job refers to himself as "powerless" and "feeble" because of his obvious physical afflictions and his loss of property. He speaks of himself as "one without wisdom" because his friends kept insisting they were right and he was wrong. We can detect a note of sarcasm in Job's words. If the friends were so strong, why could they not give him support? If they were so intelligent, why could they not enlighten him? Surely in both respects they had failed miserably!

In this speech Job specifically addressed Bildad. The pronoun "you" occurs five times, and the possessive "your" occurs once in verses 2 to 4. In each instance it is in the singular number in Hebrew, which differentiates between the singular and the plural in the form of the verb as well as the pronoun *you* and the possessive *your*. In modern English there is no such distinction; the words *you* and *your* are the same in the singular and the plural. On the other hand, in the English of the King James Version four centuries ago, that distinction was made. The King James Version uses "thou," "thee," and "thy" in the singular and "ye," "you," and "your" in the plural. In these verses, by using the singular form, Job is addressing Bildad in particular. In only three previous speeches had Job used the singular form in addressing his friends: to Eliphaz in 16:3 and to Zophar in 12:7,8 and 21:3. In all other instances he addressed the three as a group.

In contrast to verses 2 and 3, which are translated as exclamations, verse 4 is best understood as a question. Yet in that verse too Job speaks sarcastically: "Who has helped you utter these words? And whose spirit spoke from your mouth?" Job's words strongly imply that such words could not come from God, but rather from some human or demonic source.

Did Job possibly suspect that his so-called friends were acting as servants of Satan? Were they unknowingly aiding in Satan's attempts to destroy Job as he was struggling with his many problems? Would Job finally yield to the temptation of cursing God as Satan had predicted (1:11; 2:5) and as Job's wife had suggested (2:9)? Would Satan win his wager with God that Job would curse and deny him? For an answer to those questions, we must look to the conclusion of this book. Meanwhile, Job continued his speech by praising the majestic greatness of God.

Job speaks of God's majestic power

5 "The dead are in deep anguish,
   those beneath the waters and all that live in them.
6 Death is naked before God;
   Destruction lies uncovered.
7 He spreads out the northern skies over empty space;
   he suspends the earth over nothing.
8 He wraps up the waters in his clouds,
   yet the clouds do not burst under their weight.
9 He covers the face of the full moon,
   spreading his clouds over it.
10 He marks out the horizon on the face of the waters
    for a boundary between light and darkness.
11 The pillars of the heavens quake,
    aghast at his rebuke.
12 By his power he churned up the sea;
    by his wisdom he cut Rahab to pieces.

¹³ **By his breath the skies became fair;**
   his hand pierced the gliding serpent.
¹⁴ **And these are but the outer fringe of his works;**
   how faint the whisper we hear of him!
   Who then can understand the thunder of his power?"

As mentioned earlier, many scholars maintain that these words were not spoken by Job. They feel these words are instead a continuation of Bildad's short speech (25:1-6) and that the words of Job (26:1-4) are out of place here. Using their cut-and-paste technique, some scholars rearrange the chapters by placing Job 26:1-4 after this section (verses 5-14) and immediately before 27:2-7. They also reassign 27:8-23 to Zophar so that he could have a third speech. They feel that those words fit Zophar's thinking better than Job's. By playing fast and loose with these chapters, such critics are doing violence to God's sacred Word.

It is unnecessary to attribute these words (verses 5-14) to Bildad. In fact, Job could very well have spoken them. Job was aware as well as Bildad of God's greatness and power. If Bildad could praise God's majestic greatness, why couldn't Job? Job had lived in a close personal relationship with his God. He reverenced and worshiped God, and God commended him for his godliness. Although all of his friends spoke words praising God, Job in these verses praised him more eloquently than any of the three friends. Only God himself surpassed Job in describing God's power and majesty (chapter 38). These verses (26:5-14) invite comparison with other great chapters in the Bible that proclaim the greatness of God the Creator and Preserver of this universe; for example, Psalm 104 and Isaiah chapter 40.

Job describes God as the one who has complete power over the dead. When death beckons, all must yield. Even

"Destruction lies uncovered." The word "Destruction" is *Abaddon* in the Hebrew text. That very word in its untranslated form is used by John in Revelation 9:11: "They had as king over them the angel of the Abyss, whose name in Hebrew is Abaddon, and in Greek, Apollyon." There the name is attributed to Satan. God has full power over death, the grave, hell, and Satan.

In physical terms Job describes God's miraculous work of creating the heavens, the earth, waters above as well as below, and the clouds. In verse 9 the NIV reads, "He covers the face of the full moon." The word translated "the full moon" might preferably be rendered "his throne," that is, God's throne. The Bible elsewhere speaks of heaven as God's throne; for example, Isaiah 40:22; 66:1.

The horizon is described as the boundary between the light that shines on the earth and the darkness that inhabits the waters. The expression "pillars of the heavens" possibly refers to the mountains that can be seen from great distances. They appear as if they hold up the heavens.

Frequently, the Old Testament writers describe God as a great warrior conquering the forces of evil. The sea is regarded as the personification of the dark and evil powers of nature. In poems of ancient Canaanite and Near Eastern mythology, the gods are described as fighting against and subduing forces of nature such as the sea and its monsters. Using some of the same vocabulary, but without the crude polytheistic connotations of pagan mythology, Job describes the true God as the one who overcomes such forces of evil. The word "Rahab" in verse 12 must not be confused with the name of the former prostitute who kindly helped Israelite spies at Jericho (Joshua 2). In Hebrew the two words are written differently. This Rahab referred to in verse 12 is not a person but rather the personification of all evil forces. The "gliding serpent" in verse 13 may be another designation for a sea monster that also pictures an evil enemy.

God has power over the clouds and the skies. He gives us rain and sunshine. We well know the importance of each in the right amount. In our country and other parts of the world, people have often experienced drought and floods. Such experience should help us realize that we are dependent on God for our livelihood and welfare. Do we remember to thank him for the blessings of rain and sunshine?

Our Lord God is unique. He is entirely different from the false gods of heathen religions. Whereas in most such religions the god of power and the god of wisdom are different and separate beings, the one true God is both all-powerful and all-wise. In him all attributes are combined.

The final verse of this section summarizes the greatness of God's power. In this grand universe we get only a slight glimpse of the majestic greatness of our Creator-God. Appropriately, Job closes this section with a rhetorical question: "Who then can understand the thunder of his power?" The only possible answer is, "No one except God himself!" To him alone be all glory for ever and ever!

Job insists he is telling the truth

27 And Job continued his discourse:

² "As surely as God lives, who has denied me justice,
   the Almighty, who has made me taste bitterness of soul,
³ as long as I have life within me,
   the breath of God in my nostrils,
⁴ my lips will not speak wickedness,
   and my tongue will utter no deceit.
⁵ I will never admit you are in the right;
   till I die, I will not deny my integrity.

⁶ **I will maintain my righteousness and never let go of it;**
my conscience will not reproach me as long as I live.

At this point we might have expected Zophar to deliver his third speech, for in the previous chapter (26) Job had replied to Bildad's brief remarks (chapter 25). However, there is no statement introducing Zophar as the speaker.

The first six verses are clearly the words of Job, as we will see. He was the one who repeatedly maintained that he was telling the truth. He also appealed to God to give him a hearing so he could prove he was not guilty of the charges raised against him and that he had done nothing to deserve the severe suffering he was experiencing. It is also significant that none of his three friends in their speeches directly addressed God or appealed to God to hear them. We get the distinct impression that to them, God was an abstract power distant from their personal lives. On the other hand, Job had a close relationship with God and spoke to God in intimate terms, at times even accusing God of picking on him. We see an example of that in verse 2. In the remaining verses of this chapter, which many scholars assign to Zophar and others assign to Bildad, we are convinced that Job is still the speaker.

This chapter is introduced with the words "and Job continued his discourse." This formula differs from that of all he previous speeches. The words suggest that Job paused for a few moments to give the third friend, Zophar, the opportunity to respond, for he had spoken only twice. But Zophar apparently had nothing more to say. The last words of his second speech suggested a finality: "Such is the fate God allots the wicked, the heritage appointed for them by God" (20:29). Similarly, we can detect from the closing words of the other two speakers that they had nothing more to say (Eliphaz, 22:30; Bildad, 25:6).

On the other hand, Job still had much to say. After the final speech of his friends, Job's speeches continue through the next six chapters (26–31). His friends had accused him, and he felt compelled to defend himself.

Job's words in this chapter begin with an oath: "As surely as God lives." That expression is an invitation to God to curse Job if what he says is not true. It also expresses Job's hope that God will hear him and render a verdict favorable to him. In the words that follow, however, Job boldly complains that God has denied him justice, that the Almighty has made him taste bitterness of soul. Those words remind us of Naomi's statement when she returned from Moab to Bethlehem with her daughter-in-law Ruth. She said, "The Almighty has made my life very bitter. . . . The Lord has afflicted me; the Almighty has brought misfortune upon me" (Ruth 1:20,21).

Under great suffering and loss, many good Christians have expressed themselves in words like these: "Why does God make me suffer so much? Does God really love me?" Like Job, in the weakness of our flesh we sometimes complain, whereas even in our suffering and sorrow we really ought to thank God for his blessings.

Even while Job was complaining, he still confessed that God had given him life and breath. The Hebrew words translated as "life" and "breath" can both be translated as "breath." They are synonyms. The first word is the same in Hebrew as the word translated as "breath" in Genesis 2:7: "The Lord God formed the man from the dust of the ground and breathed into his nostrils the breath of life, and the man became a living being." In the chapter before us, Job confesses that God had created him and given him life and breath. Job was no evolutionist.

His words continue, "My lips will not speak wickedness, and my tongue will utter no deceit." Similarly, the author of the book of Job had earlier given this testimony: "In all this, Job did not sin in what he said" (2:10), or more literally, "with his lips."

Job continues by saying, "I will never admit you are in the right." Several English versions translate the opening words more literally: "Far be it from me to admit you are right." That is a very strong expression. The King James Version renders those words "God forbid that I should justify you."

Job continues, "Till I die, I will not deny my integrity." His greatest concern was his integrity. Again those words echo what is earlier stated about Job in this book. The author describes him as "blameless" (1:1). In his conversations with Satan, the Lord twice referred to Job as "blameless" (1:8; 2:3). In Hebrew the word *blameless* is of the same root as the word *integrity*.

In the closing verse of this section, Job tells his friends, "I will maintain my righteousness and never let go of it; my conscience will not reproach me as long as I live." The word "righteousness" also recalls earlier descriptions of Job.

Job gives further details of his godly conduct when he defends himself in chapter 29. In defending himself, Job was saying nothing more than what the sacred writer and God himself had said about him. He could therefore speak confidently. In spite of his disastrous outward circumstances, Job clung to his faith in the God who seemed so distant even though he was really so near.

The end of the wicked is disastrous

There is a great difference of opinion among the scholars who refuse to accept Job as the speaker throughout the verses of this chapter. In general, most of them attribute verses 1 to 6 to Job, but after those verses there is a wide difference of opinion. Some hold that Zophar is the speaker in verses 7 to 10, Job in verses 11 and 12, and Zophar again in verses 13 to 23. Others are of the opinion that Zophar is the speaker in verses 11 to 23, still others in verses 13 to 23. Some scholars even assign verses 13 to 23 to Bildad. Most contemporary scholars, however, deny that Job is the speaker in the last 11 verses. They say so in spite of the fact that the text continues uninterruptedly after the first verse, which directly assigns the chapter to Job.

The chief reason those scholars refuse to credit those verses to Job is that he appears to express the point of view previously held by the friends and not his own previous line of argument. He now states that the evildoers will come to a disastrous end. We might ask, Did Job suddenly change his mind? Had he finally become convinced by the arguments of his friends without openly admitting it? No, rather he, like his friends, realized that the final destiny of evildoers will be disastrous. They may appear to prosper for a time, but finally there will be a day of reckoning. Job did not flip-flop or contradict himself.

There are some scholars today who believe that Job did speak all the words in this chapter. In his book *The Word Becoming Flesh,* Horace Hummel takes that position. He aptly states that "in these chapters Job, indeed, affirms the divine visitation upon evildoers every bit as stoutly as the friends have done hitherto. What he does, however, is to deny just as stoutly that the principle is applicable in his case, and, furthermore, he appears to suggest that its most immediate applicability might be to his own tormentors (possibly even quoting their own words against themselves)" (pages 469,470).

Indeed, it is not inconsistent with his thinking for Job to state that God punishes wickedness. But Job was not willing to concede that he himself was such a wicked person.

⁷ "May my enemies be like the wicked,
   my adversaries like the unjust!
⁸ For what hope has the godless when he is cut off,
   when God takes away his life?
⁹ Does God listen to his cry
   when distress comes upon him?
¹⁰ Will he find delight in the Almighty?
   Will he call upon God at all times?

¹¹ "I will teach you about the power of God;
   the ways of the Almighty I will not conceal.
¹² You have all seen this yourselves.
   Why then this meaningless talk?

Job begins this section by uttering a curse against his enemies. He asks four questions, all of which imply a negative answer. The godless person can have no hope after death, for he has rejected God. Only through faith in Jesus Christ is there deliverance from death. God will not listen to the cry of the wicked who reject God in times of prosperity and call upon him only in times of trouble. A true believer worships God in times of prosperity as well as adversity. In his most prosperous times Job had prayed to God and offered sacrifices to him (1:5). A godless person finds no delight in the Almighty nor calls upon him at all times (verse 10). For him, God is of use only when he finds himself in deep trouble.

Turning again to his three friends, Job addressed them: "I will teach you about the power of God; the ways of the Almighty I will not conceal. You have all seen this yourselves. Why then this meaningless talk?" His friends had intended to teach Job. They had all the answers—so they thought—but their efforts only irritated Job (26:2-4). God himself later verified that when he said to Job's friends, "You have not spoken of me what is right, as my servant Job has" (42:7).

Now it was Job's turn to teach them, and he did. That Job, not one of the three friends, is speaking here is clear, for he uses the plural form of the pronoun *you*. If Zophar had spoken, he would have addressed Job in the singular. While Job's words sound very similar to those of his friends, particularly those of Zophar in chapter 20, they take on an even greater significance from the mouth of Job, since he had previously stated that the wicked often prosper during their lives. Now Job was looking beyond the immediate to their final destiny.

¹³ "Here is the fate God allots to the wicked,
    the heritage a ruthless man receives from the Almighty:
¹⁴ However many his children, their fate is the sword;
    his offspring will never have enough to eat.
¹⁵ The plague will bury those who survive him,
    and their widows will not weep for them.
¹⁶ Though he heaps up silver like dust
    and clothes like piles of clay,
¹⁷ what he lays up the righteous will wear,
    and the innocent will divide his silver.
¹⁸ The house he builds is like a moth's cocoon,
    like a hut made by a watchman.
¹⁹ He lies down wealthy, but will do so no more;
    when he opens his eyes, all is gone.
²⁰ Terrors overtake him like a flood;
    a tempest snatches him away in the night.
²¹ The east wind carries him off, and he is gone;
    it sweeps him out of his place.
²² It hurls itself against him without mercy
    as he flees headlong from its power.
²³ It claps its hands in derision
    and hisses him out of his place.

As previously stated, most modern scholars assign these verses to Zophar, and some assign them to Bildad. However, earlier scholars—including Franz Delitzsch, August Pieper, Ludwig Fuerbringer, and P. E. Kretzmann—held that Job was the speaker also in these verses. Today as well, scholars who are committed to the inerrancy of the Bible believe that Job spoke these words. In this volume of The People's Bible, we take that position. Furthermore, we believe that Job was not sarcastically repeating the statements of his friends but that he believed as well as they that the final destiny of the godless would not be successful but disastrous.

God will bring the wicked and ruthless to a bitter end. In even stronger language than that of Zophar in chapter 20, Job here describes the downfall of the ungodly. Their evil deeds will adversely affect their children and widows. Job is, of course, generalizing. We need not conclude that in every instance during this lifetime, the survivors of the ungodly will meet such a fate. In many instances they do not, just as Job had previously pointed out. But unless they repent, they will suffer eternal loss. In comparison to that, any gain they might achieve in this life is insignificant.

In verse 16 Job uses an interesting expression: "Though he heaps up silver like dust." There is a fascinating double meaning in the word "dust." In the Old Testament, dust sometimes expresses great abundance. On one occasion God told Abraham, "I will make your offspring like the dust of the earth, so that if anyone could count the dust, then your offspring could be counted" (Genesis 13:16). At other times the word *dust* signifies destruction and decay and is used in connection with death. In a psalm Moses addresses God, "You turn men back to dust, saying, 'Return to dust, O sons of men'" (Psalm 90:3). No matter how much wealth a godless person accumulates, it will have no lasting value for him.

Job continues by stating that a righteous person rather will benefit from the efforts of the wicked. The flimsiness of the wicked person's acquisitions is compared to a moth's cocoon (or a spider's web, as in some translations) and a hut made by a watchman. In biblical times temporary shelters were erected in fields during harvest times. Isaiah compares the disobedient people of Judah to such a hut or shelter that stands desolate in a vineyard or in a melon patch (Isaiah 1:8).

"He lies down wealthy, but will do so no more; when he opens his eyes, all is gone." In the parable of the rich farmer, Jesus spoke of the uncertainty of wealth and the suddenness of death. God addressed that materialistic person, "You fool! This very night your life will be demanded from you. Then who will get what you have prepared for yourself?" (Luke 12:20). Those are sobering words.

No matter how wealthy or influential or highly honored a person may become, if he defies God or rejects God, he can have no true peace with God. Job describes the death of such a person as a flood and tempest and an east wind that will snatch him, hurl him, and sweep him away. For the ungodly, death can have only terrors.

In his description of the final misfortune of the wicked, Job goes beyond his friends in the sharpness of his language. He closes this part of his speech by picturing death as an enemy that gleefully claps his hands and maliciously hisses when the evildoer meets his end. By making the picture even more severe than his friends had, Job emphasizes that the way of the evildoer leads to destruction. But Job firmly maintains that he himself is not such an evildoer.

True wisdom comes from God, who alone can work wonders in nature

Job chapter 28 is a fascinating chapter. In a striking manner it describes the ancient craft of mining. It mentions precious metals and rare jewels that remind us of the jewels mentioned in passages like Revelation 21:18-21. It describes characteristics of animals and birds and compares them to human beings. Above all, this chapter gives glory to God for his incomparable wisdom and power.

Chapter 28 is also very challenging and difficult. As we can see by comparing various English translations, there is a difference of opinion among scholars in translating some of the Hebrew words for jewels. Such is also the case in the list of jewels described in the book of Revelation. There are a few portions of verses 1 to 11 that are a challenge to the interpreter. It is particularly difficult for a person who has not had firsthand experience in mining to understand and appreciate everything Job says here.

Although the vocabulary and contents of this chapter are challenging, the biggest problem is its relationship to the rest of the book of Job. Certain critical scholars regard this chapter as an intrusion. They deny that it even belongs in the book of Job. In their opinion, it fits better into the book of Proverbs, possibly following chapters 8 and 9, two chapters that also treat the subject of wisdom. They take such a position despite the fact that this chapter occupies the place between the 27th and 29th chapters of Job in the Hebrew text as well as in all ancient and modern translations of the book!

Even among scholars who accept this chapter as a part of the book of Job, there are many who deny that Job was the speaker. A few are of the opinion that one of the three friends spoke these words. Since some of the thoughts are similar to speeches given by Bildad (for example, chapter 20), they claim that he spoke these words. Others assign them to Zophar, since he had previously spoken only twice.

The most common view, however, is that none of the participants in the dialog spoke these words but that they are comments from the author of the book. That interpretation has some merit. The general tone of this chapter is calm and deliberate. It lacks the passionate and argumentative style of Job and his three friends. It appears to be the author's reflection on the subject of wisdom. The subject matter of this chapter is also similar to that of chapter 38, in which God reminds Job that in wisdom and power he is incomparably greater than Job. Why then, one might ask, would Job speak these words since he needed to be reminded of them later? For those reasons and others, most recent commentators, conservative as well as liberal, have assigned this chapter to the author of the book rather than to Job. They regard it as an interlude between the first part of the book (chapters 1–27) and the last (chapters 29–42).

As attractive as that theory may seem, there is one important objection. The text itself does not give any evidence that Job had stopped speaking or that someone else now delivered this discourse. Only in the prologue (chapters 1,2) and the epilogue (chapter 42), both in prose form, does the author serve as spokesman. In all other instances, each speaker is introduced and continues until the next speaker takes his turn. If the author were the speaker in chapter 28, there would have been some indication that Job had stopped speaking or that someone else had begun. Such is not the case here, and we refuse to assume that such introductory words had dropped out of the text.

Job could very well have spoken these words under the direction of God. The fact that God later reminded Job of some of the same truths should not rule out Job as the speaker in this chapter. In his intense suffering Job often wavered. At times he contradicted previous statements. Sometimes he blamed God and accused God of being unfair. When he complained, Job needed to be reminded that God's thoughts and ways are far above human understanding. In the words that follow, we believe Job is the speaker. We learn that the wisdom and accomplishments of man are remarkable but that God's wisdom and accomplishments are infinitely greater.

Human investigation has not discovered true wisdom

28 ¹"There is a mine for silver
       and a place where gold is refined.
² Iron is taken from the earth,
   and copper is smelted from ore.
³ Man puts an end to the darkness;
   he searches the farthest recesses
   for ore in the blackest darkness.
⁴ Far from where people dwell he cuts a shaft,
   in places forgotten by the foot of man;
   far from men he dangles and sways.

We might well ask, "Where did Job get all this information?" While we cannot answer that question decisively, we are told in the opening verses of this book that Job was "the greatest man among all the people of the East" (1:3). We can assume that he was not only very wealthy but also well informed. As a big operator, he must have had some knowledge of the mining craft, precious metals, and gems.

From archaeology, history, and ancient literature, we learn that mining was an ancient occupation. Many centuries before the time of Job, the Egyptians engaged in mining. From earliest times they worked the Sinai Peninsula as a mining district. There were also gold mines in Nubia, the name of which means "gold country" in Egyptian. In Genesis 41:42 we are told that Pharaoh put a gold chain about Joseph's neck. Much earlier in the book of Genesis, Moses tells us about the land of Havilah "where there is gold. (The gold of that land is good)" (2:11,12). Ancient writers, including the great Greek poet Homer, often mention gold and silver. We get the impression that gold and silver were fairly plentiful, and yet they were precious.

In ancient times people also mined and smelted copper and iron. Even though their methods and implements may seem crude in comparison with our modern technology, they had the basic knowledge, capacity, and tools to carry on mining. In most cases, those who worked in the mines were slave laborers. Yet through sheer physical effort, they were able to draw from the bowels of the earth large amounts of precious metals.

Verses 1 and 2 list in order four metals: silver, gold, iron, copper. Those verses also briefly describe the process of mining, refining, and smelting those ores.

In strikingly vivid language Job describes the work of a miner as he keeps digging in the dark recesses of the earth. While this sounds modern, it is true that the miners in ancient times also had to go beneath the ground to dig out the ore. We might ask, "How could they see?" They must have had some type of lamps or torches.

Verse 4 further describes the work of the miner who is suspended by some kind of rope and sways back and forth. In the meantime, people who are walking on the earth above him may be completely unaware of his presence below them and of his efforts and hard work. We must truly marvel at the great effort and skill of miners even in ancient times. A human being can dig out great treasures from the earth—what an achievement!

And yet he is completely incapable of unearthing the true wisdom of God. Only God himself has such wisdom, and only he can communicate to mankind such true wisdom in measure, as we learn in this chapter.

> ⁵ **The earth, from which food comes,**
> **is transformed below as by fire;**

> ⁶ sapphires come from its rocks,
>   and its dust contains nuggets of gold.
> ⁷ No bird of prey knows that hidden path,
>   no falcon's eye has seen it.
> ⁸ Proud beasts do not set foot on it,
>   and no lion prowls there.
> ⁹ Man's hand assaults the flinty rock
>   and lays bare the roots of the mountains.
> ¹⁰ He tunnels through the rock;
>   his eyes see all its treasures.
> ¹¹ He searches the sources of the rivers
>   and brings hidden things to light.

These verses picture a number of interesting contrasts. On the one hand, the earth is the source of our food. Grain, vegetables, and fruits spring from the ground. And yet that same earth also produces precious metals and gems. Job declares, "The earth, from which food comes, is transformed below as by fire." That is a difficult statement. Perhaps the best explanation is that man's work in digging out and mining the ore is like a ravaging fire.

A precious stone is mentioned in verse 6. In the text the NIV has the word "sapphires," as do most English translations. That word is essentially the same in the original Hebrew, which reads "sappir." A footnote suggests "lapis lazuli," an opaque blue gemstone that was found in the ancient Near East. Some scholars favor that translation since there is some question whether or not the stone we know as the sapphire was found there.

Another interesting contrast can be seen in verses 8 to 11. The birds are known for their keen sense of sight, whereas the beasts are known for their courage and strength. Yet they have no inkling of what is going on in the mines below them, nor do they have the intelligence or skill to do what human beings accomplish in the mines. Job describes the miner in a vivid manner: "He tunnels through the rock; his eyes see all its treasures." Those tunnels probably were horizontal courses from which the ore was dug.

A footnote to verse 11 offers an alternate reading: "He dams up the sources of the rivers." P. E. Kretzmann briefly explains those words: "stopping the dripping or the seams of water which threaten to fill up the pits and galleries of the mines" (*Popular Commentary,* Old Testament, Volume 2, page 38).

The skill and achievements of mankind are truly remarkable. And yet the discovery of true wisdom is far beyond human intelligence and skill. It is also of such great value that it cannot be attained even at the price of the most precious gems and jewels. That raises an important question, a question that is repeated in a later verse (20).

Human wealth cannot purchase wisdom

12 **"But where can wisdom be found?**
   Where does understanding dwell?
13 **Man does not comprehend its worth;**
   it cannot be found in the land of the living.
14 **The deep says, 'It is not in me';**
   the sea says, 'It is not with me.'
15 **It cannot be bought with the finest gold,**
   nor can its price be weighed in silver.
16 **It cannot be bought with the gold of Ophir,**
   with precious onyx or sapphires.
17 **Neither gold nor crystal can compare with it,**
   nor can it be had for jewels of gold.
18 **Coral and jasper are not worthy of mention;**
   the price of wisdom is beyond rubies.
19 **The topaz of Cush cannot compare with it;**
   it cannot be bought with pure gold.

"Where can wisdom be found? Where does understanding dwell?" This verse may be regarded as a conclusion to the preceding verses or as an introduction to the verses that follow. In fact, it is a transitional verse, and it also serves as the theme of this entire chapter. It is so important that it is repeated almost verbatim in verse 20. The closing verse (28) also speaks of wisdom and summarizes the message of the chapter. We will consider the nature of this wisdom in more detail in our discussion of the last section of this chapter (verses 20-28).

The wisdom of which Job speaks is valuable beyond any human comprehension, and it cannot be found in this world. Nor does it exist in the depths of the sea. Job goes on to say that a person cannot acquire it with the most precious metals or jewels: gold, silver, onyx, sapphires, crystal, jasper, rubies, or topaz. It is interesting to note that the word "gold" is mentioned five times in these five verses (15-19). It is significant that in those five occurrences Job used four different Hebrew words for "gold." Each word describes the gold from a particular viewpoint. The "gold of Ophir" is mentioned several times in the Old Testament. Although the location of Ophir cannot be precisely identified, it was famous for its gold.

There is a difference of opinion among translators regarding the identification of some of the jewels mentioned in these verses. In our discussion of verse 6, we mentioned that the word translated as "sapphires" could perhaps be translated better as "lapis lazuli." In verse 17 the NIV translates the second jewel with the word "crystal"; some translations use the word *glass*. In verse 18 the NIV renders the second word "jasper;" others have *crystal*. The NIV has "rubies" for the last word of verse 8; others have *pearls*. That the word "rubies" is preferable is suggested by its use in another Old Testament passage: "Their princes were brighter than snow and whiter than milk, their bodies more ruddy than rubies, their appearance like sapphires" (Lamentations 4:7). The word *ruddy,* which means "reddish," suggests "rubies" as the translation of that Hebrew word, for rubies, not pearls, are red.

Job has listed some of the most precious metals and gems. Yet none of them, not even all of them together, are of sufficient value to acquire the true wisdom of which he is speaking. One might then ask, "If wisdom is not found in any of those places (skill in mining and purchase with jewels), where can one find it?" Job repeats that question in the opening verse of the section that follows and also gives the only true answer.

God alone is the source of true wisdom

²⁰ "Where then does wisdom come from?
   Where does understanding dwell?
²¹ It is hidden from the eyes of every living thing,
   concealed even from the birds of the air.
²² Destruction and Death say,
   'Only a rumor of it has reached our ears.'
²³ God understands the way to it
   and he alone knows where it dwells,
²⁴ for he views the ends of the earth
   and sees everything under the heavens.
²⁵ When he established the force of the wind
   and measured out the waters,
²⁶ when he made a decree for the rain
   and a path for the thunderstorm,
²⁷ then he looked at wisdom and appraised it;
   he confirmed it and tested it.
²⁸ And he said to man,
   'The fear of the Lord—that is wisdom,
   and to shun evil is understanding.'"

Job again asks, "Where then does wisdom come from? Where does understanding dwell?" Verse 20 is virtually identical to verse 12. Its repetition gives it emphasis so that it takes on the nature of a refrain. It also serves as the main theme and leads to the third part of this chapter, which reminds us that God alone is the source of true wisdom. Apart from God, such wisdom is inaccessible to mortals.

Verse 22 speaks of Destruction and Death. This verse is difficult to interpret. Does it speak of hell as the place of torment? Or does it refer to the state of the dead who have passed from this life to the next without regard to whether their souls are in heaven or in hell? Franz Delitzsch remarks in his commentary, "No creature, whether in the realm of the living or the dead, can help us get wisdom. There is but One who possesses a perfect knowledge concerning wisdom, namely Elohim (God), whose gaze extends to the ends of the earth, and who sees under the whole heaven" (Volume 2, page 111). It seems best to understand this verse to speak simply of those who have passed from this life to the next. The terms "Destruction" and "Death" appear to describe the condition of decomposition after death without regard to the eternal destiny of those who have died.

In contrast to man, God has perfect wisdom. Such wisdom was his when he created the universe. In his commentary on Job, Norman C. Habel states, "Thus wisdom both precedes creation (Proverbs 8:22ff.), and is revealed to God in the very creation process itself" (page 400).

In the book of Proverbs, Solomon declares,

> By wisdom the Lord laid the earth's foundations,
> by understanding he set the heavens in place;
> by his knowledge the deeps were divided,
> and the clouds let drop the dew. (3:19,20)

In greater detail, wisdom speaks in Proverbs chapter 8:

The LORD possessed me at the beginning of His way,
Before His works of old.
From everlasting I was established
From the beginning, from the earliest times of
    the earth.
When there were no depths I was brought forth,
When there were no springs abounding with water.
Before the mountains were settled,
Before the hills I was brought forth;
While He had not yet made the earth and the fields,
Nor the first dust of the world.
When He established the heavens, I was there,
When He inscribed a circle on the face of the deep,
When He made firm the skies above,
When the springs of the deep became fixed,
When He set for the sea its boundary,
So that the water should not transgress His command,
When He marked out the foundations of the earth;
Then I was beside Him, as a master workman;
And I was daily His delight,
Rejoicing always before Him,
Rejoicing in the world, His earth,
And having my delight in the sons of men.
    (verses 22-31, New American Standard Version)

These words from the eighth chapter of Proverbs strongly suggest that in this passage wisdom is not merely an attribute but a person. Moreover, that person is superhuman, for he existed from eternity, was active in creation, and is one with God the Father. He is no mere mortal. He is the one whom God addresses in Psalm 2:7: "You are my Son, today [that is, from eternity] I have become your Father." He is therefore none other than God the Son, who from eternity has existed with the Father and the Holy Spirit as one true God. Together they form the Holy Trinity. A careful reading of Genesis 1:1-3 suggests the Trinity: the Father (verse 1), the Holy Spirit (verse 2), and the Son (verse 3). The words "and God said" (Genesis 1:3) suggest the Word. Of him we read in John 1:1-3: "In the beginning was the Word, and the Word was with God, and the Word was God. He was with God in the beginning. Through him all things were made; without him nothing was made that has been made." All Christians who accept the Bible as God's Word identify this passage with Jesus Christ, the Son of God.

Jesus is also given the title "wisdom" in the New Testament. In one passage Paul refers to him as the one "in whom are hidden all the treasures of wisdom and knowledge" (Colossians 2:3). Paul also directly calls Christ "wisdom." In one passage he states, "We preach Christ crucified: . . . Christ the power of God and the wisdom of God" (1 Corinthians 1:23,24). Later in the same chapter, he also declares, "Christ Jesus . . . who has become for us wisdom from God" (verse 30). There is, therefore, also New Testament evidence for identifying this wisdom with Jesus Christ.

We have reason to believe that Job also had in mind the Son of God when he described God as creating and establishing this universe through wisdom. In earlier passages in Job (9:33; 16:19-21; 19:25-27), we saw indications of Job's faith in the Savior to come as his Redeemer and Intercessor. Job could very well have had the Redeemer in mind as he also spoke these words. It was the triune God who created this world, an event that Job describes in verses 25 to 27 of chapter 28. In chapter 38, in considerably greater detail, God himself reminds Job that he created this vast universe.

The concluding verse serves as a capstone to this chapter. God tells man, "The fear of the Lord—that is wisdom, and to shun evil is understanding." The first word in the Hebrew is an interjection, rendered in the King James Version by the word "Behold." The word draws attention to the importance of the statement that follows: "The fear of the Lord—that is wisdom, and to shun evil is understanding."

You may notice that the word "Lord" here is written with only the first letter capitalized, not all four. In the original Hebrew it is "Adonai," the title meaning "Lord," and not the name *Jehovah* or *Yahweh,* which is expressed by capitalizing all four letters (Lord). The title *Lord* emphasizes his sovereign majesty. We human beings are to regard him as Lord and Master. We are to show him fear in the sense of reverence and respect. We are to yield our will to his. In so doing, we will, by his grace, shun evil and try to conform our lives to his will. Through daily repentance and faith we will receive forgiveness for our sins. Through the use of his Word and sacraments, we will be kept in daily fellowship with our God.

May we follow the example of Job as he is earlier described in this book: "This man was blameless and upright; he feared God and shunned evil" (1:1). May we through the Word receive the true wisdom that leads to eternal life. God grant this!

Job recalls his former prosperity and honor

29 Job continued his discourse:

² "How I long for the months gone by,
    for the days when God watched over me,
³ when his lamp shone upon my head
    and by his light I walked through darkness!
⁴ Oh, for the days when I was in my prime,
    when God's intimate friendship blessed my house,
⁵ when the Almighty was still with me
    and my children were around me,

⁶ **when my path was drenched with cream**
and the rock poured out for me streams of olive oil.

In chapters 29 to 31, Job is still the speaker. He appears to be directly addressing his three friends. They had brought many unjust and severe accusations against him, so he felt compelled to defend himself. In this closing speech Job contrasts his previous prosperity with his present adversity and again protests his innocence of various flagrant sins and crimes.

Again, as in 27:1, Job's speech is introduced with the words "Job continued his discourse." During the three rounds of their dialogue, Job's speeches were each introduced with the words "Then Job replied." In his two long closing speeches (chapters 27,28 and 29–31), we assume that Job paused to give his friends the opportunity to respond if they so wished. Apparently, they had nothing more to say, so Job continued.

Job's opening words express a yearning for his prosperous past: "How I long for the months gone by." What a stark contrast between the Job of the past and the Job of the present! Before, he was healthy, wealthy, and the most highly respected man of the community. Now he had lost almost everything, was forsaken by most of his acquaintances, and had to listen to the cruel words of his so-called friends. His former prosperity was only a memory. In the days of his prosperity he had enjoyed a close relationship with God, his family, and his community, but now those relationships seemed over.

Job first mentions God, whom he acknowledges as the one who had brought him his great success. In days past God had watched over Job. He had felt God's fatherly concern and loving care. It was God who had blessed him both spiritually and temporally. The expressions "lamp" and "light" are symbols of God's guidance and blessings. In the past God had directed him and blessed him.

Job wishes he could still experience those blessings. He repeats an urgent wish: "Oh, for the days when I was in my prime." Does Job here refer to his youth or to his more mature years? The verses that follow favor the latter interpretation. Verse 5 tells us that Job already had his children, who at that time were probably grown up. He refers to the time of his greatest affluence, perhaps shortly before disaster struck. In those days Job enjoyed a close personal relationship with God, a relationship that he sorely missed now as he was suffering intensely. Job describes his former prosperity in vivid language: "When my path was drenched with cream and the rock poured out for me streams of olive oil." Job's household was filled with abundance.

Milk products and olive oil were two commodities that were both healthful and useful. Job had so much milk or cream that he could use them to bathe his feet if he wished. In ancient times people used olive oil for cooking, as an ointment for their bodies, and for fuel in their lamps. Olive oil is still considered to be one of the most healthful oils for cooking, and it can serve many other purposes. The expression "the rock poured out for me streams of olive oil" could refer either to the rocky hillsides on which olive trees stood or to the olive presses used for extracting the oil.

As he lived prosperously on his large estate, Job enjoyed his relationship with his God and his family. He was also an active leader in his community.

> 7 **"When I went to the gate of the city**
> **and took my seat in the public square,**
> 8 **the young men saw me and stepped aside**
> **and the old men rose to their feet;**
> 9 **the chief men refrained from speaking**
> **and covered their mouths with their hands;**
> 10 **the voices of the nobles were hushed,**
> **and their tongues stuck to the roof of their mouths.**

> [11] Whoever heard me spoke well of me,
>   and those who saw me commended me,
> [12] because I rescued the poor who cried for help,
>   and the fatherless who had none to assist him.
> [13] The man who was dying blessed me;
>   I made the widow's heart sing.
> [14] I put on righteousness as my clothing;
>   justice was my robe and my turban.
> [15] I was eyes to the blind
>   and feet to the lame.
> [16] I was a father to the needy;
>   I took up the case of the stranger.
> [17] I broke the fangs of the wicked
>   and snatched the victims from their teeth.

In days past Job regularly went from his large estate to the city nearby. The "gate" of the city was the place where people would gather to visit, transact business, or conduct trials. In the fourth chapter of the book of Ruth, we read about the business transaction that Boaz conducted at the city gate of Bethlehem before he married Ruth. In Proverbs chapter 31 the writer praises a woman of good and noble character. In one verse we read, "Her husband is respected at the city gate, where he takes his seat among the elders of the land" (verse 23).

Those words also remind us of Job as he speaks in this chapter. He tells us of the good old days when he went to the city gate and took his seat in the public square. Everyone respected him. Young men showed their respect by stepping aside. Even men who were older than Job rose to their feet. We are reminded of a situation in our time. When the president of the United States gives his annual message, the members of Congress show their respect by rising to their feet and applauding. Thus young and old, leaders and nobles showed honor and respect to Job. They stood in silence before him and waited for him to speak. In the concluding verses of this chapter, Job again reminds his friends of the high regard in which he was held by young and old.

Not only by his wise words but also by his actions, Job proved himself to be a man of sterling qualities. He was considerate of those who were in need. He states, "I rescued the poor who cried for help, and the fatherless who had none to assist him. The man who was dying blessed me; I made the widow's heart sing." Job not only helped them out of their troubles, he restored their sense of worth.

In these words he defends himself against the accusation of Eliphaz's last speech. From Job's afflictions and sufferings, Eliphaz had falsely concluded that Job had been guilty of lovelessness toward his fellow human beings. "You demanded security from your brothers for no reason; you stripped men of their clothing, leaving them naked. You gave no water to the weary and you withheld food from the hungry, though you were a powerful man, owning land—an honored man, living on it. And you sent widows away empty-handed and broke the strength of the fatherless" (22:6-9). How cruel and unjust those words were! Job attempts to set the record straight by declaring that he helped the unfortunate.

God had twice described Job as "blameless and upright, a man who fears God and shuns evil" (1:8; 2:3). Now in his own defense, Job says of himself, "I put on righteousness as my clothing; justice was my robe and my turban." In similar language the Bible elsewhere describes virtues as garments that beautify the wearer. Using similar language, Peter urges us, "Clothe yourselves with humility toward one another" (1 Peter 5:5). In his daily life, Job's righteousness and justice were as plain to see as the clothes he wore. Wouldn't we all do well to imitate Job in that respect?

In saying he was "eyes to the blind and feet to the lame," Job shows that he went out of his way to help the handicapped. He was concerned for those who were in need. If Job were alive today, there can be no doubt that he would give full support to special facilities for the handicapped.

Job refers to himself as "a father to the needy." As a good father has loving concern for his children, so Job had in mind the welfare of the needy. He made it his business to find out about those who were helpless and friendless. He was a protector of those who needed it. Strangers and aliens in particular were vulnerable to prejudice and persecution. When Job became aware of such injustice, he looked into it and made sure such an outsider received fair treatment.

In those days there also were evil men who took advantage of others, making them victims of crooked dealings. Such people sometimes resorted to violence. Job took a firm stand against them. Using strong language, he declares, "I broke the fangs of the wicked and snatched the victims from their teeth." He had a sense of justice and the strength of character to enforce it. He was a leader of men. He hoped to continue such service to his fellow men and to enjoy a full and useful life, as we learn from the verses that follow.

> ¹⁸ **"I thought, 'I will die in my own house,**
> **my days as numerous as the grains of sand.**
> ¹⁹ **My roots will reach to the water,**
> **and the dew will lie all night on my branches.**
> ²⁰ **My glory will remain fresh in me,**
> **the bow ever new in my hand.'**

Since Job was such a righteous and godly man, it isn't strange that he expected to live a long and prosperous life, uninterrupted by misfortune or tragedy. He hoped to continue to enjoy his home and family. That wish he expresses in the opening verse of this section: "I thought, 'I will die in my own house, my days as numerous as the sand.'" The word "house" literally means "nest." It suggests the quiet seclusion of a bird with its young as they are sheltered in a tree.

If you compare various English versions, you will notice that some have a different translation for the last words in verse 18. Instead of "grains of sand," they have the word *phoenix.* The same Hebrew consonants with slightly different vowels may read either "sand" or "phoenix," a bird mentioned in ancient literature. According to legend, this bird lived for several hundred years and would eventually die by burning itself in its nest, and then from its ashes a new bird would spring to life. That is a fanciful and questionable interpretation. We strongly prefer the translation of the NIV: "My days as numerous as the grains of sand." The Bible frequently uses that expression to indicate a large number.

Job uses another interesting figure of speech to express his hope for continued blessings: "My roots will reach to the water, and the dew will lie all night on my branches." Perhaps we don't appreciate the significance of those words, for most regions of the United States have sufficient rainfall. In the area where Job lived, the climate was dry, almost desert-like. Fresh green shrubs were not common except in oases, and the people were dependent on dew to give the plants sufficient moisture. Job expressed the hope that his life could be like a fresh green shrub or tree. Earlier, Bildad had expressed the opposite thought when he described the wicked man, presumably Job: "His roots dry up below and his branches wither above" (18:16).

On the same optimistic note, Job continues, "My glory will remain fresh in me, the bow ever new in my hand." He hoped that people would continue to regard him with respect for his wisdom, judgment, and leadership. The expression "bow" is used in the Bible to indicate strength and agility. Thus the patriarch Jacob on his deathbed prophesied concerning his son

Joseph, "His bow remained steady, his strong arms stayed
limber" (Genesis 49:24).

> ²¹ **"Men listened to me expectantly,**
> **waiting in silence for my counsel.**
> ²² **After I had spoken, they spoke no more;**
> **my words fell gently on their ears.**
> ²³ **They waited for me as for showers**
> **and drank in my words as the spring rain.**
> ²⁴ **When I smiled at them, they scarcely believed it;**
> **the light of my face was precious to them.**
> ²⁵ **I chose the way for them and sat as their chief;**
> **I dwelt as a king among his troops;**
> **I was like one who comforts mourners.**

Some commentators are of the opinion that these five
verses are misplaced in this chapter. They feel that this section ought to come between verses 10 and 11, and print it
accordingly in their translation of the text. While we admit
that these verses might well fit in that order, there is no evidence for that position from the Hebrew manuscripts or the
early Greek translation known as the Septuagint. Furthermore, by moving these five verses, we would lose the force
of Job's speech. In this chapter Job closes his description of
the good old days by again stating that when he appeared
and when he spoke, people showed him great respect.
They awaited his words with attention and realized they had
nothing to add after he had spoken.

Verse 24 is difficult. There is considerable variety in the
English translations. Most likely, the meaning is that people
felt highly honored as well as comforted when Job smiled at
them. In our modern terms, his smile "made their day."
They appreciated Job's kind and cheerful disposition.

Verse 25 summarizes Job's speech. He was a true leader
who had the qualities of a chief, a king, and a counselor. He
was an outstanding man.

When we read this chapter. we may be inclined to think that Job is bragging about himself. Before we draw that conclusion, we must remember that Job had been severely and unjustly accused by his three friends. He felt compelled to defend himself. Considering the injustice of their attacks, it is remarkable that in this speech Job avoids attacking them in return. His language is calm and temperate as he factually reports what his status was during the years of his prosperity. While he speaks in some detail about his reputation and achievements, he glorifies God, who had blessed him so richly. He is not indulging in boasting. He can support his statements with facts.

In this chapter Job speaks of the past, when he enjoyed prosperity and prestige. In the chapter that follows he will speak of the present, when he experienced a reversal as he sat with his unfeeling friends and lamented his miserable condition.

Job experiences misery and disgrace

30 "But now they mock me,
   men younger than I,
   whose fathers I would have disdained
      to put with my sheep dogs.
² Of what use was the strength of their hands to me,
      since their vigor had gone from them?
³ Haggard from want and hunger,
      they roamed the parched land
      in desolate wastelands at night.
⁴ In the brush they gathered salt herbs,
      and their food was the root of the broom tree.
⁵ They were banished from their fellow men,
      shouted at as if they were thieves.
⁶ They were forced to live in the dry stream beds,
      among the rocks and in holes in the ground.

⁷ **They brayed among the bushes**
   and huddled in the undergrowth.
⁸ **A base and nameless brood,**
   they were driven out of the land.

The words of Job in this chapter stand in sharp contrast to his words in the previous chapter. Before he experienced his great misfortune, Job was healthy, prosperous, influential, and highly respected. Now he was sickly, impoverished, lonely, and despised. He who had been master of a large estate was now excluded from society as he was sitting amid ashes outside the city. Formerly the noblest men, old and young, had shown Job the greatest respect and honor. Now even the dregs of society mocked and insulted him.

Earlier in a spirit of sincere resignation, Job had described the reversal of his fortune with beautiful words: "The LORD gave and the LORD has taken away; may the name of the LORD be praised" (1:21). Now in his closing speech, Job at greater length expresses the same truth. In chapter 29 he related some of the many blessings God had showered upon him: wealth, honor, influence, and leadership. In this chapter he paints a stark picture of his present condition. Before, the most respectable people honored him. Now the most contemptible people despise him. Job was an outcast among outcasts.

These opening verses of this chapter describe an ironic situation: Job, "the greatest man among all the people of the East" (1:3), is mocked and ridiculed by young men who were of the lowest classes of society. In those days it was a time-honored custom for the young to honor and respect their elders. Through Moses, God commanded the Israelites, "Rise in the presence of the aged, show respect for the elderly and revere your God. I am the LORD" (Leviticus 19:32). God added those closing words to impress upon the people the importance of that command.

Before he experienced his misfortune, people had shown Job the deepest respect. But now, when he really needed them, where were they? Surely not at his side keeping him company or showing him sympathy. Most of them either ignored him or ridiculed him. We might also ask, Where was Job's wife? Had she also forsaken him? Following his misfortune, Job mentions her when he laments, "My breath is offensive to my wife" (19:17). From those words we might conclude that she could not bear to look at him or be with him. As for his three friends, of what help were they? They might as well have ignored him. Their pompous manner and scolding words only irritated him and added to his discomfort.

When young men from the lowest classes of society mocked and insulted Job, it must have been most humiliating. They added insult to injury. Their actions provoked a bitter response from Job. Earlier (24:5-12) Job had sympathetically described the deplorable conditions of the poor and destitute who were victims of cruel oppressors. Now he speaks differently. These people were of a different kind. They were undisciplined vagabonds, a nuisance to society.

In sharp and sarcastic language, Job describes those young rowdies as "men younger than I, whose fathers I would have disdained to put with my sheep dogs." Those words are usually understood to mean that Job would not put their fathers in charge of his sheep dogs. We could understand those words to have an even stronger meaning: that Job wouldn't have their fathers do the work of the dogs who watch the sheep. How much less, then, would Job have given those young rascals such responsibility.

Speaking of those ruffians and their fathers in caustic language, Job goes on to describe their unhealthy and frail physical condition, their activities as vagabonds, their unappetizing and unhealthful diet on which only the destitute would live, their antisocial behavior, and their open-air homes in streambeds, rocks, holes, and bushes. He calls them "a base and nameless brood," children of people of low character and worthless reputation, people "driven out of the land" by respectable people.

From these verses we learn that long ago, at the time of Job, there were people who were destitute. Some were innocent victims of cruel and heartless people who took advantage of them, as we learn from the section previously referred to (24:5-12). Others apparently pursued their vagrant lifestyle as a matter of choice, as we can learn from the present chapter.

That is also true today. There are many victims of circumstances to whom our hearts must go out. We surely feel sorry for a father who has lost his job and has a difficult time providing for his family. We sympathize with a wife whose husband has deserted her and their children. We will do what we can to help such unfortunate people. But there are also those who refuse to work when they have the opportunity. There are men and women who are addicted to drugs and alcohol and who engage in crime to support their habit. There are vagrants and panhandlers who look for handouts instead of doing an honest day's work.

Job's words in these verses have a strikingly up-to-date sound. Human nature has not essentially changed.

> 9 **"And now their sons mock me in song;**
>   **I have become a byword among them.**
> 10 **They detest me and keep their distance;**
>   **they do not hesitate to spit in my face.**
> 11 **Now that God has unstrung my bow and afflicted me,**
>   **they throw off restraint in my presence.**
> 12 **On my right the tribe attacks;**
>   **they lay snares for my feet,**
>   **they build their siege ramps against me.**

¹³ **They break up my road;**
   they succeed in destroying me—
   without anyone's helping them.
¹⁴ **They advance as through a gaping breach;**
   amid the ruins they come rolling in.
¹⁵ **Terrors overwhelm me;**
   my dignity is driven away as by the wind,
   my safety vanishes like a cloud.

In the previous verses Job described the characteristics and habits of the outcasts. In these verses he pictures their spiteful words and actions against him. As he sat outside the city, those boorish young men mocked and ridiculed him. As they looked at his repulsive and emaciated body, they kept their distance and show their utter contempt by spitting in his face. Not only did they ridicule the unfortunate man; they attacked him. He mentions that they did so on his right side, which in Old Testament passages represents the position of power and honor.

The last line of verse 13 is difficult. It has been understood and translated various ways. The NIV renders it "without anyone's helping them." That would obviously be true since his enemies are many and Job is alone. Those words could also be translated "there is none to help against them." We prefer that translation since Job feels helpless as he is confronted by his aggressive enemies. He needs help. He is also overcome by terrors, and he has lost his dignity and safety. No longer does he serve as chief or king (29:25), but he is suffering great disappointment and deep humiliation.

Job pictures himself as a person who is overcome by fierce and strong enemies who abuse him. To have human enemies is unfortunate enough, but, even worse, Job feels

211

that God is attacking him. He accuses God of having unstrung his bow. Some translate the first line of verse 11 thus: "Now God has loosened my cord and afflicted me." They interpret the cord as the cord of his tent or the cord of his loincloth. A strung bow is also a symbol of strength. In either case, bow or cord, the meaning is the same. Job is complaining that God has deprived him of his strength. Again we must remember that Job was unaware of the fact that God permitted Satan to afflict Job and test his loyalty to God. In the verses that follow, particularly 18 to 23, Job continues his complaint against God.

> [16] "And now my life ebbs away;
>   days of suffering grip me.
> [17] Night pierces my bones;
>   my gnawing pains never rest.
> [18] In his great power God becomes like clothing to me;
>   he binds me like the neck of my garment.
> [19] He throws me into the mud,
>   and I am reduced to dust and ashes.
>
> [20] "I cry out to you, O God, but you do not answer;
>   I stand up, but you merely look at me.
> [21] You turn on me ruthlessly;
>   with the might of your hand you attack me.
> [22] You snatch me up and drive me before the wind;
>   you toss me about in the storm.
> [23] I know you will bring me down to death,
>   to the place appointed for all the living.

In this part of his lament, Job complains against God, who, he feels, has not listened to his pleas for deliverance and justice. He feels his life is slipping away. His deep emotional strain has drained Job of all zest for life. He wishes he could die. At night he cannot sleep, but instead he feels gnawing pains. His sufferings are physical, mental, emotional, and spiritual.

While the word "God" is not in the Hebrew text of verse 18, the NIV is justified in inserting it, for God is the implied subject. As a result of his severe physical affliction, Job had become grossly misshapen. No doubt he had lost so much weight that he was a bag of bones, and he had also suffered boils so that parts of his body swelled. No wonder his three friends had difficulty recognizing him when they came to visit him (2:12). Job's clothes no longer fit him.

Continuing his complaint, Job accuses God of throwing him into the mud and reducing him to dust and ashes. The expression "dust and ashes" also occurs in the last chapter of the book, where Job humbly addresses God, "Therefore I despise myself and repent in dust and ashes" (42:6). Abraham used the same expression when he repeatedly prayed for Sodom and addressed God, "I am nothing but dust and ashes" (Genesis 18:27). The word *dust* reminds us that man is mortal and will return to the dust from which he was taken. The word *ashes* implies that man is sinful and is in need of sacrifice for his sins. Such sacrifice Jesus Christ has already made for us.

In verses 18 and 19, Job speaks about God. In verses 20 to 23, he directly addresses God. He boldly complains that God does not answer his cry for help and justice but merely looks at him. In even stronger language he continues, "You turn on me ruthlessly." Job accuses God of attacking him, snatching him up and driving him before the wind, and tossing him about in the storm. Those are very strong words.

His words reach a climax when he addresses God, "I know you will bring me down to death, to the place appointed for all the living." The first two words, "I know," remind us of the familiar words previously spoken by Job, "I know that my Redeemer lives" (19:25). But what a contrast there is between those two verses! In those earlier words, Job confidently confessed his faith in his future resurrection. In these words (verse 23) he expresses his belief that God will soon bring him down to death, the place appointed for all the living. Some interpreters see the last line of this verse as a suggestion of the resurrection of the dead. That is possible, but its parallel relationship with the first line (speaking of death) appears to make that interpretation questionable.

In previous speeches Job complained that God had terrorized and abused him (6:4; 13:25-27; 16:9-14; 19:6-12). He accused God of acting in an arbitrary manner, picking on him without any reason. As he wrestled with the question "Why does a righteous person suffer?" he felt he had the right answer: God is arbitrary. In drawing that conclusion, Job was wrong. He sinned in charging God with injustice, for God is perfect and just.

In his booklet *Faith on Trial,* Roland Cap Ehlke discusses that difficult problem:

> Some people would use the apparent injustice of the world as an argument against the very goodness and power of God. Either God is not good or he is not almighty, they contend. For if God is good, he will want to prevent unjust suffering. And if God is almighty, he will be able to prevent it. So if he is both good and almighty . . . then why does God allow suffering?

> This is the logical dilemma Job is trapped in.

Then, under the heading "Wrong Reasoning," Rev. Ehlke continues,

> Convincing as this thinking appears to be, it still is wrong. For one thing, it is presumptuous. How can man presume to judge God? Our intelligence and experience are very limited, our vision

shortsighted. But God knows everything—past, present and future. Surely he knows better than we do what is just and unjust in the long run, in eternity.

Secondly, the accusation that God is unfair overlooks the very nature of Christian faith. Our faith is not based on what we can reason from experience. Rather, it rests in the promises of God. As Hebrews 11:1 explains, "Now faith is being sure of what we hope for and certain of what we do not see." (page 39)

[24] "Surely no one lays a hand on a broken man
  when he cries for help in his distress.
[25] Have I not wept for those in trouble?
  Has not my soul grieved for the poor?
[26] Yet when I hoped for good, evil came;
  when I looked for light, then came darkness.
[27] The churning inside me never stops;
  days of suffering confront me.
[28] I go about blackened, but not by the sun;
  I stand up in the assembly and cry for help.
[29] I have become a brother of jackals,
  a companion of owls.
[30] My skin grows black and peels;
  my body burns with fever.
[31] My harp is tuned to mourning,
  and my flute to the sound of wailing.

By his words in the first verse Job implies that when he cries out for help in his distress, he should not have to suffer harm. And yet, had not God permitted him to suffer severe afflictions? In spite of his sufferings, Job's plea for deliverance had gone unheeded. Job had wept and sympathized with those who were in trouble and had grieved for the poor. Was it really fair that he himself should now be deprived of sympathy and help when he had given it so generously to others? In the previous chapter he had listed some of the good deeds he had done for the unfortunate (29:12-17). Could he not expect others to return the favor now that he was in such dire straits? But no, that was not to be. He sadly remarks, "Yet when I hoped for good, evil came; when I looked for light, then came darkness." It just didn't seem right.

The last five verses of this chapter are filled with striking imagery describing the physical and emotional effects of his suffering. He complains, "The churning inside me never stops." Job expresses his sad loneliness in the words "I have become a brother of jackals, a companion of owls." For the last word a better translation is "ostriches." The jackal makes a mourning sound, while the ostrich gives out a hissing moan. Job was a sad and lonely man.

Two verses paint Job's condition in extremely physical terms. First he says, "I go about blackened, but not by the sun," and then he adds, "My skin grows black and peels; my body burns with fever." Those verses give us some clue to the nature of his physical ailment and have led some commentators to conclude that Job suffered from elephantiasis or some form of leprosy (see the commentary on page 26). Job's darkened skin did not result from his exposure to the sun but from his severe skin disease. His skin was peeling, and his body was burning with fever. The man was really very sick! Who could blame him for complaining? Would you or I do any better?

Job had rescued the poor who cried for help (29:12), yet no one would give him a hearing as he stood up in the assembly and cried for help. In his distress he must have ventured from his solitary place occasionally in quest of a sympathetic ear, but to no avail. His cries for help went unheeded.

In the closing verse of this chapter Job laments, "My harp is tuned to mourning, and my flute to the sound of wailing."

The harp and flute were instruments that people used for music of joyful praise to God, as we know from many psalms. For Job they became instruments suitable for dirges and lamentations.

In Job's deep humiliation and intense suffering, we see similarities to our Lord's suffering. Jesus came down from highest exaltation to deepest degradation and humiliation. Job faced the false accusations of Eliphaz, Bildad, and Zophar. Jesus faced the verbal attacks of the scribes, Pharisees, and Sadducees. Job faced the indifference of his former friends and colleagues who now ignored him. Jesus faced the cold indifference of the people who had even witnessed his miracles and of the disciples who forsook him and fled. Job was mocked and humiliated by the young vagabonds described in the opening verses of this chapter. Jesus was falsely accused, mocked, and crowned with thorns as he stood before Caiaphas, Pilate, Herod, and the angry Jews. Job felt the heavy hand of God pressing down upon him as he looked forward to nothing better than death. Jesus felt the heavy hand of God pressing down upon him as he bore the sins of all others and trudged his weary way to the cross to die for the sins of the world. As Isaiah had prophesied, "It was the LORD's will to crush him [Jesus] and cause him to suffer" (Isaiah 53:10). Indeed, "God made him who had no sin to be sin for us, so that in him we might become the righteousness of God" (2 Corinthians 5:21).

There are truly many striking parallels between the suffering of Job and the suffering of Jesus. But there are also many striking differences. Although Job had not committed special sins that merited such great suffering, he was nevertheless a sinner like the rest of us. On the other hand, Jesus was sinless, yet he bore the sins of all and suffered more intensely than anyone—yes, even Job. Jesus bore the sins of all—

yours and mine, also Job's. And although at first Job did not complain, in due time when he felt his afflictions so intensely, he did complain bitterly, as everyone else would complain under those conditions—except Jesus. Of him, Peter declares, "Christ suffered for you, leaving you an example, that you should follow in his steps. 'He committed no sin, and no deceit was found in his mouth.' When they hurled their insults at him, he did not retaliate; when he suffered, he made no threats. Instead, he entrusted himself to him who judges justly" (1 Peter 2:21-23).

Let Jesus, then, be our perfect example when we must undergo persecution and suffering. And when we do, let us also remember that Jesus already suffered for us and atoned for our sins. He has removed our heavy burden and given us his burden, which is light, and his yoke, which is easy (Matthew 11:30). Job was a great man, but he was only human and also sinful. Jesus is true God as well as true man, and he is sinless.

With these remarks we conclude the second of the three chapters in this final lengthy discourse by Job. Following this lament, Job once more protests his innocence of certain specific wrongs and sins against his fellow human beings.

Job claims he is innocent of various wrongs and crimes

Job's last long speech is clearly divided into three parts, each distinct from the other two. Chapter 29 contained a glowing account of his days of prosperity. In contrast, chapter 30 pictured his suffering and disgrace after disaster had struck. Finally, in this chapter (31) he earnestly and passionately denies that he is guilty of certain sins and crimes. In strong language he states that if he had committed certain crimes, he would be obligated to suffer dire consequences. Many of his statements begin with the word *if*. (No fewer than 19 times does the word *if* occur in these 40 verses.)

By repeatedly beginning these statements with the word *if,* Job is emphatically denying that he is guilty of those sins. As we will see when we consider the verses, he is denying not only the outward actions but even wrong motives, attitudes, and desires.

The question naturally arises, Did Job claim that he was sinless? It may seem as if he did. In verse 33, however, he admits his sin: "If I have concealed my sin as men do, by hiding my guilt in my heart." There he speaks of his sin and guilt. And yet his manner of speaking in this chapter comes dangerously close to self-righteous boasting. But we can defend Job's words to a measure when we try to understand his intense suffering and the unkind words of his friends. Job was a desperate man when he uttered these words, the last words he spoke except for two brief replies to the Lord (40:4,5; 42:2-6). His last recorded words reveal that Job had learned to bow to God in deep humility.

Job denies lust

31 **"I made a covenant with my eyes**
not to look lustfully at a girl.
² For what is man's lot from God above,
his heritage from the Almighty on high?
³ Is it not ruin for the wicked,
disaster for those who do wrong?
⁴ Does he not see my ways
and count my every step?

Job had a remarkable understanding of the true nature of sin. Although he may not have been an Israelite, his religion corresponded closely to the true religion of the Old Testament. The sins against the Sixth Commandment go much deeper than the overt act of adultery or fornication. In the

Sermon on the Mount, Jesus states, "Anyone who looks at a woman lustfully has already committed adultery with her in his heart" (Matthew 5:28).

In the opening verse of this chapter, Job declares, "I made a covenant with my eyes not to look lustfully at a girl." The last word, "girl," may also be translated as "virgin" or "maiden" and refers to one who is unmarried. On the other hand, Job speaks of a married woman in verse 9. In this opening verse Job strongly maintains that he has made up his mind not to yield to the temptation of lustfully looking at an attractive girl.

He is aware of the serious consequences of such lust: God on high will severely punish him. God sees all of Job's ways and watches his steps. Indeed, he can read Job's heart. Job refuses to place himself into the category of the wicked and consequently suffer the disastrous fate they suffer.

Job denies deceit

> ⁵ "If I have walked in falsehood
>   or my foot has hurried after deceit—
> ⁶ let God weigh me in honest scales
>   and he will know that I am blameless—
> ⁷ if my steps have turned from the path,
>   if my heart has been led by my eyes,
>   or if my hands have been defiled,
> ⁸ then may others eat what I have sown,
>   and may my crops be uprooted.

In this section Job begins a long series of oaths introduced by the word "if." That is a strong manner of protesting innocence. To his silent friends Job repeatedly denies that he is guilty of falsehood and deceit. He pictures his life in terms of walking, language that is typical of both the Old and New Testament. His words express strong confidence that God will find him innocent. Using another figure of speech, he declares, "Let God weigh me in honest scales and he will know that I am blameless." The Old Testament frequently condemns the use of false scales (Amos 8:5; Proverbs 11:1; 20:10,23). Job knows that God's scales are perfectly honest, and he asks God to weigh him in them. So confident of his innocence is Job.

In a series of four oaths Job calls down evil upon himself if he is guilty of a sin or crime. In each of those instances the word "if" is followed in the next verse by the word "then." We find such a succession in verses 7 and 8, 9 and 10, 21 and 22, and 38 and 39. Job so confidently protests his innocence of falsehood that he is willing to give up everything he has worked for.

The words "steps," "heart," and "hands" express all aspects of his desire, attitude, and activity. Verse 8 describes his work and activity in the familiar terms of farming: Job has sown, but others will reap his crops. For him it would be a total loss of his investment if he were guilty of crooked dealings.

Job denies adultery

> ⁹ "If my heart has been enticed by a woman,
>   or if I have lurked at my neighbor's door,
> ¹⁰ then may my wife grind another man's grain,
>   and may other men sleep with her.
> ¹¹ For that would have been shameful,
>   a sin to be judged.
> ¹² It is a fire that burns to Destruction;
>   it would have uprooted my harvest.

In his troubled state of mind Job does not speak in neat and logical order. In verses 1 to 4 his subject is lust for a maiden. Then, after speaking of deceit (5-8), he again speaks of lust for a woman, this time the wife of another man. Under no circumstances would Job even consider committing adultery with another man's wife. Although like all human beings Job had a sinful heart and could be tempted, he made every effort to discipline himself and resist that temptation. That woman was another man's wife and belonged to him alone as a sexual partner, just as Job's wife belonged to him alone. Job was so sure of his own innocence in this matter that he said, "Then may my wife grind another man's grain, and may other men sleep with her."

Job took his marriage vows very seriously, calling adultery something "shameful, a sin to be judged."

"It is a fire that burns to Destruction; it would have uprooted my harvest." In the NIV the word "Destruction" is capitalized. The Hebrew word is *Abaddon,* the very word Saint John uses in Revelation 9:11 when he speaks of the king of hell, Satan, as we noted in our comments on 26:6.

The Bible elsewhere describes adultery as a sin that burns like a fire. Solomon warns us against that sin in these words: "Can a man scoop fire into his lap without his clothes being burned? Can a man walk on hot coals without his feet being scorched? So is he who sleeps with another man's wife; no one who touches her will go unpunished" (Proverbs 6:27-29). Job was no adulterer.

Job denies mistreating his servants

> ¹³ "If I have denied justice to my menservants
> and maidservants
> when they had a grievance against me,
> ¹⁴ what will I do when God confronts me?
> What will I answer when called to account?
> ¹⁵ Did not he who made me in the womb make them?
> Did not the same one form us both within our mothers?

In the opening chapter we read that Job had a large number of servants (1:3). A man in that position might easily be tempted to regard them as mere property and not individual human beings. But not Job. Like him, they were human beings who had their rights. And although he tried to treat them fairly, there might have been occasions when they had a reasonable complaint. Job would not close his ears to their complaints but would give them due attention. And why? Because there was someone with higher authority than Job. He states, "What will I do when God confronts me? What will I answer when called to account?" The servants were accountable to Job, but he was accountable to God. He therefore felt a heavy responsibility to be as fair and reasonable toward his servants as he could possibly be, to maidservants as well as menservants.

Job gives another reason why he treated his servants fairly and humanely: "Did not he who made me in the womb make them? Did not the same one form us both within our mothers?" Job is, of course, speaking of God. The prophet Malachi uses similar language: "Have we not all one Father? Did not one God create us?" (Malachi 2:10) The embryo is not merely the result of a sexual act between a man and a woman. It is a wonderful creation of God. In striking language David refers to his conception in Psalm 139:13-16. I suggest that you read that passage. In verse 16 of that psalm, the words "my unformed body" could better be translated as "my embryo," an early stage in one's life within the mother's womb.

Job states that he sees no essential difference between himself and his servants, even the lowliest among them. Both he and they were once embryos in their mothers' wombs. They are as fully human as he. They too have human rights and privileges.

Job denies neglecting the poor and weak
¹⁶ **"If I have denied the desires of the poor**
or let the eyes of the widow grow weary,

¹⁷ **if I have kept my bread to myself,**
    not sharing it with the fatherless—
¹⁸ **but from my youth I reared him as would a father,**
    and from my birth I guided the widow—
¹⁹ **if I have seen anyone perishing for lack of clothing,**
    or a needy man without a garment,
²⁰ **and his heart did not bless me**
    for warming him with the fleece from my sheep,
²¹ **if I have raised my hand against the fatherless,**
    knowing that I had influence in court,
²² **then let my arm fall from the shoulder,**
    let it be broken off at the joint.
²³ **For I dreaded destruction from God,**
    and for fear of his splendor I could not do such things.

Having spoken of his own servants, Job now turned his attention to others outside his household who were in need: the poor, the fatherless, and the widows. He had previously declared that he helped and befriended them (29:12,13). Earlier Eliphaz had accused Job of refusing to help the weary, the hungry, the fatherless, and widows (22:7-9). Now in these verses Job firmly denied that false charge. Job was not a miser. He regularly shared his food with others. People were welcome at Job's table. Others were welcome guests not only on the more festive occasions when the menu included meat, but even on ordinary days when simpler fare (bread) was served. These words remind us of the household of Martin Luther, at whose table many guests were frequently gathered, fed, and entertained. Both Job and Luther extended hospitality to others.

Job makes special mention of the fatherless and the widow. He mentions that the fatherless grew up in Job's household. That could refer to the household of Job's father or to Job's own household or both. Moreover, from his birth, literally from his mother's womb, Job showed helpful concern for the widow. He uses a form of exaggeration to emphasize the fact that from his earliest days he helped others less fortunate than he.

Job's generosity also revealed itself in his concern for the physical comfort of others. From his flock of sheep he would gladly supply the wool to make warm clothing to protect them from cold.

In a strong oath Job continues, "If I have raised my hand against the fatherless, knowing that I had influence in court, then let my arm fall from the shoulder, let it be broken off at the joint." Job was a man of great prominence and influence, as we know from his words in a previous chapter (29:7-10,21-25). By a gesture he easily could have influenced the court to make a decision against an unfortunate person. But Job didn't. He firmly denies that he had ever exerted such damaging influence, and he confirms his innocence in the strongest terms. A similar oath is expressed by the psalmist when he says, "If I forget you, O Jerusalem, may my right hand forget its skill. May my tongue cling to the roof of my mouth if I do not remember you, if I do not consider Jerusalem my highest joy" (Psalm 137:5,6).

Job concludes this section by stating the reason he made every effort to be generous and fair to others: "For I dreaded destruction from God, and for fear of his splendor I could not do such things." If Job sinned against his fellow human beings, he knew that he was also sinning against God. It is God who has commanded us to love our neighbor. Job was keenly aware of his responsibility toward others, and he knew that God would call him to account if he failed to help them when they were in need.

The essential message of God's law is to love God and our neighbor. The apostle John reminds us that it is impossible for us to love God if we hate our fellow human beings:

"If anyone says, 'I love God,' yet hates his brother, he is a liar. For anyone who does not love his brother, whom he has seen, cannot love God, whom he has not seen. And he has given us this command: Whoever loves God must also love his brother" (1 John 4:20,21).

Job denies greed and idolatry

²⁴ "If I have put my trust in gold
   or said to pure gold, 'You are my security,'
²⁵ if I have rejoiced over my great wealth,
   the fortune my hands had gained,
²⁶ if I have regarded the sun in its radiance
   or the moon moving in splendor,
²⁷ so that my heart was secretly enticed
   and my hand offered them a kiss of homage,
²⁸ then these also would be sins to be judged,
   for I would have been unfaithful to God on high.

People who have acquired a large amount of money and property can be in danger of loving and trusting in their riches. The apostle Paul warns us, "People who want to get rich fall into temptation and a trap and into many foolish and harmful desires that plunge men into ruin and destruction. For the love of money is a root of all kinds of evil. Some people, eager for money, have wandered from the faith and pierced themselves with many griefs" (1 Timothy 6:9,10). We do not have to be rich to love money. People who are poor or of average wealth can also easily yield to that temptation. We must all pray for God not to let money become our god. Jesus warns us, "You cannot serve both God and Money" (Matthew 6:24).

Since Job was wealthy, he must have had to fight the temptation to place his confidence in wealth. It was only because he lived in a close relationship with God that he succeeded to the extent that he did in resisting that temptation. Verses 24 and 25 express a strong denial of false trust in riches, which is a form of idolatry. There is a great temptation to make money one's god and to worship it.

Job renounces another form of idolatry in verses 26 and 27—the worship of the sun and the moon. In ancient times worshiping the sun, the moon, and other celestial bodies was very prevalent. Because the sun is so important for life and growth on this earth, from earliest times people have worshiped it as a god. The Egyptians wrote many poems addressed to the sun-god. Among the Greek gods were Apollo and Helios, gods of the sun. Other nations also had their sun gods. The moon has fascinated people from earliest times because of its ever-changing phases and its control of ocean tides. The Greeks regarded Artemis (Diana) and Selene as goddesses of the moon. Thinking that the stars exerted a strong influence upon human beings, the ancients developed the false science of astrology. Today there are millions of people who faithfully read their horoscopes and who use astrology as a guide for their lives. Faith in astrology is inconsistent with true faith in God and is really a form of idolatry.

In these verses (26-28) Job disavows any such confidence in the celestial bodies. He refuses to express his adoration by extending them a kiss, which was a common practice in ancient times. For Job to do so would have been a form of hypocrisy. Job would not secretly worship the sun and moon while he outwardly acknowledged the Lord to be his God.

Job denies gloating over his enemy's misfortune and concealing his own sin

> [29] "If I have rejoiced at my enemy's misfortune
>   or gloated over the trouble that came to him—

> ³⁰ I have not allowed my mouth to sin
>   by invoking a curse against his life—
> ³¹ if the men of my household have never said,
>   'Who has not had his fill of Job's meat?'—
> ³² but no stranger had to spend the night in the street,
>   for my door was always open to the traveler—
> ³³ if I have concealed my sin as men do,
>   by hiding my guilt in my heart
> ³⁴ because I so feared the crowd
>   and so dreaded the contempt of the clans
>   that I kept silent and would not go outside.

Our human nature tempts us to gloat over the misfortune of others, particularly our enemies. We are inclined to say, "That served him right. He had it coming." Job was above such petty vengefulness, and he denies such sinful rejoicing. He would not let such personal animosity enter his heart or pass his lips. He would not so much as utter a curse against his enemy. Job's words remind us of Solomon's statement in Proverbs, "Do not gloat when your enemy falls; when he stumbles, do not let your heart rejoice" (24:17).

These verses (Job 31:29,30; Proverbs 24:17) express love for one's enemy from a negative point of view: not rejoicing at his misfortune. Another passage in the book of Proverbs expresses such love from a positive point of view: "If your enemy is hungry, give him food to eat; if he is thirsty, give him water to drink. In doing this, you will heap burning coals on his head, and the LORD will reward you" (25:21,22). In showing kindness to our enemy by returning good for evil, we may cause him to repent and change his ways. Paul quotes that passage in Romans 12:20 when he urges us not to seek revenge. In his Sermon on the Mount, Jesus exhorts us, "Love your enemies and pray for those who persecute you" (Matthew 5:44). Job made a sincere effort to show love and kindness to others, including his enemies.

Verse 31 of this chapter has been translated and interpreted in various ways. In the light of the preceding verses, it is best to understand these verses as expressing Job's hospitality to others. From his own flocks Job prepared and served meat to many people—not only his family, servants, and guests but also strangers. In those days people did not eat meat every day as many do today but rather on special occasions. However, since he was well-to-do, Job probably served meat more frequently than most other hosts. From his words we can conclude that no one left Job's table hungry.

Nor did Job turn people away when they sought a place to sleep. At times his estate may well have resembled a hotel. He remarks, "No stranger had to spend the night in the street, for my door was always open to the traveler." In ancient times hospitality toward strangers was more common than today, when we are rather distrustful of strangers and when motels and hotels are available almost everywhere. But even at his time, Job stood out as an unusually generous and hospitable person.

From his words in this chapter we might conclude that Job was a smug, self-righteous person who felt he had no faults or shortcomings. Such was not the case. Job was a sinner, and he admitted it, as we learn from his words, "If I have concealed my sin as men do, by hiding my guilt in my heart." The first line of that verse may also be translated as "If I have concealed my sin as Adam did." The Hebrew word is the same for "Adam" and "man" or "men." Adam hid from God after he had sinned (Genesis 3:8). He tried to conceal his sin from God. That is also characteristic of people today.

Even though Job probably was not a member of the people of God, the Hebrews, he undoubtedly was familiar with the account of the fall of Adam and Eve into sin. But Job also knew his own human nature and battled against the temptation to cover up and hide his own sin and guilt. Job feared God, and he did not permit his fear of the crowd or the disapproval of his fellow men to turn him away from God. When he feared God, he didn't need to fear men.

Job attests to his innocence

³⁵ ("Oh, that I had someone to hear me!
   I sign now my defense—let the Almighty answer me;
   let my accuser put his indictment in writing.
³⁶ Surely I would wear it on my shoulder,
   I would put it on like a crown.
³⁷ I would give him an account of my every step;
   like a prince I would approach him.)—

Job had repeatedly complained that God would not hear him. Now he expresses the urgent wish that someone would give him a hearing. That "someone" is God, whom he calls "the Almighty" and "my accuser." Job wishes that God would put down in writing the exact charge he had against Job and the reason why he permitted Job to suffer so severely. Again we must remind ourselves that Job was entirely unaware of the role of Satan, who had appeared before God and asked for permission to torment Job.

Job states, "I sign now my defense." More literally, the Hebrew reads, "Behold—my sign." In the original the word for "sign" is *tau,* the last letter of the Hebrew alphabet. In an early form of its writing, the letter *tau* was written like the English letter *X*. Then as now, the *X* was regarded as a valid signature of an illiterate person. Although Job was not illiterate, he used that word to indicate that he meant what he said and would verify it with his own signature.

Job also felt that if God would give him an honest hearing, God would declare him innocent. Job would proudly wear that declaration of innocence as a badge of honor on his shoulder and as a crown on his head. Like a prince, he would confidently approach God.

Job concludes his declaration of innocence

³⁸ **"if my land cries out against me**
   and all its furrows are wet with tears,
³⁹ **if I have devoured its yield without payment**
   or broken the spirit of its tenants,
⁴⁰ **then let briers come up instead of wheat**
   and weeds instead of barley."

The words of Job are ended.

Although many commentators place these verses earlier in this chapter, we are convinced that they belong here. We must keep in mind that Job was not following a neat and logical outline as he was speaking. Rather, in his disturbed state of mind he spoke as his thoughts and feelings moved him. It is not strange, therefore, that again at the close of his speech he would express an oath invoking severe consequences upon himself if he had been guilty of certain sins that he denied.

In these three closing verses he introduces two statements with the word "if" and expresses the result in a statement introduced by "then." He had used that same formula three times before: in 7 and 8, 9 and 10, and 21 and 22.

In verse 38 he personifies the land and calls it to witness any crimes he may have committed. In the Old Testament, God established a close relationship between a people's moral behavior and their right to occupy a land. He clearly reminded the Israelites of that fact in Leviticus 18:24-28 and other passages. It was also wrong for people to assume possession of other people's property without paying for it, to expect laborers to work without payment or support, or to have "broken the spirit of its tenants." Those words may have an even stronger meaning: "snuff out the life of its owners," as some translations read. That is what King Ahab did when, at the instigation of his wicked wife Jezebel, he had Naboth falsely accused and killed and then took Naboth's vineyard.

Job firmly denies any such wrongdoing and is willing to suffer the consequences should he be found guilty of it. He concludes, "Then let briers come up instead of wheat and weeds instead of barley." He invokes upon himself the curse with which God cursed the ground following the sin of Adam and Eve: "Cursed is the ground because of you. . . . It will produce thorns and thistles for you" (Genesis 3:17,18). The Lord also called the ground to witness against Cain after Cain had murdered Abel: "Your brother's blood cries out to me from the ground. Now you are under a curse and driven from the ground, which opened its mouth to receive your brother's blood from your hand. When you work the ground, it will no longer yield its crops for you" (Genesis 4:10-12).

This chapter closes with the statement "The words of Job are ended." This was his last speech. Job had nothing to say in reply to Elihu's four speeches in the six chapters that follow (chapters 32–37). Only twice did he humbly and briefly respond to God's speeches (chapters 38–41).

Job had finished speaking. Now it was Elihu's turn.

PART THREE

The Speeches of Elihu
(32:1–37:24)

The next six chapters contain the longest uninterrupted series of speeches by one person in the book of Job. There are four speeches, each introduced by a statement naming Elihu as the speaker.

This section is the most controversial of all the book's parts. Most liberal scholars are of the opinion that these six chapters were not originally a part of the book of Job but were later additions by an editor. They maintain that Elihu serves no role in the development of the plot but merely repeats in his own words statements that the three friends of Job had previously made. They also state that Elihu's remarks in his last speech (chapters 36,37) make God's statements in chapter 38 superfluous.

We strongly disagree with that view and will attempt to support our position in our commentary on these chapters. We feel that Elihu plays a significant role in the development of the plot in the book of Job and that his remarks are more helpful to Job than those of his three friends. We will also try to show that Elihu's speeches do not render God's speech unnecessary but rather prepare the reader for the Lord's profound utterances recorded in the four chapters that follow (38–41). But now let's make the acquaintance of the young man who so suddenly appears on the scene.

Elihu is introduced

32 **So these three men stopped answering Job, because he was righteous in his own eyes. ²But Elihu son of Barakel the Buzite, of the family of Ram, became very angry with Job for justifying himself rather than God. ³He was also angry**

Job and his three friends

with the three friends, because they had found no way to refute Job, and yet had condemned him. ⁴Now Elihu had waited before speaking to Job because they were older than he. ⁵But when he saw that the three men had nothing more to say, his anger was aroused.

Several questions pop into the reader's mind as Elihu suddenly appears upon the scene. How well did Elihu know Job and the three friends? Had they engaged in conversation at any previous time? How did Elihu find out about Job's great losses and illness? How long had Elihu been sitting there? Did any of the previous speakers notice him or pay attention to him as he was impatiently waiting for his turn to speak? Why is Elihu mentioned in neither the beginning nor the end of the book but only in these six chapters (32–37)? Were his words simply ignored, or were they so profound that they settled the matter under discussion? The reader might ask many more questions regarding Elihu's role in this conversation, but they must remain unanswered since the book itself gives us no such information.

These opening verses do, however, give us more complete information about Elihu's ancestry than that of any of the other characters in the book. The author refers to Job's friends only briefly as "Eliphaz the Temanite, Bildad the Shuhite and Zophar the Naamathite" and adds that "they set out from their homes and met together by agreement to go and sympathize with him and comfort him" (2:11). Even Job himself is introduced simply as a man who lived in the land of Uz (1:1). In contrast, the author introduces Elihu as the "son of Barakel the Buzite, of the family of Ram" (32:2).

The name Elihu means "my God is he," or "he is my God." Several other men in the Old Testament bore the same name: Samuel's great-grandfather (1 Samuel 1:1), a chief of the tribe in Manasseh (1 Chronicles 12:20), a temple gate-keeper (1 Chronicles 26:7), and a brother of David (1 Chronicles 27:18).

Elihu and his father, Barakel, were descendants of a man named Buz. That was the name of a son of Abraham's brother Nahor, and he is mentioned with his older brother, Uz, in Genesis 22:21. We cannot know for sure whether that person was an ancestor of Elihu, but the name makes it a possible identification, as the name *Uz* also suggests the land in which Job lived (1:1). If that is true, Elihu might have been a distant relative of Job. Could that possibly account for the fact that Elihu addresses Job by his first name whereas the three friends never do? Whether or not the name *Ram* in the expression "of the family of Ram" is to be identified with the ancestor of David mentioned in Ruth 4:19, we cannot know for sure. More than one person could have borne the same name.

From the opening verses of this chapter, we can learn a number of things about Elihu. In the first place, the author tells us that Elihu was younger than the other men. That is also the first thing Elihu says in his speech that follows, in verse 6. We can also learn that Elihu was courteous. He showed respect to his elders by refraining from speaking until they had spoken. But the author also informs us that Elihu was impulsive and hot-tempered. Three times we are told that he became angry: with Job (verse 2) and with Job's friends (verses 3,5).

Elihu was angry with Job for justifying himself rather than God and with the friends for failing to refute Job and yet condemning him. A footnote on verse 3 in the NIV suggests that the earlier reading was "and so had condemned God," but that the Hebrew scribes toned it down to read "and so had condemned Job." The essential meaning is the same whether we read "God" or "Job," since God had commended Job for his pious character, and so by condemning Job, the three friends also condemned God. The translation in the text of the NIV is therefore a good one: "and yet had condemned him." It can refer both to Job and to God.

There is a great difference of opinion among scholars concerning the character of Elihu. Some regard him as an impulsive, cocksure know-it-all who claims to have all the answers and recklessly makes charges against his elders without adding anything of substance to the discussion. Others are of the opinion that he is more sensitive to Job's problem than the other three, adds a new and refreshing dimension to the discussion, and offers a solution that the three older men failed to suggest. There is probably some truth in both views, but to this writer the latter opinion is preferable.

In our study of these speeches, we will try to come to grips with what Elihu says and see to what extent he either hinders or helps the attempt to answer the problem of Job's suffering. We will also consider what Elihu has to say about the justice and the goodness of God and its role in the life of Job and others.

Elihu's first speech

Elihu explains why he now must speak

⁶So Elihu son of Barakel the Buzite said:

"I am young in years,
   and you are old;
that is why I was fearful,
   not daring to tell you what I know.
⁷ I thought, 'Age should speak;
   advanced years should teach wisdom.'
⁸ But it is the spirit in a man,
   the breath of the Almighty, that gives him understanding.

> ⁹ **It is not only the old who are wise,**
> **not only the aged who understand what is right.**

We do not know how long Elihu had been sitting there listening to the other four men take turns speaking. Had he been there from the very beginning? Perhaps. He must have heard at least a fair part of their conversation, since he made comments about it. At any rate, by the time they had finished, he was churning inside, impatiently waiting to speak his piece.

Aware of his youth, Elihu begins his speech in a respectful and courteous manner. Comparing his youth and inexperience to their age and experience, his words have almost a self-disparaging tone. We are reminded of similar statements by other men of the Old Testament. For example, when Gideon was called by God to deliver Israel from the Midianites, he asked, "How can I save Israel? My clan is the weakest in Manasseh, and I am the least in my family" (Judges 6:15). Before Samuel anointed Saul king over Israel, Saul modestly declared, "Am I not a Benjamite, from the smallest tribe of Israel, and is not my clan the least of all the clans of the tribe of Benjamin?" (1 Samuel 9:21).

In spite of his youth, Elihu felt the strong urge to speak. His words suggest that God has given him insight and wisdom to make a significant contribution to the discussion. He states, "But it is the spirit in man, the breath of the Almighty, that gives him understanding." Those men ought not write him off as having nothing to contribute just because he is young. In verse 9 he continues by stating that the elderly do not necessarily have a corner on wisdom and understanding.

> ¹⁰ **"Therefore I say: Listen to me;**
> **I too will tell you what I know.**
> ¹¹ **I waited while you spoke,**
> **I listened to your reasoning;**

> while you were searching for words,
> ¹²   I gave you my full attention.
> But not one of you has proved Job wrong;
>   none of you has answered his arguments.
> ¹³ Do not say, 'We have found wisdom;
>   let God refute him, not man.'
> ¹⁴ But Job has not marshaled his words against me,
>   and I will not answer him with your arguments.

There is general agreement that Elihu's style of speaking is rather pompous, verbose, and repetitive. "I," "me," and "my" dominate the early part of Elihu's discussion, occurring more than 50 times. Many scholars label him an arrogant young man; others regard him as a young man who speaks the truth bluntly but with deep conviction. Perhaps there is some truth in both views. Unquestionably, Elihu was excited when he spoke. That can partly account for his wordiness. He was convinced he had a message, and so he urged them to listen to him. His excitement is apparent in his language. One expression that Elihu uses is not translated in the NIV, the word *behold,* or *look.* The word well expresses Elihu's emotional state of mind.

In these verses Elihu tells the three friends that they had miserably failed to convince Job that he was wrong. They had not refuted his arguments. They were on the wrong track when they dogmatically and repeatedly stated that his severe afflictions were a punishment for certain especially great sins. By their silence they now admitted that they had gotten nowhere in convincing Job of those special sins.

In verse 14 Elihu declares, "But Job has not marshaled his words against me, and I will not answer him with your arguments." Whether or not Elihu had been present from the beginning of the dialogue, Job had not directed his words against him. During the course of the discussion Elihu was an outsider and had the advantage of viewing their argument more objectively and impartially than they. In his line of argument Elihu would use a different approach and suggest a different solution. To what extent he succeeded will be evident as the discussion progresses.

> ¹⁵ **"They are dismayed and have no more to say;**
>   **words have failed them.**
> ¹⁶ **Must I wait, now that they are silent,**
>   **now that they stand there with no reply?**
> ¹⁷ **I too will have my say;**
>   **I too will tell what I know.**
> ¹⁸ **For I am full of words,**
>   **and the spirit within me compels me;**
> ¹⁹ **inside I am like bottled-up wine,**
>   **like new wineskins ready to burst.**
> ²⁰ **I must speak and find relief;**
>   **I must open my lips and reply.**
> ²¹ **I will show partiality to no one,**
>   **nor will I flatter any man;**
> ²² **for if I were skilled in flattery,**
>   **my Maker would soon take me away.**

Previously Elihu had expressed his need to answer Job and the friends. In these closing verses of chapter 32, he expresses his strong compulsion to answer them. Speaking to Job individually he comments about the friends, "They are dismayed and have no more to say; words have failed them. Must I wait, now that they are silent, now that they stand there with no reply?"

Elihu just can't wait any longer; he must say his piece. He says he will tell what he knows. He declares, "For I am full of words." The reaction of one commentator to that remark is a sarcastic "How true!" On the basis of what he says in these verses, Elihu has been accused of being obnoxiously forward and arrogant. Some commentators refer to him as a young upstart and a windbag, particularly because of what he says in verses 18 to 20.

We would do well to treat Elihu more charitably. We ought to make allowance for youthful impulsiveness and try to understand his words as expressing a sincere attempt to contribute something worthwhile to the discussion. It seems only proper to give Elihu the benefit of the doubt and think of him as one who tried to help Job and the three friends rather than parade his knowledge and wisdom.

In vivid language Elihu pictures himself as filled with new wine that is ready to ferment and burst a wineskin. Unless he speaks, he will explode. He concludes his long introduction by assuring the four men that he is not prejudiced for or against any of them and that he intends to suggest a solution that is fair to all. He also firmly maintains that he has neither the desire nor the ability to resort to flattery. His concluding words are in the form of an oath: "For if I were skilled in flattery, my Maker would soon take me away." Those words remind us of a statement of Job in the previous chapter, when he declared, "For I dreaded destruction from God, and for fear of his splendor I could not do such things" (31:23).

After his long and somewhat rambling introduction, Elihu proceeds to address Job directly. As we read the opening verses in the chapter that follows, we can immediately sense that the tone of Elihu's speech is more direct and personal than that of the friends.

Elihu requests that Job would listen to him

33 "But now, Job, listen to my words; pay attention to everything I say.

²I am about to open my mouth;
  my words are on the tip of my tongue.
³My words come from an upright heart;
  my lips sincerely speak what I know.
⁴The Spirit of God has made me;
  the breath of the Almighty gives me life.
⁵Answer me then, if you can;
  prepare yourself and confront me.
⁶I am just like you before God;
  I too have been taken from clay.
⁷No fear of me should alarm you,
  nor should my hand be heavy upon you.

For the first time in the book someone addresses Job by name. His three friends had not done so even once in their speeches. That tells us something about their personalities as well as their message. In their approach and style they were cold and objective. On the other hand, Elihu speaks to Job in a personal manner and mentions him by name a number of times. We can imagine that he looked Job directly in the eye as he spoke his opening words: "But now, Job, listen to my words; pay attention to everything I say."

Elihu's language betrays his excited state of mind. As we have mentioned, Elihu frequently uses an interjection that can be translated as "behold" or "look," a word the NIV omits. In the first 12 verses of this chapter that word is found in the Hebrew text five times, introducing verses 2, 6, 7, 10, and 12. Perhaps Elihu's awareness of his youth accounts for his excitement as well as his aggressiveness. Whether or not he was trying to compensate for his youth, his words give the impression of an impulsive and cocksure personality.

Elihu's manner of speech is verbose and repetitious, but before we judge him too severely, we must keep in mind that his speeches, like the speeches of the other men, are given in the form of poetry. One of the chief characteristics of Hebrew poetry is repetition. We can detect such repetition in each of the opening verses. Repetition serves the important purpose of reinforcing the message of the speaker or writer by stating a similar thought in different words. That was particularly important when people communicated orally, as did the participants in the book of Job. The poetic form also lends artistic beauty to the words. In its poetic style the book of Job is universally acknowledged to be a literary masterpiece.

Chapter 32 introduces Elihu's first speech; chapter 33 concludes it. Elihu expresses his strong disapproval of the course of the previous discussion, which seemed to be going nowhere. He had waited impatiently to speak. Now he had his chance, and he turned to Job. We might think that a young man would be reluctant to speak in such a frank manner to Job, the most distinguished member of the community, even though Job now found himself in humiliating circumstances. But Elihu showed no such reluctance. He spoke without fear or favor, as if he were addressing an equal.

Elihu protests his sincerity. He makes a significant statement: "The Spirit of God has made me; the breath of the Almighty gives me life." As we can also infer from Genesis 1:1-3 and John 1:1-3, the three persons of the Holy Trinity were active in the work of creation. In this verse the Holy Spirit is specifically mentioned as being active in the creation of Elihu. In the second line of the verse the word "breath" is parallel to "Spirit" and could also be capitalized.

After challenging Job to engage in a dialogue with him, Elihu mentions that he, like Job, is a creature of God. He states, "I am just like you before God; I too have been taken from clay." The last expression, "taken from clay," suggests being nipped or pinched off from clay, as a sculptor or potter might nip off a piece of clay as he is working. As Adam was created from dust, or clay, so all his descendants share that common bond that unites them and shows their total dependence on God, their Creator. Because Elihu too was only a mortal, he appealed to Job not to be intimidated by his words. Those words, as we will see, are rather sharp and severe.

Job is mistaken in complaining to God

> ⁸ **"But you have said in my hearing—**
> **I heard the very words—**
> ⁹ **'I am pure and without sin;**
> **I am clean and free from guilt.**
> ¹⁰ **Yet God has found fault with me;**
> **he considers me his enemy.**
> ¹¹ **He fastens my feet in shackles;**
> **he keeps close watch on all my paths.'**

These verses imply that Elihu must have heard the discussion from early on, if not from the beginning. He states that he heard with his own ears what Job had said. He claims to quote Job in verses 9 to 11. The opening words he attributes to Job are particularly blunt: "I am pure and without sin; I am clean and free from guilt." Did Job really say that? In his recorded speeches we fail to find those words. He had complained, "Even if I were innocent, my mouth would condemn me; if I were blameless, it would pronounce me guilty" (9:20). Those are hardly words of a man who claims to be "pure and without sin" or "clean and free from guilt." It is true that Job had declared, "Although I am blameless, I have no concern for myself; I despise my own life" (9:21). But even there Job was not claiming to be sinless but rather innocent of the false charges his friends leveled against him. There is a difference between claiming to be pure and sinless and defending oneself against a specific charge.

Elihu continues to quote Job in Job's complaint against God: "Yet God has found fault with me; he considers me his enemy. He fastens my feet in shackles; he keeps close watch on all my paths." In his deep affliction Job had spoken words similar to those. He had accused God of severely tormenting him. In two different speeches Job had made statements similar to those of which Elihu accused him. In 19:11, speaking of God, Job had complained, "His anger burns against me; he counts me among his enemies." Earlier he had addressed God, "You fasten my feet in shackles; you keep close watch on all my paths by putting marks on the soles of my feet" (13:27).

Elihu was partly right in his accusation of Job, but in his youthful passion he made the mistake of overstating his case, of saying too much.

God speaks in various ways to rescue people from destruction

¹² "But I tell you, in this you are not right,
   for God is greater than man.
¹³ Why do you complain to him
   that he answers none of man's words?
¹⁴ For God does speak—now one way, now another—
   though man may not perceive it.
¹⁵ In a dream, in a vision of the night,
   when deep sleep falls on men
   as they slumber in their beds,
¹⁶ he may speak in their ears
   and terrify them with warnings,
¹⁷ to turn man from wrongdoing
   and keep him from pride,
¹⁸ to preserve his soul from the pit,
   his life from perishing by the sword.
¹⁹ Or a man may be chastened on a bed of pain
   with constant distress in his bones,

²⁰ **so that his very being finds food repulsive**
  and his soul loathes the choicest meal.
²¹ **His flesh wastes away to nothing,**
  and his bones, once hidden, now stick out.
²² **His soul draws near to the pit,**
  and his life to the messengers of death.

Young Elihu speaks plainly to Job, telling Job that he is not right and then making a statement that no one would dare contradict: "God is greater than man." Job had expected an answer from God. He had waited for the opportunity to enter into a dialogue with God. Elihu chides Job and adds, "For God does speak—now one way, now another—though man may not perceive it." Elihu's words imply that God had already been speaking to Job, but Job hadn't realized it.

Elihu states that God speaks in dreams and visions. Earlier Eliphaz had spoken of a dream in which someone stood before him and declared that God is more righteous than man (4:12-17). Job himself suffered from frightening dreams. He complained to God, "You frighten me with dreams and terrify me with visions" (7:14). Now Elihu is possibly telling Job that God was using those troubling dreams as a means of teaching him a lesson. God often did communicate important future events to people through dreams and visions. He spoke in that manner to Abraham (Genesis 15:12-15) and Jacob (Genesis 28:12-15). Not only did Joseph (Genesis 37:5-12) and Daniel (Daniel 10:4-11) have dreams and visions, but God also gave them the ability to interpret the dreams of the cupbearer, the baker, Pharaoh, and Nebuchadnezzar.

Elihu tells Job that God may use dreams and visions so that "he may speak in their ears and terrify them with warnings." Through such dreams God will admonish and instruct people so that they learn lessons from their experiences in life. God will do so for their own good, to turn people from doing wrong and from becoming proud. Thereby God will also preserve people from dying in their sins and facing destruction, both in this life and in the next.

Elihu mentions another manner in which God speaks to people: suffering and affliction. In vivid language Elihu describes a person's affliction on a sickbed. He speaks of the aches and pains of a sick person, the lack of appetite and strong dislike for even the best food. In his extreme affliction Job could very well relate to those words, and so can anyone else who has been very sick. Such illness and lack of food can ultimately lead to starvation and death, as Elihu graphically states: "His flesh wastes away to nothing, and his bones, once hidden, now stick out. His soul draws near to the pit, and his life to the messengers of death." Those words describe Job's condition. His gaunt and disease-wracked body must have been a gruesome sight. Try to imagine how Job himself must have felt! In his speeches he had expressed the wish to die, and no doubt he felt very close to death as he sat listening to the cold words of his unfeeling friends.

In his words describing human suffering, Elihu indirectly refers to Job's own suffering. But unlike the three friends, Elihu does not state that Job's suffering was the consequence of some special sin he had committed. Rather, Elihu reminds Job and the three friends that suffering is a wholesome learning experience. God can use suffering as a means of bringing a person to the realization of his own sin, his helplessness, his need for forgiveness, and his need to trust in God, who loves him. Solomon reminds us: "My son, do not despise the LORD's discipline and do not resent his rebuke, because the LORD disciplines those he loves, as a father the son he delights in" (Proverbs 3:11,12; also quoted in Hebrews 12:5,6).

God redeems his people from their affliction

²³ "Yet if there is an angel on his side
  as a mediator, one out of a thousand,
  to tell a man what is right for him,
²⁴ to be gracious to him and say,
  'Spare him from going down to the pit;
  I have found a ransom for him'—
²⁵ then his flesh is renewed like a child's;
  it is restored as in the days of his youth.
²⁶ He prays to God and finds favor with him,
  he sees God's face and shouts for joy;
  he is restored by God to his righteous state.
²⁷ Then he comes to men and says,
  'I sinned, and perverted what was right,
  but I did not get what I deserved.
²⁸ He redeemed my soul from going down to the pit,
  and I will live to enjoy the light.'
²⁹ "God does all these things to a man—
  twice, even three times—
³⁰ to turn back his soul from the pit,
  that the light of life may shine on him.

These verses are the high point of Elihu's four speeches. Job had accused God of being cruel to him; Elihu replies that God is loving, that God redeems and restores people from the clutches of suffering and sin.

Elihu mentions sin in verse 27. Sin is the cause of all sufferings and ills in this world. If sin had not entered the world, there would be no trouble, sorrow, suffering, sickness, or death. From his words to Job we know that Elihu was aware of the problem of sin, its consequences, and its only remedy, God's forgiveness. He speaks of God's grace and a ransom for the sinner. He also declares that the sinner "prays to God and finds favor with him" and "he is restored by God to his righteous state." The grateful sinner rejoices and declares, "I sinned, and perverted what was right, but I did not get what I deserved. He redeemed my soul from going down to the pit, and I will live to enjoy the light."

Those words go far deeper than expressing deliverance from physical troubles. They describe the wonderful truth that God has redeemed and delivered the sinner from his spiritual troubles. God has forgiven his sins and pronounced him innocent. God has done all this for man "to turn back his soul from the pit, that the light of life may shine on him." The redeemed and forgiven sinner can enjoy this during this life and for all eternity in the life to come.

We might well ask, Who is the individual described in verse 23, the one called an "angel" and a "mediator"? Most modern scholars believe he is either an angel or a man. But there is a problem with that interpretation. As we read the verses that follow, that individual is described as one who performs a function that an ordinary angel or a human being would be incapable of performing. That individual is more than an ordinary angel or a mere mortal. We believe that he is none other than our Savior Jesus Christ, to whom Elihu here refers under the inspiration of God the Holy Spirit.

Verse 23 contains two words which appropriately describe the Son of God: "angel" and "mediator." The Hebrew word translated as "angel" can also be translated as "messenger." We find that word in the name of the prophet Malachi, which means "my messenger." The expression "angel of the LORD" occurs several times in the Old Testament. In some passages that "angel" refers to someone who is far greater than an ordinary created angel. He is none other than God, and in some passages he is directly called God, as when he appeared to Moses (Exodus 3:1-6), Gideon (Judges 6:11-23), and the parents of Samson (Judges 13:3-22). In Old Testament times

God frequently revealed himself in human form in the person of the Son of God, who later also became true man, born of the virgin Mary.

Another term that describes Jesus Christ is the word "mediator." In a true sense, Jesus Christ the God-man is the mediator between God and men, as Saint Paul states in 1 Timothy 2:5. In verses 23 and 24, Elihu describes this angel and mediator: "Yet if there is an angel on his side as a mediator, one out of a thousand, to tell a man what is right for him, to be gracious to him and say, 'Spare him from going down to the pit; I have found a ransom for him.'" We ask, could those words refer to anyone other than Jesus Christ?

Those words describe a superhuman task, that of redemption. The psalmist confesses, "No man can redeem the life of another or give to God a ransom for him—the ransom for a life is costly, no payment is ever enough—that he should live on forever and not see decay" (Psalm 49:7-9). On the other hand, Saint Peter declares, "For you know that it was not with perishable things such as silver or gold that you were redeemed from the empty way of life handed down to you from your forefathers, but with the precious blood of Christ, a lamb without blemish or defect" (1 Peter 1:18,19).

Also, the expression "one out of a thousand" is appropriate to describe Jesus Christ. As our Savior and Redeemer, he stands apart from all the angels and is truly "one out of a thousand."

The verses that follow can hardly apply to anyone else than Jesus Christ, particularly verses 24, 26, and 28. Those verses describe the work of our Savior as the mediator between God and men in giving his own life as a ransom for us and in redeeming us from sin, death, and the power of the devil.

Verse 25 abounds in striking imagery. Speaking of the redeemed and forgiven sinner, Elihu states, "Then his flesh is renewed like a child's; it is restored as in the days of his youth." That verse suggests the resurrection of our bodies, which Paul describes thus: "For the perishable must clothe itself with the imperishable, and the mortal with immortality" (1 Corinthians 15:53).

In an article bearing the title "Salvation by Grace: The Heart of Job's Theology," Alfred von Rohr Sauer caught the meaning of this passage and expressed it well in the following words: "Who, when he hears these prophetic words, is not impelled to think of the one Mediator between God and man, namely, the man Christ Jesus?" (from *Concordia Theological Monthly,* Volume 27, Number 5, May 1966, page 264).

Elihu again asks Job to listen

³¹ **"Pay attention, Job, and listen to me;**
　　be silent, and I will speak.
³² **If you have anything to say, answer me;**
　　speak up, for I want you to be cleared.
³³ **But if not, then listen to me;**
　　be silent, and I will teach you wisdom."

Again addressing Job by name, Elihu concludes this speech with another plea for Job to listen and take to heart what he is saying. Although he offers Job the opportunity to answer him, Elihu tells Job plainly that he has more to say.

Elihu's second speech

Elihu rebukes Job

34 Then Elihu said:
　　² **"Hear my words, you wise men;**
　　listen to me, you men of learning.

251

³ **For the ear tests words**
      as the tongue tastes food.
⁴ **Let us discern for ourselves what is right;**
      let us learn together what is good.
⁵ **"Job says, 'I am innocent,**
      but God denies me justice.
⁶ **Although I am right,**
      I am considered a liar;
   although I am guiltless,
      his arrow inflicts an incurable wound.'
⁷ **What man is like Job,**
      who drinks scorn like water?
⁸ **He keeps company with evildoers;**
      he associates with wicked men.
⁹ **For he says, 'It profits a man nothing**
      when he tries to please God.'

In this second speech Elihu appeals to his listeners to pay attention to what he is saying. The fact that he addresses them as "wise men" and "men of learning" implies that he is speaking to the three friends as well as to Job. It is possible that others were also present. The nature of the subject matter was such that it might well have attracted more people than the five men who had been engaged in the conversation.

Elihu urges the listeners to pay close attention to what he is saying. His words in verse 3, "For the ear tests words as the tongue tastes food," sound remarkably similar to Job's statement in 12:11. Whether or not Elihu was rubbing it in when he spoke those words we cannot tell, but from his words thus far we can safely say that tact was not Elihu's strongest suit.

In verses 4 to 9, Elihu launches into his strongest attack on Job. To the reader it appears presumptuous for such a young man as Elihu to speak so harshly against a man of Job's character and reputation. Again, unlike the three friends, Elihu refers to Job by name. Presuming to reason with Job, Elihu rather sharply attacks him. After having listened to at least part of the conversation between Job and his three friends, Elihu may have imagined he was assuming the role of a mediator. In this speech, however, he acted less like a judge than a prosecuting attorney.

It is true that Job had spoken sharply in his complaints against God. For that we cannot defend him. He had said that God had denied him justice (27:2). He had also earlier complained, "The arrows of the Almighty are in me, my spirit drinks in their poison; God's terrors are marshaled against me" (6:4). Elihu refers to those statements.

Yet he seems to be overstating his case when he quotes Job as saying "Although I am right, I am considered a liar." If we read those words as saying that God considered Job a liar, there is no evidence that Job had ever made such a statement. Job had complained that God had not answered him or explained why he had to suffer so greatly, but he had not accused God of calling him a liar.

Elihu's words in verses 7 to 9 are especially sharp and unkind. They appear to contradict his previous statement that he would be an impartial judge in the long controversy between Job and his friends, as he had earlier indicated. He had said, "I will show partiality to no one, nor will I flatter any man" (32:21). Elihu pictures Job as one who drinks scorn as a thirsty person gulps down water. He tells Job that by his complaints against God, Job had lowered himself to the level of evildoers and wicked men. Then Elihu closes this sharp attack against Job by asserting that Job had said, "It profits a man nothing when he tries to please God."

In his impulsiveness, Elihu falsely accused Job of saying that "it profits a man nothing when he tries to please God."

Such words are typical of unbelieving cynics. But Job was not an unbelieving cynic. He was a righteous man experiencing extreme suffering. Under those circumstances he uttered strong statements that suggested that it would profit a man nothing when he tries to please God.

These words of Elihu are in some respects even harsher than those of Job's three unfeeling friends. Their accusations of Job were less personal than Elihu's. As we saw in the previous chapter, however, Elihu offered an important insight into the problem of suffering, an insight that the three friends had failed to mention: God uses affliction to teach the sufferer important lessons so that he will trust more firmly in God. In the words that follow, Elihu does not further pursue that matter but rather speaks at considerable length about the justice and wisdom of God.

God is just and wise in his governance of the world

> ¹⁰ "So listen to me, you men of understanding.
> Far be it from God to do evil,
> from the Almighty to do wrong.
> ¹¹ He repays a man for what he has done;
> he brings upon him what his conduct deserves.
> ¹² It is unthinkable that God would do wrong,
> that the Almighty would pervert justice.
> ¹³ Who appointed him over the earth?
> Who put him in charge of the whole world?
> ¹⁴ If it were his intention
> and he withdrew his spirit and breath,
> ¹⁵ all mankind would perish together
> and man would return to the dust.

Addressing Job and his friends as "men of understanding," Elihu again appeals to them to listen to him. They must certainly agree that God would do no evil. And when he states that God "repays a man for what he has done," Elihu says exactly what the three friends had maintained.

Job had questioned God's justice, since he had to suffer such great afflictions without knowing the reason why. Again we must remind ourselves that, like the three friends and Elihu, Job was unaware of Satan's role in bringing about his severe affliction. In his intense sufferings Job complained and even accused God of mistreating him, but by God's grace he did not lose his faith in God, nor did he curse him, as Satan had predicted.

In verse 13 Elihu asks a rhetorical question: "Who appointed him [God] over the earth? Who put him in charge of the whole world?" Obviously, no one. God is the absolute sovereign over this vast universe which he created. He is not answerable to anyone for what he does. Later, God himself tells Job, "Who has a claim against me that I must pay? Everything under heaven belongs to me" (41:11).

Speaking of God, Elihu continues, "If it were his intention and he withdrew his spirit and breath, all mankind would perish together and man would return to the dust." God is the author and giver of all life. Our spirit and breath came from him, and we are completely dependent on him for every breath we draw. Not only we human beings but every living thing depends on God for its life. On this verse P. E. Kretzmann offers the following comment: "Man is completely dependent upon the providence of God, and yet God does not use His majestic power in an arbitrary manner" (*Popular Commentary,* Old Testament, Volume 2, page 47).

To Job it appeared as if God acted in an impulsive and arbitrary manner when God permitted him to suffer so greatly. To us too it may sometimes seem as if God is unjust when he allows us to suffer great misfortunes such as sickness, accidents, or the loss of a dear one. God's wisdom, however, is infinitely greater than ours. His thoughts and ways are far beyond our limited human understanding. He has also given his believers the assurance that "in all things God works for the good of those who love him, who have been called according to his purpose" (Romans 8:28). Not only is God wise and just, he is also loving and merciful.

> 16 "If you have understanding, hear this;
> listen to what I say.
> 17 Can he who hates justice govern?
> Will you condemn the just and mighty One?
> 18 Is he not the One who says to kings, 'You are worthless,'
> and to nobles, 'You are wicked,'
> 19 who shows no partiality to princes
> and does not favor the rich over the poor,
> for they are all the work of his hands?
> 20 They die in an instant, in the middle of the night;
> the people are shaken and they pass away;
> the mighty are removed without human hand.

Elihu again interrupts his speech by pleading with Job and the friends to listen to what he says. Resuming the theme of God's wisdom in governing this world, he asks Job a question that really answers itself: "Can he who hates justice govern? Will you condemn the just and mighty One?" No way! To do so would be presumptuous.

Verse 18 has been translated and interpreted two ways. In some versions and commentaries the translation is somewhat as follows: "Does one say to a king 'worthless,' and to nobles 'wicked ones'?" That refers the words "king" and "nobles" to God and suggests that it would be entirely out of place to call God "worthless" or "wicked." While that interpretation is possible, it is preferable to follow the translation and interpretation of the NIV and most other English translations.

The text then reads, "Is he not the One who says to kings, 'You are worthless,' and to nobles, 'You are wicked' . . . ?" That interpretation is also supported by the verses which follow: "Who shows no partiality to princes and does not favor the rich over the poor, for they are all the work of his hands." Even the highest and mightiest are not great in the sight of God. He has neither the need nor the desire to cater to them. Like the poorest and lowliest of people, the high and mighty are the work of his hands. In comparison to God, even the greatest and most powerful of men are as nothing.

Speaking of human beings, Elihu continues, "They die in an instant, in the middle of the night; the people are shaken and they pass away; the mighty are removed without human hand." How true! Every day we read and hear about people, some famous and others unknown, who are suddenly snatched from life in this world. Murders, automobile accidents, airplane crashes, fires, and other calamities suddenly and swiftly take their toll. Such calamities show no preference for the rich, the powerful, or the famous. Elihu's words are indeed true and sobering. When God permits death to strike, it claims its victims regardless of their earthly condition or situation. How important it is, therefore, for us to be prepared for the time of our death, whenever it may come! With Moses, we ought to pray, "Teach us to number our days aright, that we may gain a heart of wisdom" (Psalm 90:12).

> ²¹ **"His eyes are on the ways of men;**
> **he sees their every step.**
> ²² **There is no dark place, no deep shadow,**
> **where evildoers can hide.**
> ²³ **God has no need to examine men further,**
> **that they should come before him for judgment.**
> ²⁴ **Without inquiry he shatters the mighty**
> **and sets up others in their place.**

²⁵ **Because he takes note of their deeds,**
   he overthrows them in the night and they are crushed.
²⁶ **He punishes them for their wickedness**
   where everyone can see them,
²⁷ **because they turned from following him**
   and had no regard for any of his ways.
²⁸ **They caused the cry of the poor to come before him,**
   so that he heard the cry of the needy.
²⁹ **But if he remains silent, who can condemn him?**
   If he hides his face, who can see him?
   Yet he is over man and nation alike,
³⁰   **to keep a godless man from ruling,**
   from laying snares for the people.

Elihu further explains why God is all-wise and all-just in his governance of the world. Elihu says, "His eyes are on the ways of men; he sees their every step." God's omniscience qualifies him to be impartial. He sees and knows all. Not a single step of a human being can escape his notice. That fact can serve as both a warning and a comfort to us human beings. On the one hand, God sees and knows all our sins of thought, desire, word, and deed. How frightening! On the other hand, he is fully aware of all our troubles and needs. He keeps a watchful eye over us by day and by night, protects us from all danger, and keeps us in his loving care. How comforting!

Elihu further states, "There is no dark place, no deep shadow, where evildoers can hide." In one of the most profound of the psalms, David eloquently expresses the same thought. Addressing God, he declares, "If I say, 'Surely the darkness will hide me and the light become night around me,' even the darkness will not be dark to you; the night will shine like the day, for darkness is as light to you" (Psalm 139:11,12).

In one of our familiar hymns, the author John Ellerton expresses the same thought:

> Grant us thy peace, Lord, through the coming night;
> Turn thou for us its darkness into light.
> From harm and danger keep thy people free,
> For dark and light are both alike to thee.
>
> (CW 321:3)

Job had wished for the opportunity to appear before God. In verse 23 of this chapter, Elihu tells him that such an appearance would be unnecessary. God does not need to set a time for such a hearing, nor does man need to request such an appointment. In his infinite wisdom God can immediately render a judgment. He is also all-powerful and is able to shatter the mighty and replace them with others. He can overthrow them and punish them as evildoers and make a public spectacle of them. Throughout the centuries wicked and godless rulers have been brought low and humiliated, and many who went to their grave in honor will reap the rewards for their wickedness to all eternity. "Do not be deceived: God cannot be mocked. A man reaps what he sows" (Galatians 6:7). That applies also to cruel and unjust rulers. Punishment from God will fall upon wicked tyrants also because God listens to the plaintive cry of the poor and needy whom they oppress.

Verses 29 and 30 are rather difficult to understand and interpret. It seems best to understand them to say that God sometimes seems to withdraw his influence from the course of events on earth. Apparently, men like Stalin and Mao Tse-tung carried on in their cruel and ruthless manner without real opposition. Often we find that wicked men are in control and that evil prevails. God seems to hide his face, be silent, and let things run their course. Yet in spite of appearances, God is really in control.

His apparent slowness to act does not deny his sovereignty or power. He may punish or chastise a nation by allowing a wicked man to conquer it or rule over it, as he did on a number of occasions in Israel in Old Testament times. But he will not permit evil to continue to dominate beyond a certain point. In the end, right will prevail.

Elihu was convinced that God is a God of justice, and in the verses that follow he again appeals to Job to take that to heart.

Job must acknowledge God's justice and wisdom

> ³¹ "Suppose a man says to God,
>   'I am guilty but will offend no more.
> ³² Teach me what I cannot see;
>   if I have done wrong, I will not do so again.'
> ³³ Should God then reward you on your terms,
>   when you refuse to repent?
> You must decide, not I;
>   so tell me what you know.
> ³⁴ "Men of understanding declare,
>   wise men who hear me say to me,
> ³⁵ 'Job speaks without knowledge;
>   his words lack insight.'
> ³⁶ Oh, that Job might be tested to the utmost
>   for answering like a wicked man!
> ³⁷ To his sin he adds rebellion;
>   scornfully he claps his hands among us
>   and multiplies his words against God."

Elihu has emphasized the fact that God is just and wise. Elihu now appeals to Job to turn from his error and confess his guilt. Elihu is disturbed because Job had challenged God's justice and rule by suggesting that God had acted arbitrarily toward him. Job ought to admit he was mistaken. Elihu suggests that it would be unreasonable to expect God to change the rules of his government of this world to please Job.

For the third time Elihu addresses his listeners as intelligent men, and again he sharply rebukes Job. He bluntly states, "Job speaks without knowledge; his words lack insight." Although Elihu came closer than the three friends to finding the solution to Job's suffering, those words hardly reveal a sympathetic heart.

Nor do the words that follow: "Oh, that Job might be tested to the utmost for answering like a wicked man!" Hadn't Job already been tested to the utmost? He was suffering intense physical pain such as neither Elihu nor his three friends could comprehend. He felt alienated by his fellow human beings. There is no indication that his wife was at hand to sympathize or support him. He had lost his children, so they were not there to console him. His only companions were four men who sharply rebuked him. If there were others present, they were only curious onlookers. For Elihu to say "Oh, that Job might be tested to the utmost" was as ironic as it was cruel.

And yet there is some truth to what Elihu said about Job. In his closing words in this second speech, Elihu declares, "To his sin he adds rebellion; scornfully he claps his hands among us and multiplies his words against God." Job had accused God of attacking him with arrows (6:4), of making him a target (7:20), and of crushing him with a storm (9:17). He felt God was unjustly picking on him. Job had used strong language in his complaints to God. His words cannot be defended, but they can be understood when we try to realize the great suffering and loneliness the man was experiencing. Under severe afflictions even true Christians have been known to speak strong words of complaint, words they would never speak under normal circumstances. They have even uttered curses that they themselves would be shocked at hearing or speaking at other times.

Again we must remind ourselves that the real cause of Job's suffering was not any specific sin of his own. Rather, as we know from the two opening chapters, God permitted Satan to test Job severely by depriving him of his property and children and by afflicting him with intense physical suffering. As we have repeatedly observed, Job, the three friends, and Elihu were not aware of the conversation between God and Satan that is recorded in chapters 1 and 2. Job was at a loss to understand why he was undergoing such great suffering, and the other speakers were incapable of being sympathetic to him.

While many of the statements Elihu made were similar to those of the three friends, Elihu did suggest some solutions that they failed to mention. We noted some such solutions in chapter 33, and in the chapters that follow (35–37), we will learn that young Elihu had more to contribute to the discussion.

Elihu's third speech

God's exercise of justice is not in accordance with our way of thinking

35 Then Elihu said:

² **"Do you think this is just?**
    You say, 'I will be cleared by God.'
³ **Yet you ask him, 'What profit is it to me,**
    and what do I gain by not sinning?'

The opening verse of this chapter suggests that Elihu paused at the close of his second speech (chapter 34) in order to see whether or not his listeners had a response to his statements. Since no one spoke up, Elihu continued his monologue. His opening words are addressed to Job. As in the previous chapter, Elihu's words are sharp and direct. He intends to convince Job and the other listeners that Job has no case in his dispute with God. In fact, Job needs to humble himself before the Lord.

Elihu's opening statement is a question: "Do you think this is just?" The very form of the question suggests a resounding negative reply. The last half of the second verse is difficult. Translators and commentators have interpreted it in various ways. The NIV renders it "I will be cleared by God." It is true that Job had requested a hearing in the hope that God would declare him innocent of the charges made against him by his friends. In the closing chapter of the book, God did indeed tell the three friends, "You have not spoken of me what is right, as my servant Job has" (42:7).

In an earlier statement Elihu had accused Job of saying "It profits a man nothing when he tries to please God" (34:9). Now he suggests that Job had asked the question "What profit is it to me, and what do I gain by not sinning?"

We might well ask, Did Job really say that? Did his words suggest such a thought? To Elihu they evidently did. Job had uttered strong complaints to God when he saw that he, a righteous man, had to suffer so much while many of the godless appeared to prosper. He even charged God with afflicting the righteous at least as severely as the wicked. Yet from Job's spoken words we fail to find any evidence that he had said, "What do I gain by not sinning?" Although Job was aware of his own sinfulness, there is no evidence that he intended to give himself over to a sinful lifestyle. In fact, in his speech in chapter 31, he strongly denies any such intention or activity.

⁴ **"I would like to reply to you**
     and to your friends with you.
⁵ **Look up at the heavens and see;**
     gaze at the clouds so high above you.
⁶ **If you sin, how does that affect him?**
     If your sins are many, what does that do to him?
⁷ **If you are righteous, what do you give to him,**
     or what does he receive from your hand?
⁸ **Your wickedness affects only a man like yourself,**
     and your righteousness only the sons of men.

Elihu addresses these words primarily to Job, as we can learn from the forms of the verbs and pronouns, which are singular in the Hebrew in verses 5 to 8. He also includes the three friends, as we know from the last line in verse 4. Elihu appeals to the majestic greatness of God.

God is infinitely greater than human beings. He is far beyond being either helped or harmed by mortals. In the words of P. E. Kretzmann, "Neither the sins of men nor their good deeds have any effect upon the blessedness of the great God" (*Popular Commentary,* Old Testament, Volume 2, page 48). That does not mean that God is indifferent to the conduct of men. Indeed, he regards every sin as a serious violation of his holy will. Nevertheless, God's own person is not affected by the good or the evil that Job or Elihu or you or I do.

Therefore, Elihu concludes, Job ought to beware of judging God by human standards and insisting that God give him an immediate hearing.

⁹ **"Men cry out under a load of oppression;**
     they plead for relief from the arm of the powerful.
¹⁰ **But no one says, 'Where is God my Maker,**
     who gives songs in the night,

¹¹ who teaches more to us than to the beasts of the earth
    and makes us wiser than the birds of the air?'
¹² He does not answer when men cry out
    because of the arrogance of the wicked.
¹³ Indeed, God does not listen to their empty plea;
    the Almighty pays no attention to it.
¹⁴ How much less, then, will he listen
    when you say that you do not see him,
  that your case is before him
    and you must wait for him,
¹⁵ and further, that his anger never punishes
    and he does not take the least notice of wickedness.
¹⁶ So Job opens his mouth with empty talk;
    without knowledge he multiplies words."

Elihu attempts to explain why God sometimes delays in delivering people from their suffering and affliction. One of the common sayings during the Second World War was, There are no atheists in foxholes. When people are in great danger, they will cry out to God for help even though they scarcely, if ever, do so otherwise. Elihu expresses that thought in these verses. To many people, God is like an insurance policy, convenient to have when a crisis occurs. He is someone to call for help only when danger arises. When the going is good, he can be ignored.

Elihu maintains, "No one says, 'Where is God my Maker, who gives songs in the night, who teaches more to us than to the beasts of the earth and makes us wiser than the birds of the air?'" The expression "who gives songs in the night" refers to the joy that a believer can have even in the deepest affliction, for he knows that God is with him, to protect and deliver him.

We are reminded of an incident that took place over 1,900 years ago in faraway Philippi, in ancient Greece. Paul and Silas had been unjustly beaten and imprisoned. Their feet were fastened in stocks. We might think they would be complaining and crying out in bitter anguish. But, on the contrary, we read, "About midnight Paul and Silas were praying and singing hymns to God, and the other prisoners were listening to them. Suddenly there was such a violent earthquake that the foundations of the prison were shaken. At once all the prison doors flew open, and everybody's chains came loose" (Acts 16:25,26). On that remarkable occasion there truly were "songs in the night," and God delivered Paul and Silas, as well as others.

In contrast, Elihu describes people whose heart is not right with God. When they cry to him, they cry out of desperation, not out of believing hearts. Their plea is in vain. Elihu says, "Indeed, God does not listen to their empty plea; the Almighty pays no attention to it."

After having described the ungodly whose plea God does not hear, Elihu again addresses Job directly. He classifies Job with the ungodly whom he has just described. He feels that the principles he set forth in the preceding verses also apply in Job's case. He chides Job for his impatience and his insistence on receiving an answer from God. In Elihu's opinion Job has not appealed to God in true humility but rather in an arrogant and demanding spirit.

Verses 14 and 15 offer challenges to the translator and interpreter. The remarks of one commentator are helpful in bringing out the meaning of these verses. "Although Job agonizes over the fact that he *cannot see* God, Elihu wants him to realize that, nonetheless, his *case is before* God. God has known about it from the beginning. But Job cannot compel God to take any specific course by his laments and complaints" (John E. Hartley, *The Book of Job,* page 467).

In essence, Elihu tells Job, "Be patient, wait!" He might well have given himself that same advice, for Elihu himself was eager to jump into the fray. He was also rather impulsive and at times intemperate in his language. Yet he did add a needed dimension to the discussion.

In the closing verse of this chapter Elihu speaks very frankly: "So Job opens his mouth with empty talk; without knowledge he multiplies words." Although Elihu's words were very severe, Job did not challenge them. No doubt Elihu's sharp words helped Job reflect on the presumptuous nature of some of his statements in which he accused God of treating him unfairly. Job was wrong in accusing God of being unjust, and Elihu was right in rebuking Job and reminding him that he dare not judge God. God doesn't exercise justice in accordance with our way of thinking.

Elihu's speeches also must have prepared Job for the message contained in the next six chapters: two in which Elihu is the speaker and four in which God is the speaker. Those latter four chapters form the grand climax of the book of Job and lead to the happy conclusion in the closing chapter.

Elihu's fourth speech

Elihu's last speech is contained in chapters 36 and 37. This is the longest of his four speeches. As we have already observed, Elihu's previous speeches reflect an attitude of impatience and sharpness. In contrast, his words in this closing speech are more temperate and gentle, although he still speaks in a bold and confident manner.

Again, as in previous speeches, he opens by appealing to his listeners to give him their full attention. Realizing that he has already spoken at some length, he asks them to bear with him while he addresses them in his final speech.

God is wise and powerful in his dealings with mankind

36 Then Elihu continued:

² "Bear with me a little longer and I will show you
   that there is more to be said in God's behalf.
³ I get my knowledge from afar;
   I will ascribe justice to my Maker.
⁴ Be assured that my words are not false;
   one perfect in knowledge is with you.

Elihu is convinced that Job has unjustly accused God of treating him unfairly. Therefore he feels compelled to speak in God's behalf. Although he is young, Elihu claims to have a considerable amount of knowledge, and he intends to use that knowledge to ascribe justice to his Maker. In this closing speech he appeals to history and nature. He declares that God is wise, powerful, and loving in his dealings with mankind (36:1-21) and in his control over the world of nature (36:22–37:24).

He assures his listeners that his words are not false. Does he possibly have in mind Job's earlier statement to his friends? Job had accused them, "You, however, smear me with lies" (13:4). Speaking of himself, Elihu also boldly asserts, "One perfect in knowledge is with you." In a forthright manner, Elihu maintains that his arguments are valid and convincing. He is speaking particularly to Job, since the word "you" is in the singular in the Hebrew.

⁵ "God is mighty, but does not despise men;
   he is mighty, and firm in his purpose.
⁶ He does not keep the wicked alive
   but gives the afflicted their rights.
⁷ He does not take his eyes off the righteous;
   he enthrones them with kings
   and exalts them forever.

⁸ But if men are bound in chains,
   held fast by cords of affliction,
⁹ he tells them what they have done—
   that they have sinned arrogantly.
¹⁰ He makes them listen to correction
   and commands them to repent of their evil.
¹¹ If they obey and serve him,
   they will spend the rest of their days in prosperity
   and their years in contentment.
¹² But if they do not listen,
   they will perish by the sword
   and die without knowledge.
¹³ "The godless in heart harbor resentment;
   even when he fetters them, they do not cry for help.
¹⁴ They die in their youth,
   among male prostitutes of the shrines.
¹⁵ But those who suffer he delivers in their suffering;
   he speaks to them in their affliction.

After his introductory remarks, Elihu now launches into his speech, in which he emphasizes God's wisdom and power in dealing with human beings. Because he is all-wise, God is perfectly just and fair in his dealings with men. He is also kind and compassionate. And because he is all-powerful, God is capable of carrying out his purposes. He is able to bring the wicked to a disastrous end. On the other hand, he gives the humble and the afflicted their rights. He does not forget those who are righteous. Elihu states, "He does not take his eyes off the righteous; he enthrones them with kings and exalts them forever."

Those words remind us of two Old Testament heroes, Joseph and Daniel. Both men suffered unjustly, faced severe temptations, and were eventually exalted to important positions. Although most believers will not be exalted to such prominent and influential positions as were Joseph and Daniel, God will deliver the righteous at the time and in the manner that he knows best.

Elihu speaks of affliction in a twofold manner: as wholesome discipline for the righteous and as well-deserved punishment for the ungodly. He first points out the positive side of affliction (verses 8-11) and then the negative side (verses 12-15).

Elihu uses the expressions "chains" and "cords of affliction" to describe the troubles that overtake the righteous. Chains can be both restraining and painful. So also can the afflictions that a child of God must endure. Those afflictions, however, can serve a beneficial purpose. They can help keep a person from wandering on forbidden pathways, and they can also bring one to realize his own helplessness and turn to God for help.

Speaking of God, Elihu declares, "He tells them what they have done—that they have sinned arrogantly. He makes them listen to correction and commands them to repent of their evil." Unlike the three friends, Elihu emphasizes the fact that for the believer, suffering is a form of God's loving discipline designed to help the afflicted become aware of his sin, repent, and become stronger in his faith. Elihu had already stated that fact in more detail (33:19-33). Now again in his fourth speech he re-emphasizes it.

In verses 11 and 12 Elihu effectively contrasts the fortunes of those who listen to God and those who do not listen to him. He states, "If they obey and serve him, they will spend the rest of their days in prosperity and their years in contentment. But if they do not listen, they will perish by the sword and die without knowledge." Elihu proposes an important choice: either listen and prosper, or refuse to listen and perish.

Elihu pictures the negative side of affliction. He tells Job and the friends how the godless react to suffering. They store up anger in their hearts, and in so doing, they place themselves under God's righteous wrath. When they reap the reward of their evil deeds, they show no remorse nor do they cry out to God for help. In newspaper and television reports, we frequently see examples of such hardened people today—people who murder others and mutilate the bodies of their victims. In many instances they give no indication that they are sorry for having committed such horrible crimes. Even the sure prospect of death in the electric chair seems to make no impression on some criminals.

In verse 14 Elihu states, "They die in their youth, among male prostitutes of the shrines." Some translations tone down the expression "male prostitutes" by using words like "dissipation," "youthful shame," or "perverts." However, the translation "male prostitutes" expresses the Hebrew word precisely. In ancient times wild sexual orgies accompanied the practice of many heathen religions. Both male and female prostitutes participated in the revelry, which included both homosexual and heterosexual activities. These lewd activities still take place today in certain occult groups. Such a profligate life often leads to disease and an early death.

After having described the godless in such strong terms, Elihu again turns his attention to the godly, whom he had described in verses 7 to 11. "But those who suffer he delivers in their suffering; he speaks to them in their affliction." In chapter 33 Elihu had at greater length described suffering as a wholesome discipline to strengthen the faith of the righteous. He had stated that God speaks also through suffering. Job had complained that God would not answer him or explain why he was suffering so much. On the other hand, the three friends had insisted that Job's suffering was punishment for some special sins on his part. While Elihu also saw suffering as punishment and correction, he regarded it primarily as wholesome chastening to test and strengthen Job's faith.

In his booklet *Faith on Trial,* Roland Cap Ehlke states, "Could it not be, implies Elihu, that God uses troubles to bring about good? Perhaps he sends pain into our lives to turn us to him *before* we fall into sin, not only (as the friends contended) to punish and correct us *after* we have already fallen" (page 45).

In the verses that follow, Elihu again directly addresses Job. His language is sharper and less temperate than in the rest of this final speech.

> 16 "He is wooing you from the jaws of distress
>   to a spacious place free from restriction,
>   to the comfort of your table laden with choice food.
> 17 But now you are laden with the judgment due the wicked;
>   judgment and justice have taken hold of you.
> 18 Be careful that no one entices you by riches;
>   do not let a large bribe turn you aside.
> 19 Would your wealth
>   or even all your mighty efforts
>   sustain you so you would not be in distress?
> 20 Do not long for the night,
>   to drag people away from their homes.
> 21 Beware of turning to evil,
>   which you seem to prefer to affliction.

The six verses in this section pose difficulties for the translator and interpreter. With the possible exception of 19:23-27, no other section of the book is more difficult to translate. A comparison of English translations will attest to that. We have attempted to express the meaning on the basis of our understanding of the text.

Addressing Job in particular in verse 16, Elihu first describes Job as one caught in "the jaws of distress." In both the Old and the New Testament the words translated as "distress," "affliction," or "tribulation" give the picture of someone in a tight squeeze. The opposite meaning is expressed by the word translated as "a spacious place." Elihu describes such a place as "free from restriction" and adds, "to the comfort of your table laden with choice food."

Was Elihu consciously hinting at Job's future restoration, described in the closing chapter? Probably not. At this time only God knew that Job would be doubly blessed at the end. The words, however, are surely a fitting description of Job's former affluent life as well as his greater affluence after his restoration. We can be confident that Job did not live on bread and water after God so richly blessed him at the conclusion of this great human drama.

Elihu harshly and rather unjustly classifies Job with the wicked in verse 17. His words sound much like those of Job's three friends.

He is convinced that God has acted justly and is lovingly testing Job to draw him from his error of blaming God and accusing God of treating him unfairly. Elihu was certainly right in defending God's justice. Nor would any of the other participants in this discussion disagree with him in that matter. Earlier the friends had maintained that God is just. Even Job had admitted that. But in his suffering he had yielded to the temptation of accusing God of picking on him.

We must remind ourselves that none of the men engaged in this discussion knew the real reason for Job's terrible ordeal—that God had permitted Satan to afflict Job to test his faith. Yet although Elihu was unaware of that, he contributed more than the others toward solving the problem of Job's great suffering.

Verse 18 is particularly difficult. The NIV translates it, "Be careful that no one entices you by riches; do not let a large bribe turn you aside." That translation suggests that Job might be tempted to desire more money now that he had lost so much, and that by means of a large bribe he might pay a ransom for himself so that he could be relieved of his suffering. Such an attitude, says Elihu, would only turn him away from God.

While that interpretation is possible and has some support from the reference to wealth in the next verse, another translation appears to this writer to be preferable. The New American Standard Version, a modern revision of the King James Version, translates verse 18, "Beware lest wrath entice you to scoffing; And do not let the greatness of the ransom turn you aside." Commenting on this verse, P. E. Kretzmann states, "Job should not let the heat of his afflictions mislead him by its greatness and thus become guilty of presumptuous mocking" (*Popular Commentary,* Old Testament, Volume 2, page 50). In this verse the word translated as "bribe" is the same word in the Hebrew as the word for "ransom" in Job 33:24. There Elihu quotes the angel, whom we identified as the Son of God, as saying, "I have found a ransom for him."

Elihu then asks Job whether his wealth will be able to sustain him so that he no longer need suffer his affliction. The obvious intended reply is no.

Elihu states, "Do not long for the night, to drag people away from their homes." What does Elihu mean by those words? Does the word "night" symbolize death? It probably does. At any rate, in his introductory speech Job had poured forth a long and bitter lament in which he wished he had never been born. In striking imagery he repeated that wish throughout the entire chapter. In verse after verse Job repeatedly wished for darkness rather than light, death rather than life. Now Elihu warns Job not to wish to die but rather to bear his suffering with patience.

Elihu closes this section of his speech with the warning "Beware of turning to evil, which you seem to prefer to affliction." He says that Job is mistaken in giving vent to his feelings by complaining to God and insisting on bringing his case before God. Rather, Job ought to submit humbly. Did Elihu have an inkling of the real purpose of Job's suffering—to prove that Job was a true child of God? We really don't know. But we do know that although he was unaware of the wager between God and Satan, Elihu did point to suffering as a test and not merely as punishment. In afflicting the God-fearing, God has only good in mind.

In the rest of this speech (36:22–37:24), Elihu directs the attention of his listeners to another sphere in which God manifests his great wisdom and power.

God is wise and powerful in his control over the world of nature

> ²² "God is exalted in his power.
>   Who is a teacher like him?
> ²³ Who has prescribed his ways for him,
>   or said to him, 'You have done wrong'?
> ²⁴ Remember to extol his work,
>   which men have praised in song.
> ²⁵ All mankind has seen it;
>   men gaze on it from afar.

Previous speakers have praised the great power of God. Now Elihu takes up the theme again. He also asks, "Who is a teacher like him?" God is not a cruel tyrant; he is a loving and caring teacher.

In nature as well as in his dealings with mankind, God reveals his love as well as his greatness. Nor does God need any human advice or help. Elihu asks a rhetorical question: "Who has prescribed his ways for him, or said to him, 'You have done wrong'?" Similarly, Isaiah asks, "Who has understood the mind of the LORD, or instructed him as his counselor? Whom did the LORD consult to enlighten him, and who taught him the right way? Who was it that taught him knowledge or showed him the path of understanding?" (Isaiah 40:13,14). The obvious answer is no one!

Elihu urges Job to praise God rather than blame him. We also ought to keep that in mind. It is easy to complain when things go wrong. But shouldn't we rather thank God for his many blessings and praise him for his great works? Shouldn't we follow Elihu's advice and praise God in song?

As we look at this world, God's marvelous creation, we ought to be filled with awe and give expression to it in words of praise and songs of joy. The heavens and earth and all nature are a remarkable tribute to the all-wise and all-powerful God. In the opening verse of a familiar psalm, King David eloquently expresses that truth: "The heavens declare the glory of God; the skies proclaim the work of his hands" (Psalm 19:1). Can you and I remain silent when all nature bursts into songs of praise to our great God?

In the next verses, Elihu goes into more detail in his description of the wonders of God's creation. The closing verses of this chapter and the entire chapter that follows prepare us for the profound speech of the Lord that begins in chapter 38.

> [26] **How great is God—beyond our understanding!**
> **The number of his years is past finding out.**
>
> [27] **"He draws up the drops of water,**
> **which distill as rain to the streams;**

²⁸ **the clouds pour down their moisture**
   and abundant showers fall on mankind.
²⁹ **Who can understand how he spreads out the clouds,**
   how he thunders from his pavilion?
³⁰ **See how he scatters his lightning about him,**
   bathing the depths of the sea.
³¹ **This is the way he governs the nations**
   and provides food in abundance.
³² **He fills his hands with lightning**
   and commands it to strike its mark.
³³ **His thunder announces the coming storm;**
   even the cattle make known its approach.

The verse that introduces the Lord's speech reads,
"Then the LORD answered Job out of the storm" (38:1).
Since God's discourse seems to follow immediately upon
this final speech of Elihu, the storm was probably
already brewing, and there might well have been omi-
nous clouds appearing in the sky as Elihu was speaking
these words. That must have given his words a particularly dramatic effect.

In verse 26 Elihu states, "How great is God—beyond
our understanding! The number of his years is past finding out." God is eternal, a concept that is completely
beyond our comprehension. It is truly mind-boggling!
Our poor finite minds are utterly incapable of grasping
the concept that God has no beginning and no end.

God is truly great! That thought is given expression in
the popular hymn "How Great Thou Art!" The opening
lines are especially appropriate in connection with this
chapter of Job.

> O Lord my God, when I in awesome wonder
> Consider all the works thy hand hath made,
> I see the stars, I hear the mighty thunder,
> Thy pow'r throughout the universe displayed.

Then sings my soul, my Savior-God to thee,
"How great thou art! How great thou art!"

(CW 256:1)

This section of Elihu's final speech abounds in vivid imagery. There is repeated mention of clouds, thunder, lightning, and rain. Elihu gives a word picture of the wonders of a thunderstorm with its striking audiovisual effects. In these concluding verses of chapter 36, Elihu states the purpose of thunder and lightning. At its worst a thunderstorm can be a frightening experience that can drive human beings and animals to scurry about seeking shelter. Yet it can also serve a useful purpose. Elihu describes such a purpose: "He draws up the drops of water, which distill as rain to the streams; the clouds pour down their moisture and abundant showers fall on mankind. . . . This is the way he governs the nations and provides food in abundance."

Thunder and lightning are remarkable manifestations of God's great wisdom and power. Elihu does not propound a naturalistic or mechanistic view of the universe. To him thunder and lightning are not merely natural or physical phenomena. They are sent by God, and they serve his purposes. It is God who "spreads out the clouds" and "thunders from his pavilion." He "scatters his lightning about him." He "fills his hands with lightning and commands it to strike its mark," as a sure marksman hits a target.

In the concluding verse of this chapter, Elihu makes an interesting statement: "His thunder announces the coming storm; even the cattle make known its approach." Many people who are well acquainted with domestic animals have held the opinion that cattle can sense the coming of a storm and will act in a disturbed manner.

Elihu seems to have spoken these words to the men seated around him as a storm was coming up. His comments about the storm strongly suggest that. His last speech continues without interruption into the next chapter.

37 "At this my heart pounds
and leaps from its place.
² Listen! Listen to the roar of his voice,
to the rumbling that comes from his mouth.
³ He unleashes his lightning beneath the whole heaven
and sends it to the ends of the earth.
⁴ After that comes the sound of his roar;
he thunders with his majestic voice.
When his voice resounds,
he holds nothing back.
⁵ God's voice thunders in marvelous ways;
he does great things beyond our understanding.
⁶ He says to the snow, 'Fall on the earth,'
and to the rain shower, 'Be a mighty downpour.'
⁷ So that all men he has made may know his work,
he stops every man from his labor.
⁸ The animals take cover;
they remain in their dens.
⁹ The tempest comes out from its chamber,
the cold from the driving winds.
¹⁰ The breath of God produces ice,
and the broad waters become frozen.
¹¹ He loads the clouds with moisture;
he scatters his lightning through them.
¹² At his direction they swirl around
over the face of the whole earth
to do whatever he commands them.
¹³ He brings the clouds to punish men,
or to water his earth and show his love.

No doubt that as Elihu speaks these words, he is witnessing a storm brewing. But more than that, he sees in the storm a manifestation of the majestic power of God. In this chapter Elihu anticipates statements that God himself makes even more strongly and profoundly in the next chapter.

Elihu's reaction to the storm is expressed in the opening verse of this chapter: "At this my heart pounds and leaps from its place." While that sounds like an exaggeration, it is a frank and honest expression of Elihu's feelings. Speaking to Job and his friends, Elihu continues, "Listen! Listen to the roar of his voice, to the rumbling that comes from his mouth." He urges them to give their full attention to the thunder they hear as the storm grows in its intensity.

To Elihu the thunder was not merely a natural phenomenon. Neither he nor any of the ancients had the sophisticated understanding of thunder and lightning that today's physicists and meteorologists possess. But he did understand one important fact that most modern scientists ignore: the almighty God is in full control of all the forces of nature. And so Elihu describes thunder as "the rumbling that comes from his [God's] mouth."

Likewise Elihu gives a supernatural explanation for lightning: "He [God] unleashes his lightnings beneath the whole heaven and sends it to the ends of the earth." Elihu also correctly observes that lightning precedes thunder, for light travels more swiftly than sound: "After that comes the sound of his roar; he thunders with his majestic voice." In the Hebrew the word "roar" is the same word that is elsewhere used to describe the roar of a lion. A thunderstorm can dominate the whole landscape and can frighten and captivate man and beast. It ought to lead us all to realize that we are helpless and powerless and that God is in control of all things.

Not only is God all powerful; he is great and wise beyond our comprehension. "He does great things beyond our understanding." In verses 6 to 10, Elihu speaks of winter weather. Unlike a modern meteorologist, Elihu does not give a physical explanation for snow and rain. He acknowledges that it is God who sends moisture in those forms upon the earth.

In the part of the world in which Job and his friends lived, the rainy season occurs during the winter months. Light early rains come in the fall and are followed by snow. During the spring the heavier late rains arrive to make it possible for the crops to grow. In ancient times people did not have snow-clearing equipment such as we have today. When heavy snow fell, it would interrupt the people's activities and force them to remain indoors, as Elihu reminds his listeners in verse 7. Their confinement could give them the opportunity to meditate on God as he has revealed himself in nature and also in his Word. We do well to learn from Elihu. Our busy life often tempts us to neglect God and his Word.

Elihu's description of a winter storm is vivid. Not only human beings but also animals must seek shelter during such a storm. "The animals take cover; they remain in their dens." Some animals hibernate, greatly reducing their activity and their intake of food. Others remain under cover until the weather permits them to resume their regular activity.

In the opening line of verse 9, Elihu speaks of the "tempest" that "comes out from its chamber." Although some commentators refer that to the warm south wind, the line that follows suggests that Elihu is rather speaking of the cold north wind.

Elihu describes God as the one who controls the forces of nature. He confesses, "The breath of God produces ice, and the broad waters become frozen." Elihu's description of a rainstorm is vivid. He knows that certain clouds will produce rain. But, of greater importance, Elihu realizes it is God who sends the clouds, lightning, thunder, and rain. He speaks of the thick, dark clouds that are heavy with rain. They move about not aimlessly but under God's own direction. Elihu pictures God as a skillful pilot who steers his ship through narrow straits and troubled waters. In nature God truly reveals himself as all-wise and all-powerful.

Not only does Elihu state the fact that God sends the rainclouds, but he also states the *purpose.* "He brings the clouds to punish men, or to water his earth and show his love." In the Hebrew the expression "to punish men" reads "for a rod." The word *rod* often stands for punishment or correction. It is possible that when he spoke these words, Elihu had in mind two of Job's earlier statements. Job had complained, "If only there were someone to arbitrate between us, to lay his hand upon us both, someone to remove God's rod from me, so that his terror would frighten me no more" (9:33,34). Later, speaking of the apparent prosperity of the wicked, Job had stated, "Their homes are safe and free from fear; the rod of God is not upon them" (21:9).

According to Elihu, rain serves many purposes. God can send a violent rainstorm to punish people. The Bible plainly tells us that at the time of Noah, God sent the great flood to punish the vast majority of people because of their flagrant sins. Since Job and Elihu lived at an early time, the great flood may have been fresh in their memory. It was a disastrous event of such magnitude that it must have been passed down from generation to generation. Although God has promised that he will not send such an overwhelming flood again to destroy the earth (Genesis 8:21), he still does send rainstorms. Sometimes those storms produce floods that force people to move out of their homes. That has happened to many people. When we consider such catastrophes, we dare not act like Job's three friends and judge the flood victims to be especially great sinners. Rather, like Elihu, we ought to realize that God sends storms and other forces of nature as a judgment on sin in general and as a warning to lead us to repent of our own sins.

God also sends rain to water the ground so that it will enable the grass, shrubs, trees, and crops to grow. In so doing, God reveals his providence and loving care for us.

In the opening verses of this chapter, Elihu addressed all of the listeners. Now he again turns to Job and addresses him in particular.

> ¹⁴ **"Listen to this, Job;**
>   **stop and consider God's wonders.**
> ¹⁵ **Do you know how God controls the clouds**
>   **and makes his lightning flash?**
> ¹⁶ **Do you know how the clouds hang poised,**
>   **those wonders of him who is perfect in knowledge?**
> ¹⁷ **You who swelter in your clothes**
>   **when the land lies hushed under the south wind,**
> ¹⁸ **can you join him in spreading out the skies,**
>   **hard as a mirror of cast bronze?**
> ¹⁹ **"Tell us what we should say to him;**
>   **we cannot draw up our case because of our darkness.**
> ²⁰ **Should he be told that I want to speak?**
>   **Would any man ask to be swallowed up?**

Unlike the three friends, Elihu addresses Job by name. That adds a personal touch to his statements. He urges Job to submit to God rather than to expect God to engage Job in a dialogue. Job ought to pause and consider God's wonders. When he does, he will soon learn that those wonders are far beyond Job's powers of comprehension. In effect, Elihu tells Job that if he can't understand nature, he surely can't understand God. In his closing speech Elihu asks Job questions that anticipate God's more profound questions in the next chapter.

In verses 15 and 16 Elihu speaks of the clouds and lightning. It is God who gives orders to the clouds and controls them. He also produces lightning and thunder. In a remarkable manner God balances the clouds above us and makes it possible for rain to fall. In his commentary *Job and Science*, Walter Lang states, "There is an even balance between production and use of electricity in thunderstorms and rain. This remarkable statement in Job has only recently been discovered by scientists" (page 434). Thousands of years ago Elihu touched on this balance when he spoke of "how the clouds hang poised" in the sky to produce lightning, thunder, and rain.

Verses 17 and 18 present another picture, that of sweltering in summer heat. When the south wind would blow off the desert in the summer, people in that part of the world would swelter. Life would come almost to a standstill. Neither people nor animals would want to move around.

Elihu continues by asking Job a challenging question: "Can you join him [God] in spreading out the skies, hard as a mirror of cast bronze?" People in ancient times perceived the sky to be a solid expanse of metal resembling a shining mirror. In that pollution-free environment the bright, shining sun gave the sky the brilliance of a shiny metal mirror. Elihu now challenges Job to order the clouds to cover the sky to give relief from the extreme heat on a summer day. Obviously, that would require ability far greater than Job's.

In verse 19 Elihu again refers to Job's wish to appear before God to present his case. He reminds Job that such an encounter with the almighty God would not only be useless; it would be presumptuous. And it would be disastrous, as Elihu suggests, "Would any man ask to be swallowed up?" To challenge God to a confrontation would be self-destructive. Job must not make the mistake of considering God his equal. God is infinitely greater, wiser, and more powerful.

²¹ Now no one can look at the sun,
  bright as it is in the skies
  after the wind has swept them clean.
²² Out of the north he comes in golden splendor;
  God comes in awesome majesty.
²³ The Almighty is beyond our reach and exalted in power;
  in his justice and great righteousness, he does
    not oppress.
²⁴ Therefore, men revere him,
  for does he not have regard for all the wise in heart?"

In these closing verses of Elihu's fourth and final discourse, Elihu speaks of God in his divine splendor. He
compares God to the sun in its brightness. If human beings
cannot look at the sun in its blinding brilliance, how much
less can they behold God in his dazzling splendor.

"Now no one can look at the sun, bright as it is in
the skies after the wind has swept them clean." Having
said this, Elihu goes on to picture God in golden splendor even more brilliant than the sun.

Elihu depicts God as coming out of the north. In the
Old Testament the direction *north* is often used when
expressing the threat of invasion by a powerful nation.
Speaking of Cyrus the Great of Persia, God states, "I have
stirred up one from the north, and he comes. . . . He
treads on rulers as if they were mortar, as if he were a
potter treading the clay" (Isaiah 41:25). Here in Job the
expression "out of the north" suggests conquest and
emphasizes God's great power.

Elihu states that "God comes in awesome majesty."
The whole setting of the last part of Elihu's final
speech strongly suggests that the storm which is brewing is the same storm through which God will soon
address Job. The first verse of the next chapter makes
that even clearer: "Then the LORD answered Job out of
the storm" (38:1).

In his closing words Elihu attempts to defend God against Job's charge that God is arbitrary and unjust. Elihu declares, "In his justice and great righteousness, he does not oppress."

Then he concludes, "Therefore, men revere him, for does he not have regard for all the wise in heart?" That closing verse has been translated and interpreted in two different ways. The note in the NIV suggests the other interpretation: "For he does not have regard for any who think they are wise." Although the two interpretations appear to be contradictory, both can be defended. If we interpret the last sentence as a question, as in the text of the NIV, we would understand the expression "wise in heart" in a favorable sense, referring to people whose hearts are in tune with God. If we interpret the last sentence as a statement, we would understand the expression to refer to people who are proud and conceited and wise in their own eyes. In most of the Bible versions and commentaries, those words are translated as a statement, not a question. In the context of this passage the translation given in the note in the NIV appears to be preferable to that given in the text.

Before we leave this chapter, it would be helpful to summarize Elihu's speeches. As noted in our introductory remarks on Elihu (see page 233), many scholars are of the opinion that his speeches were not originally a part of the book but were added later by an editor. They claim that his speeches contribute nothing to the book but are merely the words of an immature young upstart. They also contend that his speeches say nothing of significance that God does not say much better in the next four chapters (38–41). They maintain that Elihu's speeches were not worthy of response, for no one directly responded to them. We cannot agree with any of those views.

As we study Elihu's speeches we can learn that he did indeed contribute to the discussion. While his words may at times have been as harsh as those of the three friends, Elihu added an important dimension to the discussion. Throughout their speeches the three friends had strummed away on the same string. They had repeatedly told Job: since you are suffering so much, you must be an unusually bad sinner. They had falsely judged his character by his sufferings. Their approach was strictly motivated by the law—in fact, their own rigid and warped interpretation of the law. They had ignored the gospel. Consequently, the effect of their speeches was a feeling of irritation rather than comfort.

On the other hand, Elihu pointed out that God uses afflictions not only as a punishment for sin but also to test the faith of the believer and strengthen it. He viewed affliction as a loving discipline, not merely as God's angry punishment for wrongdoing. He also comforted Job with the gospel. He spoke of God's messenger, or angel, who would deliver the afflicted one from his troubles—not only physical but also spiritual (33:23-28). Unlike the three friends, Elihu was sympathetic with Job.

In his article "The Book of Job in Its Significance for Preaching and the Care of Souls," August Pieper gives a good summary of Elihu's speeches. We list them here in abbreviated form, numbered according to Elihu's four discourses:

1. God is good, even when he sends great afflictions to the God-fearing.
2. God is just, because he is the almighty Creator and Lord of all things.
3. God does not exercise justice in accordance with our thinking.
4. In afflicting the God-fearing, God has only good in mind.

Pieper adds two great truths: God is good, even when he smites. God is just, even when we do not understand him.

When you or I or one of our loved ones experience troubles and afflictions, may God give us the grace to remember those truths! When it appears that we have nowhere to turn, may we remember to turn to him who has promised, "Whoever comes to me I will never drive away" (John 6:37). From Elihu's speeches we can find comfort in the truth that "the Lord disciplines those he loves" (Hebrews 12:6).

The fact that Job did not answer Elihu does not imply that he ignored what his young friend had said. We can infer that Elihu had convinced him and that Job therefore had nothing to reply. We may conclude that Elihu's sympathetic approach, with his personal interest in Job and his emphasis on suffering as a wholesome discipline, had convinced Job that God was not unjustly afflicting him. Rather, God was testing and strengthening Job's faith and proving to Satan that Job was not a fair-weather believer.

Elihu's speeches are not superfluous. They are an integral part of this remarkable book. Elihu's closing speech prepares us for the great speeches of the Lord, which are contained in the four chapters that follow. Profound in content and eloquent in language, those four chapters can well be regarded as the grand climax of this profound and eloquent book.

As we will now attempt to comment on those verses, we are well aware that even our best attempts will be feeble and faltering in comparison to the words of the speaker, God himself.

PART FOUR

God's Speeches to Job
(38:1–41:34)

The four chapters that follow contain two discourses in which God addresses Job. For centuries readers of the book of Job have admired the superb literary style and puzzled over the profound contents of these four chapters.

God's speeches immediately follow the four speeches of Elihu. The Lord does not reply to those speeches nor does he make any direct reference to the speeches of Job and the three friends. He does not discuss the problem of suffering, whether it is punishment for special sins or wholesome discipline for the child of God. He does not give Job's three friends the satisfaction of agreeing with them in their accusations against Job. He does not grant Job's request for a declaration of innocence from the charges the friends had brought against Job. Only in the closing chapter does God commend Job and blame the friends. God does not put himself on the defensive as though he had to explain his actions to his lowly creatures. He does not come to defend himself but to call Job to repentance and to reinstate Job as a man even more richly blessed than before.

Instead of answering Job's questions and responding to Job's demands, God bombards Job with questions of his own. In his book *Job and Science,* Walter Lang mentions that the Lord asks Job 42 scientific questions in chapter 38 alone. In all, according to Henry M. Morris, there are about 77 questions that God directed at Job in chapters 38 to 41 (*The Remarkable Record of Job,* page 98). Those questions were intended to make Job aware of how little he really knew about this universe and eventually confess, "Therefore I despise myself and repent in dust and ashes" (42:6).

Although God spoke directly to several other Old Testament characters—including Adam, Noah, Abraham, Jacob, Moses, and Elijah—his manner of speaking to Job was unusually dramatic. He came to Job in a storm. It is difficult for us to imagine the effect that must have had on Job. God does not rebuke Job for claiming innocence and integrity. He avoids that subject altogether. Rather, God reproves Job for his boldness and presumption in thinking he can dispute with God as his equal. God is perfectly wise, just, and powerful. Who is Job to contend with God? He asks Job question after question concerning this great universe and things that are in it.

God speaks of scientific facts that are highly sophisticated even for our modern scientific age. God has a perfect knowledge of this universe, for he created it. Scientists are only gradually beginning to learn facts that God has known from eternity. So who is Job to contend with God? Did Job create the universe? Does he govern it? Does he provide for the living creatures that inhabit the earth? Job, a mere mortal, is unable to comprehend the wonders of this universe, much less create and sustain it. How then can he assume to comprehend God, the almighty Maker of this universe?

Although God speaks very plainly, cuts Job down to size, and humbles Job, he still loves Job deeply. God does not use his power as a bully would, but as a caring heavenly Father who provides for all his creatures and especially blesses his children who trust in him, including Job. In fact, in the closing chapter of the book God commends Job and blesses him with even greater prosperity than at the beginning. By his words to Job, God turns Job's attention away from his sufferings and directs it to God's power, wisdom, and love.

Throughout his intense suffering, Job desperately clung to his faith in God. As Job earlier stated, "Though he slay me, yet will I hope in him" (13:15). By God's grace Job kept his faith, even though at times it wavered and his intense suffering led him to say things he would not have said otherwise. Yet Job needed to learn an important lesson in humility. Through his two speeches the Lord made Job realize that he was totally dependent on his God and that he must humbly submit to God and realize that all blessings come from God.

We now turn to the powerful words that God addressed to Job. As we read them, let each of us take them to heart.

God's first speech

The LORD challenges Job

38 Then the LORD answered Job out of the storm. He said:
² **"Who is this that darkens my counsel**
  with words without knowledge?
³ **Brace yourself like a man;**
  I will question you,
  and you shall answer me.

It is significant in verse 1 that God is referred to by his name *the LORD* (Yahweh), the covenant-God. Throughout the greatest part of the book, he is referred to by three titles: Shaddai ("the Almighty"), and El and Eloah (both meaning "God"). Only once in those 35 chapters do we find the name *LORD* (Yahweh), in 12:9. The name *LORD* is used repeatedly in chapters 1, 2, and 42, the prose chapters. It is also used in chapter 40. From this we can conclude that Job knew the true God by his covenant name and that he stood in a covenant relationship with him.

Many critics of the book of Job claim that the book is a composite of several different units that have been spliced together. They regard chapters 1 and 2 as one unit, chapters 3 to 31 as a second, chapters 32 to 37 as a third, chapters 38 to 41 as a fourth and, finally, the closing chapter (42) as a fifth unit. They assume many different authors for the book and deny its unity.

The writer of this volume of The People's Bible rejects such a fragmentary theory. There is significant ancient evidence that the book is a unit. From earliest times scholars generally regarded the book as one work, not the patched-up result of many sources. In the ancient Greek translation known as the Septuagint, which was produced before the time of Christ, the first verse of this chapter begins with the words "After Elihu had finished speaking." Although those words are not given in the Hebrew text or in any of our modern English translations, they are evidence that the ancient translators understood the Lord's speeches to follow directly after Elihu's speeches. The speaker in chapters 38 to 41 is none other than the Lord, the God of the covenant.

By this confrontation, God is giving a final test to his servant Job. It will serve to purge Job of his pride, bring him to realize his own sinfulness and helplessness, and lead him to trust more firmly in the Lord his God.

The Lord opens his discourse with a question that is truly shattering: "Who is this that darkens my counsel with words without knowledge?" Those words are not spoken with reference to Elihu's speech, as some have suggested. God refers them to Job, whom he addresses.

He continues, "Brace yourself like a man." Literally, those words read, "Gird your loins like a man." In ancient times people didn't wear slacks, jeans, or shorts as people do today. They wore long, flowing garments which they would tie up with a sash or belt when they engaged in some physical activity. That was particularly true in the case of warfare or athletic contests. In these words God challenges Job to get ready for a contest with him. The Lord asks Job questions, which Job is to answer if he can.

God reveals his power and wisdom in the forces of nature

> ⁴ "Where were you when I laid the earth's foundation?
>   Tell me, if you understand.
> ⁵ Who marked off its dimensions? Surely you know!
>   Who stretched a measuring line across it?
> ⁶ On what were its footings set,
>   or who laid its cornerstone—
> ⁷ while the morning stars sang together
>   and all the angels shouted for joy?

God asks Job questions concerning the creation of the world. "Where were you?" he asks. If you weren't present at the creation, how can you presume to dispute with me or sit in judgment over my way of conducting the affairs of this world?

God uses physical language to describe his creation of the earth. The earth did not come into being through a long process of evolution. Rather, it is the result of God's perfect plan of creation. God speaks of himself as an architect who planned every detail, a surveyor who measured its lines and dimensions, and an engineer who sank the footings and laid the cornerstone. In ancient times the laying of a cornerstone was a festive occasion at which people expressed themselves in joyful song. Also today we conduct a special ceremony for the laying of a cornerstone in a new building.

Speaking of laying earth's cornerstone, God describes the happy occasion when "all the angels shouted for joy." The last line of that verse literally reads, "and all the sons of God shouted for joy," as we find in a note in the NIV. In this context the translation "angels" in the text of the NIV expresses the correct meaning. In the parallel construction of the verse, the preceding term "morning stars" also refers to the angels. The expression "morning stars" suggests the purity and brilliance of the angels.

About two centuries ago an English poet and artist, William Blake, produced a number of engravings based on the book of Job. The most famous is entitled "When the Morning Stars Sang Together." God is pictured with outstretched arms in the center. Below him are people seated on the earth; above him are angels with arms upraised, chanting praises.

People often ask the question, On what day were the angels created? Genesis chapter 1 doesn't answer that question, perhaps because angels are invisible beings. Verse 7 of this chapter (38) strongly suggests that God created angels on one of the first days of creation, perhaps the first day, when he created light. Some angels rebelled against God and were banished from heaven (2 Peter 2:4; Jude 6). The devil was already at work in the Garden of Eden to tempt Adam and Eve as we read in Genesis chapter 3. From these verses it appears as if the angels were present at the time God created the earth and separated the land from the water.

In the section that follows, God asks Job profound questions about another marvelous creation, the sea.

> 8 **"Who shut up the sea behind doors**
> **when it burst forth from the womb,**
> 9 **when I made the clouds its garment**
> **and wrapped it in thick darkness,**
> 10 **when I fixed limits for it**
> **and set its doors and bars in place,**
> 11 **when I said, 'This far you may come and no farther;**
> **here is where your proud waves halt'?**

These four verses comprise one long question. God asks Job, "Who created the sea?" The obvious answer is no one—except God.

About three-fourths of the earth's surface is covered by water. What a powerful force water is! We have seen instances of the devastating damage inflicted upon homes that have been struck by hurricanes and floods. How much greater was the damage caused by the flood in the days of Noah! That deluge wiped out all creatures living on earth except those in the ark. If he so willed, God could send another universal flood, but in his undeserved goodness he has promised not to do so (Genesis 8:21). God has the powerful forces of water under his control. Addressing God, the psalmist states, "You set a boundary they [the waters] cannot cross; never again will they cover the earth" (Psalm 104:9).

In verse 8 God tells Job how he restrained the sea. In describing his work of creating and controlling the sea, he uses the language of childbirth. He stopped the rushing sea with doors and bolts so that it could go no farther than a certain point. We are reminded of that whenever we observe the ocean tides. God has set a fixed limit beyond which the waters cannot go.

God describes himself as making the clouds as a garment for the sea and wrapping it in thick darkness. The picture is that of wrapping a baby. God is in control of the mighty oceans and seas. During the flood in Noah's day we read that "all the springs of the great deep burst forth, and the floodgates of the heavens were opened" (Genesis 7:11). Torrents of water came in from every direction and covered the earth so that everything perished. The Bible also tells us that the waters flooded the earth for 150 days (Genesis 7:24). But then God reversed the process. We read further, "Now the springs of the deep and the floodgates of the heavens had been

closed, and the rain had stopped falling from the sky"
(Genesis 8:2).

God can control the mighty waters of the sea more
easily than you or I can turn on a water faucet to fill a
bathtub. He who created the waters by his command also
perfectly controls them.

When Job heard these words, he had to be deeply
impressed. But God was not through speaking. He had
much more to say.

> 12 **"Have you ever given orders to the morning,**
>   **or shown the dawn its place,**
> 13 **that it might take the earth by the edges**
>   **and shake the wicked out of it?**
> 14 **The earth takes shape like clay under a seal;**
>   **its features stand out like those of a garment.**
> 15 **The wicked are denied their light,**
>   **and their upraised arm is broken.**

In this section God reminds Job of the great marvels
of the dawn, when the darkness of night yields to the
light of day. God humbles Job by asking him if he has
ever commanded morning to appear and ordered light to
replace darkness. The obvious answer is no, never! Like
Job, we also take it for granted that each morning the sun
will rise and each evening it will set. We assume there
will always be the regular sequence of night and day. We
really don't appreciate the marvelous creation of light.
God created light on the first day. The first recorded
words of God are "Let there be light" (Genesis 1:3). Every
dawn is a recreation of light. Just as we need the darkness of night for sleep, we need the light of day to
accomplish our work.

In a very striking manner the Lord describes the effects of
dawn. As a homemaker takes a tablecloth by the corners and

shakes out the food crumbs, so the rays of dawn shake out the wicked from the earth. In ancient times as now, burglars, sex offenders, and murderers felt more secure committing their crimes under the cover of darkness than in broad daylight. The light of day will more easily expose them and lead to their capture. Light makes things distinct that are indistinct in darkness.

In his comments on verse 14, one writer states, "As the morning light etches multiple designs on the horizon in an array of colors, the darkened earth begins to take shape before the human eye. The dawn lights up the hills, valleys, trees, and shrubs. Just as a lump of clay is turned into a beautiful design beneath a *seal,* so too the earth glistens in beauty beneath the sun's first rays" (John E. Hartley, *The Book of Job,* page 497).

The Bible also uses light and darkness in a moral and spiritual sense. Light has the connotation of *good* whereas darkness stands for *evil.* For example, on the night when Jesus had a conversation with Nicodemus, he said, "This is the verdict: Light has come into the world, but men loved darkness instead of light because their deeds were evil. Everyone who does evil hates the light, and will not come into the light for fear that his deeds will be exposed. But whoever lives by the truth comes into the light" (John 3:19-21).

In striking contrast to these verses are the verses that follow.

> ¹⁶ **"Have you journeyed to the springs of the sea**
> **or walked in the recesses of the deep?**
> ¹⁷ **Have the gates of death been shown to you?**
> **Have you seen the gates of the shadow of death?**
> ¹⁸ **Have you comprehended the vast expanses of the earth?**
> **Tell me, if you know all this.**

Another realm beyond the reach of man is the vast region underground and at the bottom of the sea. The Lord asks if Job has gone to those remote places and acquainted himself with them. The "springs of the sea" can include the rivers that feed into the ocean and the fountains below. People in ancient times expressed great wonder at the ocean. Even today, in spite of extensive research by oceanographers and marine experts, the ocean still holds many mysteries we can't comprehend.

In verse 17 God asks Job the penetrating double question, "Have the gates of death been shown to you? Have you seen the gates of the shadow of death?" This language suggests that when a person enters the realm of death, the gates are closed behind him. There is no turning back to life in this world. Had Job entered the gates of death at the time God spoke those words? Obviously, he had not!

There is a relationship between the word "death" in the first line and the term "shadow of death" (one word in Hebrew) in the second line of verse 17. The phrase "shadow of death" is familiar to us from Psalm 23:4. It occurs 18 times in the Old Testament, including 10 in the book of Job. Job himself used that expression eight times; here God uses it as he speaks about the realm of the dead.

God's question in verse 17 is a very profound one. It ought to make us think seriously about our own futures. We are now alive, on this side of the gates of death. We dare not ignore the fact that the time will come, perhaps sooner than we think, when we will no longer be alive. Countless others have already died, including many friends and relatives. They are now on the other side of the "gates of death." We can't ask them, and they can't tell us what it is like. It is our confident hope that those who believed in Jesus Christ as their Savior have now entered their eternal rest, awaiting the resurrection of their bodies. Such is also our hope for ourselves. But we have not yet personally experienced passing to the other side of death's gates. It is a matter of faith during our life on earth. Like Job, we must answer all of God's questions in these verses with a no.

> ¹⁹ **"What is the way to the abode of light?**
> **And where does darkness reside?**
> ²⁰ **Can you take them to their places?**
> **Do you know the paths to their dwellings?**
> ²¹ **Surely you know, for you were already born!**
> **You have lived so many years!**

By a brief but powerful decree, "Let there be light," God created light on the first day (Genesis 1:3). Now he asks if Job knows the way to the abode of light and where darkness resides. He personifies light and darkness and describes them as having a home. He concludes this section of his speech with a statement that expresses divine irony: "Surely you know, for you were already born! You have lived so many years!" Those words must have humbled Job. God would teach Job, and also you and me, to let God be God and to put ourselves in submission to him.

> ²² **"Have you entered the storehouses of the snow**
> **or seen the storehouses of the hail,**
> ²³ **which I reserve for times of trouble,**
> **for days of war and battle?**
> ²⁴ **What is the way to the place where**
> **the lightning is dispersed,**
> **or the place where the east winds are scattered over**
> **the earth?**
> ²⁵ **Who cuts a channel for the torrents of rain,**
> **and a path for the thunderstorm,**
> ²⁶ **to water a land where no man lives,**
> **a desert with no one in it,**

²⁷ **to satisfy a desolate wasteland
    and make it sprout with grass?**
²⁸ **Does the rain have a father?
    Who fathers the drops of dew?**
²⁹ **From whose womb comes the ice?
    Who gives birth to the frost from the heavens**
³⁰ **when the waters become hard as stone,
    when the surface of the deep is frozen?**

God now directs Job's attention to his marvelous manner of providing moisture to sustain his creation. In his wisdom he manages the weather for the benefit of people and animals and vegetation. He asks Job several thought-provoking questions about snow, hail, lightning, thunderstorms, rain, dew, ice, and frost. He speaks of the storehouses of snow and hail. The snowflake is a marvelous creation of God. All snowflakes have a symmetrical six-sided shape, yet each is different. The psalmist tells us that God sends snow (Psalm 147:16). A little snowflake reflects the perfect plan God used in creating this world.

An excessive amount of snow, however, can strike terror into human hearts and can even lead to death. All of us have heard of people who have lost their lives in blinding snowstorms. Snowstorms have also turned the tide of wars. The invading armies of Charles XII from Sweden, Napoleon from France, and Hitler from Germany were defeated in successive centuries chiefly on account of unusually severe winter weather in Russia during those years. Snow can indeed be a frightening enemy.

So also can hail. In verse 23 God expressly mentions that he has reserved hail for times of trouble and days of battle. There is a good example of that in the book of Joshua. When Joshua and the Israelites helped the Gibeonites in battle, they put the enemy to flight. The sacred writer tells us that as the enemy fled, "the Lord hurled large hailstones down on them from the sky, and more of them died from the hailstones than were killed by the swords of the Israelites" (Joshua 10:11).

God also controls the lightning and winds. He asks if Job can understand those marvels of nature.

The verses that follow describe God's gift of rain. Thunderstorms and torrents of rain are not mere accidents of nature. God sends them. People who have experienced severe drought are especially appreciative of rain.

But further, God's goodness and providence extend even to areas where people don't live. God sends rain so that grass, flowers, shrubs, and trees can grow in otherwise desolate areas. Job had undoubtedly seen that, and God reminds him of it in his speech.

The question might arise: "Where did these forms of moisture originate?" In verses 28 to 30 God asks four challenging questions about the rain, dew, ice, and frost. Those questions are striking in their imagery. Using the language of human conception and birth, God asks Job about the origin of those forms of moisture. Verse 28 suggests the role of a father and verse 29 the role of a mother. In verse 30 God describes the process of freezing. Water can change into several forms: steam, ice, and water again. Those natural phenomena are remarkable creations of God. Scientists as well as all others would do well to remember that.

> 31 **"Can you bind the beautiful Pleiades?**
> **Can you loose the cords of Orion?**
> 32 **Can you bring forth the constellations in their seasons**
> **or lead out the Bear with its cubs?**
> 33 **Do you know the laws of the heavens?**
> **Can you set up God's dominion over the earth?**

God now directs Job's attention to the heavenly constellations. In his second speech, Job himself had briefly mentioned some of them. Speaking of God, he had stated, "He is the Maker of the Bear and Orion, the Pleiades and the constellations of the south" (9:9). See pages 68 and 69 for the commentary on those groups of stars. In these verses God mentions one additional group of stars, referred to in verse 32 as "the constellations." In the Hebrew that word is in the plural and refers to a cluster of stars that cannot be identified with certainty.

God describes the stars comprising the Pleiades as "beautiful." He created them and other stars and describes his creation as "very good" in the opening chapter of the Bible. Like other stars and planets, they are beautiful to behold, and throughout the ages they have fascinated people.

In speaking of those four constellations, God suggests that he binds and looses them, brings them forth and leads them out, as if they were animals. Those expressions may refer to the rising and setting of the constellations. God asks if Job is able to control those constellations. The answer is obvious.

God asks more questions: "Do you know the laws of the heavens? Can you set up God's dominion over the earth?" It would be the height of presumption for Job to maintain that he could do so. Again, he must humbly confess, "No, not at all!" Only God has a perfect knowledge of the laws of heaven, for he created and established the heavens. He also created the earth and maintains it.

In the last line of verse 33 the NIV inserts the word "God's" in half-brackets, since it is not given in the Hebrew text. The line can be translated in either of two ways: "Can you set up God's dominion over the earth," as in the NIV, or "Can you set up their rule over the earth," referring to the stars. There is no contradiction between the two translations, since God created the sun, moon, and stars to rule over the earth and indicate signs and seasons (Genesis 1:16-18; Jeremiah 33:20,25). The sun determines daylight and night and is also essential for life on earth. The moon constantly passes through its various phases and also controls the ocean tides. The stars, beautiful to behold, have for centuries also served as a guide for sailors.

We now turn our attention to the concluding verses of this first half of God's first speech to Job.

> ³⁴ **"Can you raise your voice to the clouds**
>   **and cover yourself with a flood of water?**
> ³⁵ **Do you send the lightning bolts on their way?**
>   **Do they report to you, 'Here we are'?**
> ³⁶ **Who endowed the heart with wisdom**
>   **or gave understanding to the mind?**
> ³⁷ **Who has the wisdom to count the clouds?**
>   **Who can tip over the water jars of the heavens**
> ³⁸ **when the dust becomes hard**
>   **and the clods of earth stick together?**

In this final section of his discourse about the forces of nature, God asks Job several questions about the clouds and their function in providing rain. These questions must have humiliated Job, as they would also humiliate you and me. We mortals don't understand the origin and movement of clouds and their function in producing rain. Much less can we control them or make them do our bidding. Medicine men have cried out in vain to the clouds for rain. It was only because of God's almighty power in responding to Elijah's prayer that rain fell to end the drought in Israel (1 Kings 18:45). By his own power Elijah couldn't have done it. Meteorologists can predict rain, but they can't produce it. While sometimes there may be a measure of success in men's attempts to "seed" the clouds, it is a form of tampering with nature and a questionable activity.

As for lightning, scientists can study it and to a certain extent explain it, but they can't produce it. Only God can do that. There is gentle and humorous satire in God's question to Job: "Do you send the lightning bolts on their way? Do they report to you, 'Here we are'?" Poor Job! How embarrassing!

Verse 36 has been interpreted and translated in a variety of ways throughout the centuries. We refer in particular to the words translated as "heart" in line one and "mind" in line two of verse 36 in the NIV. Those two words are in a parallel construction. The best interpretation and translation of this verse is that given in our NIV text. It is the all-wise God who also gives wisdom and understanding to human beings. Only he has perfect wisdom and is able to create and control this universe.

In concluding the first part of his opening speech, God asks if Job has the wisdom to count the clouds. That question is as challenging as his statements to Abraham: "If anyone could count the dust, then your offspring could be counted" (Genesis 13:16) and "Look up at the heavens and count the stars—if indeed you can count them" (Genesis 15:5). Who can count the dust, the stars or the clouds? No one—except God himself.

God also compares the clouds to jars, or skin bottles, filled with water. In vivid language he challenges Job to tip them over to water the earth and produce dirt clods that stick together. Could Job do that? Could anyone? Surely no one—except God himself.

Verse 38 concludes the first half of God's first speech to Job. God has raised many challenging questions about this marvelous universe. Could Job do what God has done—create this marvelously well-ordered universe, govern it, and preserve it? Could any mere mortal do so? No, never! Only God can. This universe could never have come into existence through a haphazard, accidental series of changes and developments. It is the work of a perfectly wise and powerful Creator who has a loving concern for his creatures.

The last three verses of chapter 38 introduce the subject of the next chapter. They tell us about God's creatures in the animal world.

God reveals his power and wisdom in the kingdom of the animals

After he has shown Job his understanding of the forces of nature in the heavens, on the earth, and in the sea, God reveals his knowledge of the animals. By giving a brief word picture of a few animals, he asserts his lordship over the entire earth. These animals did not develop over a long period of time through a process of evolution. On the contrary, God created them and endowed them with instinct and special abilities. He also provides for their needs.

As he hears God speak these words, Job must marvel at God's wisdom and goodness in providing for his creatures. Job must also confess that no human being would be able to do what God does. Job must conclude that if God has such loving concern for the animals, he will not ignore Job's plight but will turn his loving attention to Job and help Job in the manner he knows best.

By these questions God repeatedly reminds Job that he had nothing to do with creating and preserving the animals. How then can Job presume to question the wisdom of God, who created those animals and everything in this universe?

In this fascinating section of the book, the Lord directs Job's attention to a few of his many marvelous creatures in the animal world. Each of them has its own characteristics. Although these animals lack human intelligence, God has endowed them with the necessary instincts, strength, and mobility to survive.

When the Lord spoke these words, Job had to marvel at the wisdom of the God who created these animals and gave them their individual characteristics. As we read these verses, may God the Holy Spirit also lead us to acknowledge God's wisdom instead of second-guessing him when things don't go as we'd like them to.

The lion and the raven

³⁹ "Do you hunt the prey for the lioness
    and satisfy the hunger of the lions
⁴⁰ when they crouch in their dens
    or lie in wait in a thicket?
⁴¹ Who provides food for the raven
    when its young cry out to God
    and wander about for lack of food?

God begins by directing Job's attention to the most noble of wild animals, the lion, rightly referred to as "the king of beasts." In our country we don't see lions except in zoos and circuses. In ancient times, particularly in the Middle East, it was not unusual for people to see lions out in the open. No doubt Job had seen them. People were aware of the presence of lions and treated them with great respect. Lions have always been known for their courage, fierceness, and strength.

God asks if Job provided the lions with their food. Would Job be able to catch a victim? Not very likely. And even if he did catch one, would he dare bring it to the mother lion and her hungry cubs? He would do so at the risk of life and limb. No human being can provide for a lioness and her cubs in their natural habitat. Only God can do so, and he does. He has created the majestic lion and given her the instinct and ability to catch her prey and feed her young ones. God provides for dangerous wild animals as well as domesticated animals.

God's next question concerns a creature that stands in sharp contrast to the majestic lion—the raven. One of the least attractive of birds, it is a scavenger that feeds on rotten flesh and makes a rather unglamorous croaking noise as it flies. As long as her baby birds are unable to take care of themselves, the raven searches for food to satisfy their hunger. As soon as the young ones are able to fly, the mother bird expels them from the nest and leaves them to fend for themselves. And yet, as different as ravens and lions are, they have one important thing in common: they must search for food for themselves and their young. God has given them the ability to do so.

In his Sermon on the Mount, Jesus referred to the ravens when he was teaching his disciples not to worry about little things in their daily life. He said, "Consider the ravens: They do not sow or reap, they have no storeroom or barn; yet God feeds them" (Luke 12:24). By his reference to the ravens, Jesus would teach us that God is surely aware of our needs and that it is useless and even sinful for us to worry about what we will eat or drink or wear. Rather, we ought to seek God's kingdom and righteousness (Matthew 6:33).

The mountain goat

39 "Do you know when the mountain goats give birth?
  Do you watch when the doe bears her fawn?
 ² Do you count the months till they bear?
  Do you know the time they give birth?

³ They crouch down and bring forth their young;
   their labor pains are ended.
⁴ Their young thrive and grow strong in the wilds;
   they leave and do not return.

God asks Job several questions about another of his wild creatures. The mountain goat, also known as the ibex, inhabits the steep cliffs of the wilderness. It is still found in various parts of the Middle East. It is very shy and timid. As a protection against hostile forces, God has endowed this animal with a keen sense of smell, sure and nimble feet that enable it to climb rocks and run swiftly, and a tan color that blends in well with the rocky hillside.

God has created this animal to be totally independent of any human help. The female conceives her young and carries them until the time of delivery. She gives birth to her young without any help from human beings. After their birth the young ones grow up and soon go off on their own with no help from anyone except God, who has given them their remarkable abilities so that they can survive in their strange environment.

Job could only look at those graceful creatures and marvel. He did not know how long their gestation period was. God knew. And that is the God whose wisdom Job had questioned.

The wild donkey

⁵ "Who let the wild donkey go free?
   Who untied his ropes?
⁶ I gave him the wasteland as his home,
   the salt flats as his habitat.
⁷ He laughs at the commotion in the town;
   he does not hear a driver's shout.
⁸ He ranges the hills for his pasture
   and searches for any green thing.

In the opening chapter of this book the sacred writer informs us that Job owned five hundred donkeys (1:3). In the closing chapter he tells us that the number of donkeys was doubled to one thousand (42:12). Those were domesticated animals that were useful to the owner for labor, transportation, and milk.

The donkey mentioned in these four verses of this chapter is a different breed, a wild donkey. It would be difficult if not impossible to tame him. He is a free and wide-ranging animal who inhabits desolate places, "salt flats," as we read in verse 6. Like other animals, he craves salt to supplement his diet of grass. He also shies away from venturing to a city where people might disturb his carefree lifestyle. He enjoys his unlimited freedom. He stands in sharp contrast to the slow, plodding, and submissive domesticated donkey such as was numbered among Job's livestock.

And yet the two kinds of animals had something in common. Both the wild donkey and the domesticated donkey were created by the all-wise and all-powerful God, who watches over both and provides for them. God knew all about the wild donkey. Did Job?

The wild ox

9 "Will the wild ox consent to serve you?
    Will he stay by your manger at night?
10 Can you hold him to the furrow with a harness?
    Will he till the valleys behind you?
11 Will you rely on him for his great strength?
    Will you leave your heavy work to him?
12 Can you trust him to bring in your grain
    and gather it to your threshing floor?

The Lord confronts Job with seven questions in these four verses. Again, the implied answer to each is an emphatic no. In contrast to Job's domesticated oxen, this wild ox would refuse to comply with Job's wishes. Under no circumstances would he consent to submit to or serve Job.

The King James Version translates the Hebrew word for this animal with the word "unicorn," following the ancient Greek and Latin versions. That translation is questionable and misleading, since the same word is used in Psalm 22:21, which refers to the "horns" of the wild oxen. A unicorn would have only one horn.

Most scholars identify this wild ox with the *aurochs,* an animal now believed to be extinct. According to some accounts, it was a huge animal with long horns pointed forward and was very dangerous. The ancient Egyptian king Thutmose III boasted about his exploits in hunting this wild animal. The animal is also pictured on the famous Ishtar Gate in ancient Babylon.

By these questions God points out how impossible it would be for Job to attempt to make this animal yield to his wishes. Unlike Job's domesticated oxen, this wild ox would defy any attempt to restrict his freedom by harnessing him and making him walk in a straight line. He would refuse to pull the plow to turn up the soil. Instead, he would make a quick retreat away from the field, or he would attack the man who foolishly ventured to hitch him to the plow. If Job were to depend on this wild ox, he would be unable to haul his grain into his threshing floor. This strong and unruly ox would show no inclination to yield to Job's wishes. Only God is his master—neither Job nor any other human being.

The ostrich

13 **"The wings of the ostrich flap joyfully,**
  but they cannot compare with the pinions and feathers
  of the stork.

¹⁴ **She lays her eggs on the ground**
      and lets them warm in the sand,
¹⁵ **unmindful that a foot may crush them,**
      that some wild animal may trample them.
¹⁶ **She treats her young harshly, as if they were not hers;**
      she cares not that her labor was in vain,
¹⁷ **for God did not endow her with wisdom**
      or give her a share of good sense.
¹⁸ **Yet when she spreads her feathers to run,**
      she laughs at horse and rider.

In sharp contrast to the sections that precede and follow, this passage describes a creature that appears to be stupid, awkward, and comical. In these lines God describes a female ostrich. She has a small head attached to a large body by a long, skinny neck. She has long legs and short, stubby wings that are unable to lift the big bird into flight but rather serve to enable her to run swiftly. With her unattractive physical features and her swiftness of foot, she reminds one of a camel.

In verse 13 the ostrich is compared to the stork. Both birds are large and have a long neck and long legs, but there the similarity ends. The ostrich has wings that can flap and propel her rapidly along the ground, but she can't fly, whereas the stork can fly to great heights. The ostrich lays her eggs on the ground so that they may be crushed or left as prey to wild animals. The stork has much more concern for her eggs. The ostrich shows little affection for her young and sometimes seems to disown them. Jeremiah compared the people of Judah to ostriches: "My people have become heartless like ostriches in the desert" (Lamentations 4:3). In contrast, the stork is known for her deep love and devotion for her young. The Hebrew word for "stork" is related to a word that means "kind" or "devoted." The mother stork has been known to prick her breast until she draws blood to feed her hungry baby birds.

Nevertheless, as unfavorable as the ostrich might appear to be in comparison with other birds and animals, she has certain good qualities that enable her to survive. God gave this strange bird legs that are long and strong and wings that can propel her to a remarkably high speed so that she resembles an airplane taking off. In the closing verse of this unit, God reminds Job that the ostrich can outrun a horse. The ostrich is ugly and awkward and not very intelligent, yet she is swift and strong and resourceful. God knows all the details of this remarkable creature.

The horse

> [19] "Do you give the horse his strength
>   or clothe his neck with a flowing mane?
> [20] Do you make him leap like a locust,
>   striking terror with his proud snorting?
> [21] He paws fiercely, rejoicing in his strength,
>   and charges into the fray.
> [22] He laughs at fear, afraid of nothing;
>   he does not shy away from the sword.
> [23] The quiver rattles against his side,
>   along with the flashing spear and lance.
> [24] In frenzied excitement he eats up the ground;
>   he cannot stand still when the trumpet sounds.
> [25] At the blast of the trumpet he snorts, 'Aha!'
>   He catches the scent of battle from afar,
>   the shout of commanders and the battle cry.

This eloquent passage gives us one of the most striking descriptions of an animal in all literature. The horse is no doubt the noblest of all domesticated animals. It is a creature of true beauty.

Over the years the horse has served in many capacities. The ancient Romans used horses for their chariot races. Today race horses earn thousands of dollars for their owners and gain fame for themselves as well as the jockeys who ride them. Horses are also used in harness races that attract large crowds. They gracefully go through their paces in circus acts. During the first half of this century, farmers used horses for drawing implements in their fields. From ancient times until about a century ago, horses were used in warfare. It is particularly the warhorse that God describes to Job in this section of his speech.

Did Job give the horse his strength, agility, and courage? No, not at all! It was God alone who created this majestic animal and gave him his abilities. God asks, "Do you give the horse his strength or clothe his neck with a flowing mane?" The Hebrew word translated as "a flowing mane" suggests the idea of "thunder" or "vibration." Some versions translate it accordingly. The expression no doubt refers to the horse's mane, which tosses back and forth as the horse races headlong into battle.

God also compares the warhorse to a locust as he leaps into battle and frightens others with his fierce snorting. Horses and locusts are compared elsewhere in the Bible as well. In the book of Revelation, for instance, the apostle John thus describes a vision of a swarm of locusts: "The locusts looked like horses prepared for battle" (Revelation 9:7).

God further describes the warhorse: "He paws fiercely, rejoicing in his strength, and charges into the fray." This verse pictures the warhorse as he paws the battle ground fiercely and charges into battle unafraid of the weapons of the enemy. The ancient Roman poet Virgil similarly describes the warhorse: "The hoofs' four-footed thunder shakes the crumbling plain" (*Aeneid,* VIII, 596).

When the warhorse is aroused for battle, nothing can stop him. The sight of a weapon does not deter him but rather spurs him on to dash into the fray. On his back the arrows rattle in the quiver and the spear and lance of his owner flash in the sunlight. The sound of the trumpet arouses him to action. He knows only one way to go: forward to meet the enemy. He can smell the battle and is eager to do his part and carry his master to victory.

As God described the warhorse in this vivid word picture, it must have had an overwhelming effect on Job.

From his remarks in the chapter that follows, we know that God's speech humbled Job. Although he was great among his fellow men, compared to God, Job was as nothing. God knew all his creatures intimately. But in the dark night of his grief Job actually thought God had lost sight of him!

The Lord had opened this part of his first speech by raising questions about the lion (38:39,40), the most majestic of the wild animals. He now concludes by asking Job questions about two majestic birds that soar in the skies, the hawk and the eagle.

The hawk and the eagle

> ²⁶ "Does the hawk take flight by your wisdom
>   and spread his wings toward the south?
> ²⁷ Does the eagle soar at your command
>   and build his nest on high?
> ²⁸ He dwells on a cliff and stays there at night;
>   a rocky crag is his stronghold.
> ²⁹ From there he seeks out his food;
>   his eyes detect it from afar.
> ³⁰ His young ones feast on blood,
>   and where the slain are, there is he."

The Bible mentions the hawk in only two other passages, Leviticus 11:16 and Deuteronomy 14:15. In both passages it is listed among unclean birds that the Israelites were forbidden to eat. The hawk is a bird that can swiftly swoop down on other birds and kill them.

God asks if Job has the necessary insight and intelligence to direct the hawk in its flight to the south for the winter. Obviously, Job does not have such wisdom. It is only God the Creator who has given the hawk such instinct. Migratory birds have a sure sense of timing and direction that is superior to the most sophisticated navigation instruments in our modern airplanes. It is truly amazing that the Lord has built such an unerring sense of direction and timing into the tiny head of a migratory bird. Did Job place that delicate instrument into the birds? Are their movements in flight under his direction? Certainly not! There is an immense difference between a man's limited mastery of his environment and God's total sovereignty over this universe.

The Lord also introduces his statements about the eagle with a question: "Does the eagle soar at your command and build his nest on high?" Again the answer is an emphatic no. Neither Job's intelligence nor his command can make those most graceful birds fly. The ostrich and the eagle are an interesting study in contrasts. In verses 13 to 18 we already noted the awkwardness of the ostrich as she runs along the ground flapping her wings. On the other hand, the eagle takes off into a graceful and effortless flight, soaring high into the skies. The ostrich foolishly lays her eggs in the sand where they can be broken or stolen. The eagle builds his nest on a high cliff and lays his eggs in a place that is inaccessible to most other creatures.

In his noble appearance and lofty flight, the eagle has from ancient times been regarded as the king of birds. It is not strange that the United States adopted the eagle as a national symbol. In Exodus 19:4 God describes himself as carrying the Israelites on eagles' wings. In his lament over the death of Saul and Jonathan, David states that they were swifter than eagles and stronger than lions (2 Samuel 1:23). Two Old Testament passages that make reference to the high nests of eagles are Jeremiah 49:16 and Obadiah chapter 4. The eagle's nest, hidden away in a remote place inaccessible to others, is indeed a picture of safety and seclusion.

In his graceful flight, the eagle can swoop down upon his prey with uncanny precision and incredible speed. God has endowed this majestic bird with unusually keen sight so that he can detect his victim from a distance and quickly pounce upon his prey to carry it off to his nest. There the eagle will feed his young, who remain in the nest for 8 to 12 weeks, after which the parent birds send them off to care for themselves.

The closing verse in this section states that the eagle feeds on animals he catches: "His young ones feast on blood, and where the slain are, there is he." Like the parent birds, the young eagles are carnivorous, feeding on flesh rather than vegetation. The mention of blood in this verse also suggests that the flesh they eat is freshly killed and not rotten flesh such as vultures prefer to eat.

In this speech God's description of selected animals began with the lion, king of beasts, and ends with the eagle, king of birds. In between he directed Job's attention to a lineup of interesting animals. These are only a small sampling of God's marvelous creatures. As we ponder the great mystery of God's work of creation with Job, must we not bow in deep humility and praise our almighty God? Who except the Lord could create and preserve such living beings, each with its own remarkable nature and characteristics? And when we pause to reflect that this same God created us human beings in his own image and also redeemed us through his Son, Jesus Christ, surely we must joyfully exclaim with David, "I praise you because I am fearfully and wonderfully made" (Psalm 139:14).

In effect, God had told Job, "I am wise; you know nothing. Who are you to want to contend with me?" This was bitter medicine for Job, but it was wholesome medicine.

This chapter concludes the Lord's first speech to Job. After an interlude that contains a brief dialogue with Job, God will again address Job in a speech that features two strange animals, the behemoth and the leviathan.

God's second speech

God and Job in a brief dialogue

40 The LORD said to Job:

² **"Will the one who contends with the Almighty correct him?**
Let him who accuses God answer him!"

³**Then Job answered the Lord:**

⁴ **"I am unworthy—how can I reply to you?**
I put my hand over my mouth.
⁵ **I spoke once, but I have no answer—**
twice, but I will say no more."

These five verses serve as a transition between chapters 39 and 40. A good case can be made for placing them at the end of chapter 39. And many commentators regard them as a conclusion to that chapter. Since the Hebrew text places these verses at the beginning of chapter 40, we will consider them under this chapter. These verses contain a brief dialogue between the Lord and Job and can serve as an introduction to the Lord's second speech.

God's words to Job are brief and to the point. He first asks Job, "Will the one who contends with the Almighty correct him?" In his eagerness to prove his innocence against his friends' charges, Job had wished for the opportunity to appear before God to present his case. Speaking of God, he had said, "If only I knew where to find him; if only I could go to his dwelling! I would state my case before him and fill my mouth with arguments" (23:3,4). Job couldn't understand why he had to suffer so much. He felt that God was picking on him. Job falsely regarded God as his enemy. He did not realize that God was allowing him to suffer in order to prove to Satan that Job was a true child of God and also to test and strengthen Job's faith.

Now in this dialogue God gives Job the opportunity to answer him. Job had asked for a confrontation; now he has it. He had accused God; now let him speak up. But what does Job say? He says nothing at all of what he had intended to say! He says nothing about his own righteousness, his friends' unjust criticism, or God's unfairness in dealing with him. Dazzled and humbled by God's great wisdom and power, Job can only confess, "I am unworthy—how can I reply to you? I put my hand over my mouth. I spoke once, but I have no answer—twice, but I will say no more." Job humbly bows to the Lord, who is infinitely greater and wiser. He sees himself as unworthy before the Sovereign Lord of the universe. God has magnified his own wisdom, he has exposed Job's ignorance, and Job can find nothing to say in his own defense.

After Job's humble submission, we might wonder why God does not immediately bless Job and restore his property and wealth. Why does God continue speaking to Job in such strong language in this chapter and the one that follows? The fact that God has more to say to Job indicates that he, the all-knowing God, is not satisfied with Job's repentance. Job sees himself as small and insignificant, completely overwhelmed by God's majestic greatness. Yet he does not confess that it was a sin on his part to accuse God of injustice.

Job's repentance is genuine so far as it goes, but it doesn't go far enough. He needs to acknowledge that God's thoughts and ways are far higher and greater than his own, and Job therefore must accept them even though he can't understand them. He also needs to realize that the God who has allowed him to suffer is really not his enemy but is his true friend who loves him.

Job needs to learn that God's relationship to Job is a gospel relationship, not a law relationship. In the end, Job would realize that. He would sincerely repent and in true faith submit to God, who would restore him and bless him twofold, as we learn from the closing chapter of this book. Before he would do that, however, the Lord would have more to say to Job. In the verses that follow, God proceeds to prepare Job for true repentance.

God again challenges Job

⁶Then the LORD spoke to Job out of the storm:

⁷ "Brace yourself like a man;
   I will question you,
   and you shall answer me.
⁸ "Would you discredit my justice?
   Would you condemn me to justify yourself?
⁹ Do you have an arm like God's,
   and can your voice thunder like his?
¹⁰ Then adorn yourself with glory and splendor,
   and clothe yourself in honor and majesty.
¹¹ Unleash the fury of your wrath,
   look at every proud man and bring him low,

¹² **look at every proud man and humble him,**
   crush the wicked where they stand.
¹³ **Bury them all in the dust together;**
   shroud their faces in the grave.
¹⁴ **Then I myself will admit to you**
   that your own right hand can save you.

Verses 6 and 7 are almost identical to 38:1-3, with which the Lord's first speech is introduced. In this second speech, however, he omits the question contained in 38:2: "Who is this that darkens my counsel with words without knowledge?" Instead, God confronts Job with a twofold question: "Would you discredit my justice? Would you condemn me to justify yourself?" Job had consistently maintained his innocence of the charges his friends had brought against him. He had not committed any special sins that warranted his severe suffering. Nor does God accuse him of any such special sins.

God is not taking sides with Job's three friends against Job. But God does reprimand Job for accusing him of being unfair in his dealings with Job. Job protested his innocence, but in so doing he blamed God. He assumed that his own innocence and God's righteousness were incompatible and mutually exclusive. If Job was innocent, God could not be righteous in afflicting him—so Job thought.

Elihu had suggested to Job that God can speak to a person through affliction to turn him from doing wrong and to strengthen him in his faith (33:19-30). Apparently, what Elihu had said did not fully impress Job. Job had to learn that when God afflicts a believer, he does so out of true love and concern for that individual. Job's three friends had emphasized God's *justice,* that God rewards everyone exactly according to each person's works. Job had emphasized God's *power,* also maintaining that God expressed it according to how he felt, as though he were a bully. On the other hand, the Lord, although all-just and all-powerful, emphasized his great *mystery* and *love*. God is far above human comprehension, yet he loves all of his creatures and cares for them, also including poor Job who was suffering so severely.

In his speeches God speaks sharply to Job. As in his first speech where he challenged Job's wisdom, so here he challenged Job's power. He does so to break down the sinful pride that had been building up in Job's heart. He reminds Job that God's justice embraces the whole universe, which he created and controls. The Lord has power over the universe, and he has full responsibility for everything that happens in it.

When the Lord challenges Job with these questions and statements, he does so to remind Job that it is presumptuous on Job's part to judge the Lord. Job was guilty of assuming the rights and privileges of God, who alone can render perfect judgment. The Lord asks if Job has an arm or a voice like God's. The word "arm" expresses the idea of power (Psalm 98:1), whereas "voice" suggests authority. Elihu had repeatedly spoken of the voice of God that spoke through the thunderstorm (37:1-7). It was also in a thunderstorm that God manifested his power and authority to Job.

After having asked Job if he has an arm and voice like God, the Lord challenges him to act accordingly. In verses 11 to 13, God challenges him to appear in majestic glory, to humble the proud and crush the wicked and bring about their final destruction. If Job can do that, God will admit that Job is self-sufficient and doesn't need the Lord to save him. Obviously, Job is unable to do that.

Job had accused God of injustice because he felt God had not properly dealt with the wicked. They appeared to prosper while Job suffered. Earlier Job had complained, "Why do the wicked live on, growing old and increasing in power?" (21:7)

and then continued by giving a list of examples of how the
wicked prospered while they ignored God (21:8-15). In saying those things, Job was guilty of accusing God of being
unjust. He also complained that in their death as well as in
their lifetime, the wicked fared no worse than the godly
(21:13). Job failed to realize that God will call all of the
wicked to account at the final judgment. Since Job was "playing God" in passing judgment on the Lord's governance of
this world, God challenges him to unleash his fury against the
proud and the wicked and to bring them to a disgraceful end.
If Job is able to do so, then the Lord will praise him and
admit that Job can save himself.

The Lord's first speech in chapters 38 and 39 had the
effect of humbling Job and of leading him to confess his
unworthiness (40:4,5). Yet the Lord knew that Job needed to
hear more and to learn more about God's wonderful works
and ways, so he addressed Job in the strong language of
verses 7 to 14. The Lord had still more to say, and Job had
more to learn.

In this second speech, the Lord directs Job's attention to
two large and fierce creatures, the behemoth and the
leviathan. He challenges Job to catch and control them. The
two passages that follow have captured the imagination of
readers throughout the centuries by their vivid description
and the challenge they present in identifying the animals.
Before we consider the specific passages, we will make a
number of introductory remarks about these two animals and
the various attempts people have made at identifying them.

The behemoth and the leviathan

In his final speech the Lord describes these two strange
and powerful animals at considerable length. More verses
are devoted to those two animals than to the many animals

described in his first speech. Since the language in these passages is somewhat different from that of the preceding passages, some critics claim that the accounts describing the behemoth and the leviathan were written by a different author and later inserted into the book of Job. Such a view violates the unity of the book, and we strongly object to it. We believe that the author, whoever he was, wrote the entire book under the inspiration of God the Holy Spirit.

Perhaps no other section of the book of Job has been the subject of as much discussion and controversy as these passages describing the behemoth and the leviathan. Throughout the centuries people have speculated about those creatures and have tried to identify them. We will mention four general classes of interpretation and add a few brief comments.

1. *Mythological monsters.* This interpretation held by a number of ancient Jewish scholars is also accepted by some scholars today. They point to the legends of dragons and other fierce animals in ancient folklore and identify the behemoth and the leviathan as such fictitious animals. We would reject that interpretation for two reasons: (a) The Lord describes the behemoth and the leviathan as actual animals that Job could see, not as imaginary creatures taken from folklore. (b) It would be unworthy of the Lord to resort to speaking of imaginary creatures that never existed.

2. *Wild animals in general.* This applies particularly to the behemoth. The form of the word "behemoth" appears to be in the plural, although that is not absolutely certain. Yet the animal is consistently described as one creature, not many. If the form "behemoth" is, in fact, in the plural, it rather suggests the majestic power of the creature, as the plural may occasionally be used.

3. *Animals that are still in existence.* Most commentators favor this interpretation. In their attempts to identify the

behemoth, they have suggested many animals: the hippopotamus, the rhinoceros, the elephant, the water buffalo, and the ox, among others. The overwhelming favorite is the hippopotamus. In fact, it is given in the marginal notes of many English Bible versions. There are, however, some problems that make it difficult to accept this interpretation, as we will attempt to point out in our comments.

With reference to the leviathan, there are two chief candidates: the crocodile and the whale. Most commentators identify the leviathan as the crocodile, and that word appears in the marginal notes of English versions. As in the case of the behemoth, there are certain statements that lead this writer to question that identification.

4. *Animals that once lived but are now extinct.* In many respects this appears to be the most plausible interpretation. Since Job lived long ago, possibly four thousand years ago or longer, the animals God describes might well have lived at that time but later became extinct. Even within our lifetime we know of animals that are endangered species or are no longer in existence. Some animals that lived a century or two ago now no longer exist. Surely, then, it is possible that Job saw animals that are unknown to us.

Today several conservative scholars, particularly those who have a strong interest and background in science, identify the behemoth as a grass-eating dinosaur and the leviathan as a flesh-eating dinosaur. They maintain that the dinosaurs did not become extinct millions of years ago, as evolutionists maintain, but rather lived on this earth even after the great flood and even at the time of Job.

As we all know, there are skeletal remains of dinosaurs, and those remains are proof that such large animals existed for a period of time following the creation. Yet a number of questions arise. Is it possible to reconstruct an accurate picture of those creatures from their skeletal remains? How much guesswork is involved in such an effort? Did those large animals survive the great flood of the time of Noah? If so, for how many years or centuries did they survive? Were they on earth at the time of Job? Even if we assume a very early date for Job, isn't it at best questionable to identify those animals as the animals God refers to in these passages? Nowhere does the Bible mention such animals in the account of Abraham, who was probably a contemporary of Job.

It seems best to exercise caution and refrain from making a specific identification of these creatures and to leave the question open. Suffice it to say that God is speaking of two large and formidable creatures that existed at that time—creatures Job saw—but that have possibly long since passed out of existence.

God had his special reasons for speaking of those creatures. He would further teach Job a lesson in humility and total reliance on the great God who created them and everything else in this universe. We too can profit from learning that lesson.

The behemoth

¹⁵ "Look at the behemoth,
  which I made along with you
  and which feeds on grass like an ox.
¹⁶ What strength he has in his loins,
  what power in the muscles of his belly!
¹⁷ His tail sways like a cedar;
  the sinews of his thighs are close-knit.
¹⁸ His bones are tubes of bronze,
  his limbs like rods of iron.

These four verses introduce us to the first of the two great creatures, the behemoth. They give a striking physical description of that large animal. That such an animal was in existence at the time of Job is evident from the Lord's opening statement: "Look at the behemoth." Some scholars have derived the word "behemoth" from an Egyptian word meaning "the ox of the water." It appears more likely to be the plural of the Hebrew word meaning "beast." In the case of this animal, the plural serves to emphasize his majestic greatness. This huge animal did not slowly develop through the process of evolution. God created him, as he also created Job. The Lord describes the behemoth in considerable detail. He tells Job that the behemoth "feeds on grass like an ox." It must have taken a lot of grass to satisfy his enormous appetite.

God also refers to the behemoth's great strength in his loins and belly. Those opening statements appear to describe the hippopotamus, but they could also describe some other great creature, perhaps one that is no longer in existence. Do these words refer to a dinosaur? While we might speculate, we can't draw any definite conclusions.

Verse 17 poses a problem for those who maintain that the behemoth is a hippopotamus. The text reads, "His tail sways like a cedar." We know that a hippopotamus has a short, stubby tail. Some scholars suggest that the word "cedar" refers to a short branch of a cedar tree rather than to the main trunk. Such an explanation, however, is questionable and a forced interpretation of the words. Those words suggest a long tail rather than the short tail of a hippopotamus. Later verses (19,23,24) also describe an animal that must have been larger than a hippopotamus. The name "behemoth" does not specifically identify the animal in the sense that "lion" (38:39) and "horse" (39:19) identify those animals.

In vivid language the Lord further describes the behemoth: "The sinews of his thighs are close-knit. His bones are tubes of bronze, his limbs like rods of iron." The Lord describes the sinews of the behemoth's thighs as "close-knit," literally "intertwined" so that they are reinforced. His bones are "tubes of bronze." The picture is that of metal that has been beaten into shape. Perhaps the colloquial expression "hard as nails" would be appropriate. The closing line in this section further describes this supercreature: "His limbs like rods of iron." What a formidable beast!

> ¹⁹ **He ranks first among the works of God,**
> **yet his Maker can approach him with his sword.**
> ²⁰ **The hills bring him their produce,**
> **and all the wild animals play nearby.**
> ²¹ **Under the lotus plants he lies,**
> **hidden among the reeds in the marsh.**
> ²² **The lotuses conceal him in their shadow;**
> **the poplars by the stream surround him.**
> ²³ **When the river rages, he is not alarmed;**
> **he is secure, though the Jordan should surge against**
> **his mouth.**
> ²⁴ **Can anyone capture him by the eyes,**
> **or trap him and pierce his nose?**

The Lord has described the physical appearance of the behemoth (verses 15-18). Now he speaks of the behemoth's activities and habits.

What is meant by the statement "He ranks first among the works of God"? It can't mean that God created the behemoth before he created anything else. According to Genesis 1:24, God created the land animals on the sixth day. The expression "ranks first" rather suggests the idea of "chief" or "foremost" in its size and awesome appearance. No single human being could contend with that large animal.

Although the second line of verse 19 is difficult in the Hebrew and has been translated and interpreted in various ways, the NIV expresses the thought well. God created also the behemoth. Although that huge animal might intimidate human beings, God can completely control him. God speaks as if he were holding a sword before the animal to subdue him and prevent him from making aggressive movements against his Creator. God holds him in check.

One of the problems that confront the scholars is the locale of this animal. Verses 20 and 23 appear to suggest the land of Israel with its hill country (20) and the Jordan (23). On the other hand, verses 21 and 22 give the picture of Egypt. Was Job familiar with both countries? Probably so, since he operated a large estate and may well have traveled to other countries in the Middle East. At least, Job must have been familiar with their geographical features.

The Lord reminds Job that the hills provide the behemoth with their produce. That animal's enormous appetite would send him to the hills in search of more food. Could those words imply that in the course of time the behemoth would fail to receive sufficient nourishment and become extinct? That is at least a possibility.

Although the behemoth was a creature of tremendous size and imposing appearance, it evidently was not fiercely aggressive. We read, "All the wild animals play nearby." Those smaller creatures apparently felt no need to keep their distance but were secure in the vicinity of that huge animal.

The behemoth's habitat was "under the lotus plants," and "the lotuses conceal him in their shadow." Many commentators mention that the lotuses referred to in these verses were large thorny lotus plants that grew in Israel as well as in Africa. As we mentioned before, these verses suggest both areas as possible locations. Marshes and poplars were also found in that part of the world. We can conclude from these verses that the behemoth was an animal that also enjoyed his leisure.

And yet the behemoth could not be intimidated. He would remain undaunted even in the face of the rushing waters of a river. From verse 23 we can learn that the behemoth was an amphibious animal, equally at home in the water and on the dry ground. That is certainly true of the hippopotamus, but it could also be true of certain other large animals, such as the amphibious dinosaurs.

In the final verse of this passage, God asks Job a question: "Can anyone capture him by the eyes, or trap him and pierce his nose?" The obvious answer is no. The Lord dares Job to try to do so. To capture such a huge and strong animal would require a force of many men with the necessary equipment. It's as if God is saying, "Job, I can do anything; you can do nothing. Who are you to contend with me?"

The expression "by the eyes" has been understood in various ways, and it is difficult to express it adequately in English. A superficial reading of those words might suggest grabbing the animal by the eyes in a manner similar to grabbing it by the tail, but that would be ridiculous and unworthy of the Lord's manner of speaking. Nor does the expression refer to blinding the animal, for the words do not refer to poking out his eyes. Rather, we could express the meaning in a paraphrase such as this: "Can anyone capture him while he (the behemoth) is watching?" One would do so at the greatest risk of being killed. The concluding line in this ten-verse unit reads "or trap him and pierce his nose?" The behemoth is so large and strong that it would be impossible to catch him in a trap or to pierce his nose. People in ancient times would pierce the nose of an aquatic animal to force it to breathe through its mouth and inhale water so that it would suffocate. Could Job do that to the behemoth? Never!

If Job can't control or capture one of God's creatures, how can he presume to sit in judgment over God's rule of this world? How can he sit in judgment over God's dealings with Job as an individual? How can he challenge the great Creator of this universe when he can't even stand up to some of the animals God created? In his speeches to Job the Lord is repeatedly reminding Job that God's thoughts and ways are infinitely higher and greater than those of human beings. He has reminded Job of that truth in the first three lessons in this course of instruction dealing with the physical world (38:1-38), animals and birds (38:39–39:30), and the behemoth (40:15-24). One final lesson remains—God's discourse about the leviathan.

The leviathan

41   **"Can you pull in the leviathan with a fishhook**
        or tie down his tongue with a rope?
  ² **Can you put a cord through his nose**
     or pierce his jaw with a hook?
  ³ **Will he keep begging you for mercy?**
     Will he speak to you with gentle words?
  ⁴ **Will he make an agreement with you**
     for you to take him as your slave for life?
  ⁵ **Can you make a pet of him like a bird**
     or put him on a leash for your girls?
  ⁶ **Will traders barter for him?**
     Will they divide him up among the merchants?

The question naturally arises, What kind of animal was the leviathan? Several commentators have claimed with no reservations that the leviathan was a crocodile. A few versions of the Bible have even substituted the word *crocodile* for the word "leviathan" in the text. Another suggested identification is the whale.

Certain statements in this chapter make those identifications doubtful. It is also questionable to identify the animal as a dinosaur, since we can't know for sure whether or not the dinosaurs existed at the time of Job. Again, it seems best to refrain from making a precise identification of the leviathan. We can, however, turn our attention to other Old Testament passages in which the word *leviathan* occurs.

The word "leviathan" is found only six times in the Old Testament: twice in Isaiah 27:1 and once each in Psalm 74:14, Psalm 104:26, Job 3:8 and the first verse of this chapter, 41:1. In Isaiah 27:1 he is called "the gliding serpent" and "the coiling serpent," and is referred to as "the monster of the sea." That verse also states that the Lord will punish and slay the leviathan. That passage suggests a fierce amphibious reptile which may have inhabited the earth at an earlier time. Stories of dragons in ancient folklore might well have had a historical basis. In literature from ancient Ugarit, a country north of Israel, an animal with a related name, Lotan, is similarly described. Isaiah 27:1 introduces a chapter that tells of the deliverance from Israel's enemies. Leviathan may have been a personification of Israel's enemies in that poetic passage.

Another challenging passage is Psalm 74:14, in which Asaph addresses God, "It was you who crushed the heads of Leviathan and gave him as food to the creatures of the desert." Was the leviathan actually a many-headed creature that really existed? Or is this a poetic passage picturing God's power over the hostile forces of nature in starkly concrete terms? In whatever manner we might answer that question, we are left with the distinct impression that the leviathan was a powerful creature that was also hostile and dangerous.

In Psalm 104:26 the psalmist describes the leviathan as a creature living in the sea: "There the ships go to and fro, and the leviathan, which you formed to frolic there." That passage mentions the sea. Does that possibly speak against the crocodile identification? Don't crocodiles usually swim in rivers rather than in seas or oceans?

In his opening speech Job referred to the leviathan. Cursing the day of his birth, he lamented, "May those who curse days curse that day, those who are ready to rouse Leviathan" (3:8). Those words suggest the great danger that would be involved in challenging and combating that fierce creature. That same theme is repeatedly emphasized in chapter 41 of the book of Job.

The only remaining occurrence of the word "leviathan" is in the first verse of this chapter. In all six Old Testament occurrences, the word is given without the definite article ("leviathan") in the Hebrew. The NIV uses the article in this chapter ("the leviathan") but not in 3:8, where it capitalizes the word ("Leviathan"). Some translations capitalize it also in this chapter (41). In either case, the leviathan, like the behemoth, appears to be a unique creature of great size and strength.

Immediately following his brief description of the behemoth in 40:15-24, the Lord introduces his longer discourse about the leviathan. He begins a long series of questions with the challenging words "Can you pull in the leviathan with a fishhook or tie down his tongue with a rope?" The obvious answer is no. To try to do so would be as useless as to attempt to catch an elephant in a mousetrap.

The next question similarly implies a negative answer: "Can you put a cord through his nose or pierce his jaw with a hook?" The words of these two verses have led most scholars to conclude that this animal is a crocodile. They mention that crocodiles can attain a length of almost 30 feet and that it would be virtually impossible to catch them in the manner suggested in these verses. Now while it may be impossible for one person to catch a crocodile in that manner, we do know that a number of men can do so. Even in ancient times people caught crocodiles. The ancient Greek historian Herodotus reports that men would catch a crocodile by baiting hooks with sides of pork and beating pigs along the shore so that their squeals would attract the attention of the crocodile (II, 70). We might therefore ask, was the leviathan a larger and more ferocious animal than the crocodile? The words of these verses suggest that possibility.

To catch the leviathan would be difficult, if not impossible. But just suppose Job succeeded in catching him; what would Job do with him? In verses 3 to 6, the Lord asks Job several questions that suggest situations which would be both ridiculous and comical. Could we even imagine that such a huge creature would come cowering to Job or any other human being and beg him for mercy? Would he enter into an arrangement that would make him a slave for life, like a conquered warrior submitting to his conqueror after the battle? And how absurd it would be to imagine that Job or anyone else would make a pet out of such an untamable animal and play with him as one might play with a pet bird! In many households today we can see canaries, parakeets, and similar birds kept in cages. In ancient times parents gave their children tamed birds to lead on a leash. Would Job tie the leviathan to a leash and have his girls lead the leviathan around as a pet? Forget it!

The Lord continues by turning Job's attention to the markets of the day. Members of the fishermen's guilds would meet to conduct business and sell their wares in the open markets, as we can also see today in many parts of the world. Would those merchants be able to bring the leviathan to the market? Not very likely! And even if they could do so, would they be able to sell him? Hardly! How would they cut him up and divide him? And even if they did, would the people buy him for food? Very questionable!

With this barrage of questions the Lord is impressing on Job how utterly impossible it would be for Job to contend with the leviathan and conquer him. In the verses that follow, God pursues that theme and reminds Job that God is even more powerful than the leviathan.

> ⁷ **Can you fill his hide with harpoons**
>   **or his head with fishing spears?**
> ⁸ **If you lay a hand on him,**
>   **you will remember the struggle and never do it again!**
> ⁹ **Any hope of subduing him is false;**
>   **the mere sight of him is overpowering.**
> ¹⁰ **No one is fierce enough to rouse him.**
>   **Who then is able to stand against me?**
> ¹¹ **Who has a claim against me that I must pay?**
>   **Everything under heaven belongs to me.**

In verses 1 and 2 the Lord had asserted that one can't catch the leviathan with a hook or a cord. Now God states that a person is unable to penetrate the leviathan's hide with harpoons or his head with spears. (In verses 13 to 17 the protective armor that covers the leviathan's body is described.) If this animal was a crocodile, could we say that no weapon could pierce his hide, attack his head, and kill him? Were the weapons of ancient times too dull to kill a crocodile? Or was this leviathan perhaps a creature larger and stronger than a crocodile, with a head and body that was considerably more protective? We ask those questions far more easily than we can answer them.

Verse 8 reminds us that one experience in attempting to attack the leviathan will teach Job never to try it again. In fact, he may never have that opportunity. In the verse that follows, Job is warned about the danger of such a confrontation. His attempt at subduing the leviathan would be doomed from the beginning. He would panic at the very sight of the beast. The experience would overpower him.

In his opening speech Job had spoken of "those who are ready to rouse Leviathan" (3:8). Now in the first line of verse 10, the Lord declares, "No one is fierce enough to rouse him." To attempt such a foolhardy act would be fatal. The very sight of this fierce creature would disarm even the most courageous. Who then is Job to challenge such an enemy?

After saying those words, the Lord directs Job's attention to someone far greater than even the leviathan. He adds, "Who then is able to stand against me?" The leviathan is indeed a powerful creature, but he is only a *creature*. God, on the other hand, is the *Creator* who made everything, including the leviathan.

In his previous speech concerning the behemoth, the Lord had stated, "He ranks first among the works of God, yet his Maker can approach him with his sword" (40:19). God had made the behemoth by his almighty power, and he could control him at will. Similarly, he could control the leviathan. That fierce animal could never strike fear into the heart of his Maker. He was completely under God's control. If Job can't stand up to the leviathan, how can he stand up to the Lord?

Job had asked God to repay him for his piety (19:6-10; 30:20-26). The Lord answers Job, "Who has a claim against me that I must pay? Everything under heaven belongs to me." The Lord created heaven and earth and this whole vast universe with its countless galaxies of stars and planets. How can one fail to be filled with reverent awe as he gazes into the heavens on a clear night? The Lord is infinitely greater than any of his creatures, including the behemoth and the leviathan. What right, then, does Job have to question God's justice in his dealings with people? What right does the creature have to sit in judgment over the Creator? We would do well to call to mind the words of Saint Paul, "But who are you, O man, to talk back to God? 'Shall what is formed say to him who formed it, "Why did you make me like this?"' Does not the potter have the right to make out of the same lump of clay some pottery for noble purposes and some for common use?" (Romans 9:20,21).

Saint Paul refers to verse 11 of this chapter in the concluding doxology of chapter 11 of his epistle to the Romans. He declares, "Who has ever given to God, that God should repay him?" (Romans 11:35). We need to take that to heart. With Job, we need to learn that God's ways are infinitely higher than ours. We can't understand them because we can't understand God.

As he was experiencing his great troubles and afflictions, Job couldn't understand why he had to suffer so much. What a change from his earlier days! The Lord had blessed Job with unusually great prosperity. Then God suddenly deprived Job of all that and allowed him to suffer greatly. "Why?" asked Job. God had his own reason for doing so. He did so to humble Job and to test and strengthen Job's faith.

In his dealings with you and me, there are times when we might wonder why God allows sickness, accidents, the loss of loved ones, or other afflictions to touch our lives. We might even be tempted, with Job, to accuse God of being unfair to us. But when we have such thoughts, let's remember that God has his own good reasons for sending us joy or sorrow, prosperity or hardship. Let's also remember that as surely as we are his children, he loves us and does for us what is in our best interests, even though we can't understand or appreciate it at the time. Instead of questioning him, we ought to submit to him in faith. We ought to find comfort in his Word and turn to him in prayer. We all need to grow in the virtue of patience. Job needed to learn that lesson, and so do we.

¹² "I will not fail to speak of his limbs,
   his strength and his graceful form.
¹³ Who can strip off his outer coat?
   Who would approach him with a bridle?
¹⁴ Who dares open the doors of his mouth,
   ringed about with his fearsome teeth?
¹⁵ His back has rows of shields
   tightly sealed together;
¹⁶ each is so close to the next
   that no air can pass between.
¹⁷ They are joined fast to one another;
   they cling together and cannot be parted.

In these verses the Lord gives a detailed physical description of the leviathan. He begins by stating his intention to describe that strong and graceful animal. In the first line of verse 13, God asks, "Who can strip off his outer coat?" The implied answer is no one. As we learn from the verses that follow, the leviathan is covered with a tightly fitting coat that can't be penetrated or removed.

In the NIV the last line of verse 13 reads, "Who would approach him with a bridle?" The last word in that verse poses a difficulty. Several other translations of that Hebrew expression have been suggested: "double rows of teeth," "double coat of mail," and "double armor" among others. The Hebrew expression suggests two rows of teeth set in jaws that would ordinarily be restrained by a bit and bridle. Perhaps a combination of the various translations could best express the thought of verse 13.

The next verse (14) describes the jaws and teeth of the leviathan. His jaws are vividly pictured as "the doors of his mouth." Some commentators who identify the leviathan as the crocodile make a point of saying that no lips are mentioned in this verse. That would, however, also apply to other

337

reptiles, perhaps some large reptile that was present at the time of Job. Whether this creature was a crocodile or a dinosaur is best left undecided. From the text we do know that the leviathan was a large and ferocious creature, undoubtedly of the reptile family. We are also informed that his strong jaws contained sharp teeth that could make mincemeat out of anyone foolish enough to try to pry open his mouth.

Verses 15 to 17 describe in considerable detail the outside covering of the leviathan. His scales are pictured as "rows of shields tightly sealed together" (verse 15). They are so close that "no air can pass between" (verse 16). They "are joined fast," "cling together," and "cannot be parted" (verse 17). In his commentary on Job, Walter Lang suggests that this is for the purpose of achieving "controlled humidity." How could Job or any other mortal pierce the scaly hide of such a creature? In the leviathan, God had created an animal that no man could catch or subdue.

> [18] **His snorting throws out flashes of light;**
>   **his eyes are like the rays of dawn.**
> [19] **Firebrands stream from his mouth;**
>   **sparks of fire shoot out.**
> [20] **Smoke pours from his nostrils**
>   **as from a boiling pot over a fire of reeds.**
> [21] **His breath sets coals ablaze,**
>   **and flames dart from his mouth.**

After having described the physical qualities of the leviathan, the Lord concludes with a vivid account of some of the leviathan's activities. In this four-verse section he is pictured as a fire-breathing dragon.

This passage poses a problem for the interpreter: Is this picture language, or is it to be understood literally? It is difficult to come to a definite conclusion. Scholars who identify the leviathan as a crocodile interpret these verses figuratively, or symbolically. Since crocodiles do not breathe fire or let fire-brands stream from their mouths or pour out smoke from their nostrils, they understand the words to express a symbolic meaning. They interpret verse 18 to mean that the rays of sun-light make the water from his nostrils resemble flashes of light as he snorts or sneezes. They understand the language of these four verses to express a comparison. They say they *resemble* light, fire, and smoke but are not those elements in reality. As evidence they would point to the last line of verse 18: "His eyes are *like* the rays of dawn." That statement does not say they *are* the rays of dawn. Referring to an Egyptian hieroglyph representing a crocodile's eyes as the symbol of dawn, Franz Delitzsch maintains that the leviathan is a crocodile.

Most commentators are of the opinion that the vivid language of these verses is picture language and does not describe an animal that actually breathed out fire or smoke.

But the matter isn't quite that simple. Although the last line of verse 18 is in the form of a simile, in the rest of the verses the statements are not given in that form. In a straightforward manner, the text reads, "Firebrands stream from his mouth; sparks of fire shoot out. Smoke pours from his nostrils as from a boiling pot over a fire of reeds. His breath sets coals ablaze, and flames dart from his mouth."

How are we to understand these verses? Is the Lord describing the fierce habits of the leviathan in picture language that doesn't imply real fire and smoke? Or could we justifiably understand the words in a literal sense? It is difficult to decide. In the ancient Greek translation known as the Sep-tuagint, the word "leviathan" is translated with the word from which the English word *dragon* is derived. Does that possi-bly suggest a creature like the dragon? In the ancient folklore of many nations, fire-breathing dragons are described. Were

those creatures merely the figment of the fertile imagina-
tions of ancient people? Or is it possible that there were
such animals in existence in the distant past? Were some
of the dinosaurs possibly capable of producing such fire
or smoke? Some scholars maintain that they were able to
do so.

The writer of this volume of The People's Bible is not in
a position to either affirm or deny such a possibility. We
must leave the question open and invite the reader to pursue it further through personal research or discussion with
others. Suffice it to say that the leviathan was a large and
fierce creature that could arouse fear in the hearts of those
who would come near him.

> ²² Strength resides in his neck;
>   dismay goes before him.
> ²³ The folds of his flesh are tightly joined;
>   they are firm and immovable.
> ²⁴ His chest is hard as rock,
>   hard as a lower millstone.
> ²⁵ When he rises up, the mighty are terrified;
>   they retreat before his thrashing.
> ²⁶ The sword that reaches him has no effect,
>   nor does the spear or the dart or the javelin.
> ²⁷ Iron he treats like straw
>   and bronze like rotten wood.
> ²⁸ Arrows do not make him flee;
>   slingstones are like chaff to him.
> ²⁹ A club seems to him but a piece of straw;
>   he laughs at the rattling of the lance.

In these verses the Lord continues to describe the awesome physical characteristics that make the leviathan invul-
nerable to attack. God declares, "Strength resides in his
neck." Anyone who has watched two strong bulls do battle is

soon convinced that they have great strength in their necks. To an even greater extent that is true of the leviathan. At the sight of that creature, everyone flees in panic.

The leviathan is a huge creature, yet it is not flabby. "The folds of his flesh are tightly joined, they are firm and immovable." His muscles are solid, and his skin fits tightly, like a metal casting. He is in tip-top physical condition.

Verse 24 further describes him, "His chest is hard as rock, hard as a lower millstone." In Hebrew the word translated as "chest" means "heart," as we also find it in most English versions. Either translation is acceptable. The creature is solid throughout his enormous body.

The Lord compares the leviathan's heart to a lower millstone. In ancient times people would grind their grain between two millstones. The lower millstone was stationary, whereas the upper millstone would be turned by the person who ground the grain. Because of the extra wear, the lower millstone had to be especially hard.

After having given this brief description of the leviathan's strength, the Lord reminds Job that it would be both useless and dangerous to attack the leviathan. By merely rising up, the leviathan would strike terror into the hearts of the mighty, including other animals as well as human beings.

To wound the leviathan with any kind of weapon would be impossible. A sword would bounce off him, and so would a spear or a dart or a javelin or any of the other weapons of the day. In ancient times iron and bronze were used in the manufacture of weapons. When such a weapon would be hurled at the leviathan, it wouldn't faze him at all. He could repulse it as if it were made of straw or rotten wood. One might as well throw a bundle of grain or a wooden stick at him.

Arrows of metal would bounce off his impenetrable hide. Even slingstones would be like chaff to the leviathan. One such stone from David's sling killed the giant Goliath, but it would be unable to harm the leviathan, much less kill him.

A huge club, when wielded with great force, can give a devastating blow, but to the leviathan it would have the same effect as a piece of straw. Even if someone hurled a lance at him at full force, he would only laugh and taunt his would-be attacker. In previous verses of his speeches to Job, the Lord describes other animals as laughing in the face of danger. Of the wild donkey he states, "He laughs at the commotion in the town" (39:7). He similarly pictures the ostrich: "She laughs at horse and rider" (39:18). Of the noble horse he declares, "He laughs at fear, afraid of nothing" (39:22). Similarly, the leviathan will not be intimidated but will face any opponent confidently and with laughter.

> ³⁰ **His undersides are jagged potsherds,**
>   **leaving a trail in the mud like a threshing sledge.**
> ³¹ **He makes the depths churn like a boiling caldron**
>   **and stirs up the sea like a pot of ointment.**
> ³² **Behind him he leaves a glistening wake;**
>   **one would think the deep had white hair.**
> ³³ **Nothing on earth is his equal—**
>   **a creature without fear.**
> ³⁴ **He looks down on all that are haughty;**
>   **he is king over all that are proud."**

In these closing verses of his speech the Lord pictures the leviathan as an amphibious creature, one that is at home on land as well as in the water. The creature's undersides are jagged like sharp pieces of broken pottery. When the leviathan goes on the mud he leaves a trail like a sledge that was used in ancient times. Such sledges had sharp pieces of stone that would beat out the grain at threshing time. From those words we can conclude that either the animal must have had short, stubby legs which didn't enable him to clear the ground, or he would purposely crawl along close to the ground. In either case, he would leave a clear impression in the mud.

"He makes the depths churn like a boiling caldron and stirs the sea like a pot of ointment." What a picture! As he thrashes and slashes in the deep waters, he churns them so they resemble a kettle with boiling water or a pot of ointment that may have been used for its fragrance or for its healing powers. Two words in this verse (31) are particularly significant, the words "depths" and "sea." Those words strongly suggest a large body of water, not a river such as the Nile or the Jordan. The words suggest either the Mediterranean Sea or possibly even the Indian Ocean, both of which might have been familiar to Job. This verse also makes the identification of the leviathan as the crocodile a questionable one, since the crocodile inhabited rivers more commonly than seas or oceans. If the animal wasn't a crocodile, what was it? Again we can say only one thing for sure: it was a large and ferocious animal.

In verse 32 the Lord further describes the leviathan: "Behind him he leaves a glistening wake; one would think the deep had white hair." Today we might think of a motorboat speeding along on a lake while leaving a long, foamy track behind it. In such a manner the leviathan would stir up the water as he would swim along. In the case of the leviathan, however, the place was not a lake but the ocean or sea, as we can infer from the word translated as "deep" in the last line of verse 32. The wake following the path of the leviathan was white, like the white hair of an elderly person.

Earlier the Lord had described the behemoth in unique terms: "He ranks first among the works of God" (40:19). Now in verse 33 of chapter 41 he describes the leviathan as a creature even more powerful: "Nothing on earth is his equal—a creature without fear."

Those words describe a creature that must have been larger and more ferocious than the crocodile. Was it a dinosaur? Was the leviathan possibly a supernatural creature on the order of a dragon, such as appears in ancient legends and folklore? Was the leviathan a creature that symbolized the hostile forces of evil? These are a few of the many questions people have raised about the leviathan. This writer prefers to regard the leviathan as a large and fierce creature that Job had seen and was acquainted with, at least to some extent. But as we have previously stated, we ought to refrain from precisely identifying the animal because there is too much guesswork involved.

The Lord concludes this discourse on the leviathan as abruptly as he began it. In verse 1 he had introduced him with the question: "Can you pull in the leviathan with a fishhook or tie down his tongue with a rope?" Now he closes this speech with the statement "He looks down on all that are haughty; he is king over all that are proud." A number of questions might arise as we ponder this final verse of the Lord's discourse. Do the words "he looks down" suggest that the leviathan is able to stand on his hind legs, raise his large body, and look down on others, people as well as animals? Although the NIV translation would suggest that, the Hebrew verb can more literally be translated as "he sees." From those words we therefore can't draw the conclusion that the animal was taller than other animals such as the giraffe or that he could stand up on his hind legs. Whether or not the animal could stand on his hind legs, as advocates of the dinosaur theory would suggest, we do know from this verse that the leviathan was "king over all that are proud." That would also include the lion, known to us as "the king of beasts."

As Job heard those words, did he count himself among the "proud"? In his insistence on an encounter with God, Job had shown himself to have been proud. He had demonstrated sinful pride in accusing God of being his enemy and blaming God for his sufferings. In his sinful pride Job had also presumed to judge God by human standards, not realizing that God's thoughts are infinitely higher than those of Job or any other human being.

While it may seem strange that God did not directly answer any of Job's questions in his two speeches in chapters 38 to 41, we must remember that God had in mind a much higher and nobler goal. In love God asked Job question after question to bring Job to the realization that his greatest need was to banish all thought of self-reliance and to place himself completely into the hands of God. Job needed to learn the lesson that if he can't comprehend the marvelous creations of God, how can he expect to comprehend the Creator himself? He again needed to be reminded of the truth he had earlier so nobly confessed: "The LORD gave and the LORD has taken away; may the name of the LORD be praised" (1:21).

It was for Job's benefit that God had richly blessed him with abundant prosperity. Now as he was suffering, Job needed to realize that God was also blessing him in his dire adversity as a means of strengthening his faith and drawing him even closer to God. In his speeches to Job, the Lord revealed himself as the majestic God whose thoughts and ways are incomparably greater than man can understand. But the Lord also revealed himself as the God of love who created Job, provided for him, and was deeply concerned about him.

God ended his speeches with the final verse of this chapter because in his omniscience he knew that Job had learned his lesson. Job had repented and now placed his full trust in God.

Again he could say as he had earlier confessed, "Though he slay me, yet will I hope in him" (13:15).

As a believer in the true God, Job also looked forward in faith to his Savior, the Lord Jesus Christ. In two of his speeches he gave evidence of such faith. In his second reply to Eliphaz, he had confessed, "Even now my witness is in heaven; my advocate is on high" (16:19). As true God and true man, Jesus Christ would stand as a witness for Job. As his advocate, or defense attorney, Jesus would defend Job against the vicious attacks of the devil. In his first epistle Saint John uses that beautiful picture when he says, "If anybody does sin, we have one who speaks to the Father in our defense ["an advocate" in the KJV]—Jesus Christ, the Righteous One" (1 John 2:1). Later, in his second reply to Bildad, Job nobly confessed his faith in his Redeemer and also in his own resurrection. He declared, "I know that my Redeemer lives, and that in the end he will stand upon the earth" (19:25). Then in the next verse he added, "Yet in my flesh I will see God" (verse 26). With those words Job expressed a firm hope that his Redeemer would rise from the dead and that he himself would also rise after death to be in the presence of God.

In his speech young Elihu later reminded Job of the Savior whom he called an angel, a mediator, one out of a thousand, and one who would redeem Job (33:23-28). As Elihu described him, the Savior could be none other than the Son of God who would also become true man in the fullness of time. It was therefore the Lord, the triune God, in whom Job trusted and whom he served. As a child of God, Job clung to God in faith and now no longer needed an answer to the vexing problem of his sufferings. Job was satisfied that he was in the hands of his God.

Whether or not Job ever learned of the role Satan had played in his sufferings, we do not know. But we do know that God was now ready to release Job from his sufferings, to declare him right in his discussions with his friends, and to prove to Satan that Job was a righteous man who would not renounce his faith in God.

The final chapter of this book gives us a brief dialogue between Job and the Lord and closes with the happy account of how the Lord restored Job and blessed him even more richly than in the beginning.

PART FIVE

Epilogue
(42:1-17)

The first six verses of this final chapter contain Job's reply to the Lord. In the form of poetry, those verses express Job's humble submission to his Lord and Creator. The book then concludes with a passage in narrative prose. This prose epilog informs us that God settled the dispute between Job and his friends and blessed Job with wealth and prosperity even greater than he had before his affliction.

Job humbly replies to the LORD

42 Then Job replied to the LORD:

² "I know that you can do all things;
    no plan of yours can be thwarted.
³ You asked, 'Who is this that obscures my counsel
        without knowledge?'
    Surely I spoke of things I did not understand,
    things too wonderful for me to know.
⁴ "You said, 'Listen now, and I will speak;
    I will question you,
    and you shall answer me.'
⁵ My ears had heard of you
    but now my eyes have seen you.
⁶ Therefore I despise myself
    and repent in dust and ashes."

In one of the opening verses of this book, we read that Job "was the greatest man among all the people of the East" (1:3). Not only was he God-fearing and wealthy, but he was wise, highly respected, and a leader of men, as we learn from his statements in chapter 29. Compared to others, Job ranked at the very top.

While he was suffering his deep afflictions, Job had complained that God was unjustly punishing him. Unaware of the conversation between the Lord and Satan, Job accused God of being his enemy. In sinful pride he also presumed to judge God's thoughts and ways. He needed to learn the important lesson that God is infinitely greater than him. In his speeches the Lord taught Job that lesson. It had the effect of humbling Job and bringing him to sincere repentance.

In this closing chapter Job begins his reply with a humble confession: "I know that you can do all things; no plan of yours can be thwarted." Although Job still was unable to understand God, he was now convinced that everything takes place within the framework of God's wisdom and almighty power. God is in control. He can bless, and he can afflict; he can give, and he can take away. Job had certainly experienced that, but he had to learn not to question God's governance in this world but to submit to God and acknowledge that God knows best. We also need to learn that lesson.

In the NIV text of verses 3 and 4, there are half-brackets around the opening words "you asked" and "you said." That means that the words are not given in the Hebrew text but are added in the translation to indicate that Job is quoting God's earlier statements in 38:2,3. In verse 3 Job used the word "obscures" instead of the word "darkens" that God had used, but the meaning is similar.

Job continues by making humble confession, "Surely I spoke of things I did not understand, things too wonderful for me to know." He acknowledges that God's thoughts and plans are on a completely different wavelength from Job's. Although wise by human standards, Job confesses that he is ignorant compared to God.

Job's ignorance had led him to make foolish statements and to charge God with unfairness. Job was not guilty of the charges his three friends had leveled against him, but he was guilty of judging God by human standards. God's wisdom is of a far higher order than man's wisdom, and to man it must remain a mystery. With Job, you and I must also be reminded of the words of Saint Paul: "Oh, the depth of the riches of the wisdom and knowledge of God! How unsearchable his judgments, and his paths beyond tracing out!" (Romans 11:33).

In verse 4 Job again quotes God. In his opening speech the Lord had challenged Job to answer a barrage of questions that he fired at him. The questions imply that if Job is so smart and knows so well how to run things here below, let him explain how this grand universe came into being! After God's two powerful speeches, Job realized how little he himself knew and how little he could do. Compared to God, Job was nothing. His closing words are a true confession of a man who is sincerely repentant.

Job declares, "My ears had heard of you but now my eyes have seen you." Before God appeared to him and spoke to him, Job had heard of God. He had become familiar with the true God through the spoken word of others and in worship services. He had prayed to God, praised him, and lived in close fellowship with him. And yet, he had not experienced such a direct revelation of God before the Lord appeared to him in the storm and spoke directly to him.

Job had requested a meeting with God so that he could bring his case before God (23:3-5). After Elihu's speech Job did get his wish when God appeared to him in a storm (38:1–41:34). As it turned out, the Lord did the speaking, and Job listened. Although the Lord did not directly answer Job's questions, he did impress Job with the fact that God is all-wise and all-powerful, completely in control of this vast universe. Whether or not the Lord assumed a visible form, he spoke to Job so that Job could say "my eyes have seen you." Job was now satisfied. To Job, God was now someone who loved him and had his true welfare at heart. Now Job saw God not as an enemy but as a friend. The Great Physician would soon heal the wounds Job had suffered.

Job's final recorded words give clear evidence of his sincere repentance: "Therefore I despise myself and repent in dust and ashes." In saying those words, Job is not conceding that he was wrong in his argument with his friends. He is not implying that his afflictions were due to some especially great sins he had committed. Nor does God in his speeches accuse Job of such sins. Rather, Job is yielding to the Lord and repenting of the sin of judging God by human standards.

Retracting the bold words he had addressed to God, Job states that he repents in dust and ashes. In the original Hebrew there is a striking similarity in sound between those two words. The word for "dust" is *aphar,* and the word for "ashes" is *epher.* That is just one example of the poetic literary qualities of this book.

In ancient times people gave expression to deep sorrow by sitting in ashes and throwing handfuls of dust over themselves. In the second chapter of this book, we noted that Job sat among the ashes (2:8) and that his three friends came and sprinkled dust on their heads (2:12) while they were sitting beside him without speaking a word. To express deep sorrow and repentance, people would also dress in sackcloth and sit in ashes, as we learn from several Bible passages, including Isaiah 58:5 and Jonah 3:6,8.

The Lord now recognized that Job's repentance was sincere and complete, and he was about to relieve Job of his great suffering and restore him to prosperity. But before that, he had something to say to Job's friends.

The LORD *rebukes Eliphaz, Bildad, and Zophar but accepts Job*

7**After the LORD had said these things to Job, he said to Eliphaz the Temanite, "I am angry with you and your two friends, because you have not spoken of me what is right, as my servant Job has.** 8**So now take seven bulls and seven rams and go to my servant Job and sacrifice a burnt offering for yourselves. My servant Job will pray for you, and I will accept his prayer and not deal with you according to your folly. You have not spoken of me what is right, as my servant Job has."** 9**So Eliphaz the Temanite, Bildad the Shuhite and Zophar the Naamathite did what the LORD told them; and the LORD accepted Job's prayer.**

Not only had the three friends falsely accused Job of special sins; they had also painted a false picture of God. To the friends, God seemed to be a cold and heartless being who punished sinners in exact proportion to the sins they committed. They were unwilling to concede that God would permit a person to suffer greatly in order to test that person's faith and to strengthen him. In their theology the law predominated and the gospel played an insignificant role. Their actions and words leave us with the impression that their religion was a cold, formal discipline lacking a personal relationship with God. Because of their mistaken opinions of God, the three friends needed to be reprimanded, so the Lord spoke to them in no uncertain terms.

He addressed Eliphaz, the friend who had spoken first and at greater length than the other two. Since God held Eliphaz primarily responsible, Eliphaz was probably the oldest of the three. The Lord spoke very plainly to Eliphaz: "I am angry with you and your two friends." In a number of passages, the Bible speaks of God's anger. In the psalm that bears his name, Moses twice refers to anger. He states, "We are consumed by your anger and terrified by your indignation" (Psalm 90:7). A few verses later he declares, "Who knows the power of your anger? For your wrath is as great as the fear that is due you" (verse 11). God's anger is not tainted with sin as ours is. His anger is his righteous reaction to that which is unholy and sinful. It's interesting to note that God did not say he was angry because the friends had unjustly accused Job. He said he was angry because they had not spoken of him what was right, as his servant Job had. Their false accusation of Job was, of course, a sin against Job, but more than that, it was a sin against God. They had painted a false picture of God when they attacked Job. Unknowingly, the three friends had played into Satan's hands when they attacked Job.

It is significant that in verses 7 and 8 the Lord refers to Job as "my servant Job" no fewer than four times. He had earlier given Job that same title of honor twice in his two encounters with Satan in the opening chapters of the book (1:8; 2:3).

To appease his anger, the Lord instructed Eliphaz to sacrifice seven bulls and seven rams, a truly large offering. The size of the offering reflects the seriousness of the sins of Job's friends. They had sinned not only against Job but also against God. To escape God's wrath they had to provide those fourteen animals for a sacrifice, and they did so. By a strange turn of events the three men who had heartlessly accused Job were now at his mercy. The Lord appointed Job to serve as a priest to pray for them that they might be spared.

Before disaster struck, Job had faithfully served as the priest of his household. In the opening chapter we read that he prayed for his children whenever they had held a feast, and he sacrificed a burnt offering for each of them (1:5). Now he again was to serve in the role of a priest. Job's activity as a priest strongly suggests an early date for the events of this book, in the age of the patriarchs before the establishment of the formal priesthood during the time of Moses and Aaron.

In the book of Ezekiel, Job is given the distinct honor of being ranked with Noah and Daniel as a great man of prayer. When God foretells the doom that will overtake the rebellious people of Judah, he states that even the intercessory prayers of Noah, Daniel, and Job would be of no avail to save them (Ezekiel 14:12-20). However, when Job prayed for his three friends, God answered his prayer and delivered them. Verse 9 closes with the words "and the LORD accepted Job's prayer." By accepting Job's prayer, God forgave the three friends.

God accepted Job as the priest and mediator for his friends. We might regard Job as an Old Testament reminder of the far greater Priest and Mediator, Jesus Christ. Of him we read, "There is one God and one mediator between God and men, the man Christ Jesus, who gave himself as a ransom for all men" (1 Timothy 2:5,6). Furthermore, "We do not have a high priest who is unable to sympathize with our weaknesses, but we have one who has been tempted in every way, just as we are—yet was without sin" (Hebrews 4:15). As our Great High Priest, Jesus sacrificed himself for our sins (Hebrews 7:27) and prays for us at the throne of our heavenly Father (Romans 8:34).

The LORD restores Job's prosperity and grants him a long and happy life

¹⁰After Job had prayed for his friends, the LORD made him prosperous again and gave him twice as much as he had

Job joins his family in happiness

before. ¹¹**All his brothers and sisters and everyone who had known him before came and ate with him in his house. They comforted and consoled him over all the trouble the LORD had brought upon him, and each one gave him a piece of silver and a gold ring.**

¹²**The LORD blessed the latter part of Job's life more than the first. He had fourteen thousand sheep, six thousand camels, a thousand yoke of oxen and a thousand donkeys.** ¹³**And he also had seven sons and three daughters.** ¹⁴**The first daughter he named Jemimah, the second Keziah and the third Keren-Happuch.** ¹⁵**Nowhere in all the land were there found women as beautiful as Job's daughters, and their father granted them an inheritance along with their brothers.**

¹⁶**After this, Job lived a hundred and forty years; he saw his children and their children to the fourth generation.** ¹⁷**And so he died, old and full of years.**

After Job had served as priest and mediator for the three friends, the Lord made him prosperous again. The King James Version gives a literal translation of the Hebrew: "The LORD turned the captivity of Job." Elsewhere in the Old Testament that expression is frequently used of Israel and Judah after the people had been held captive under the power of others. (See, for example, Psalm 14:7; 85:1; 126:4 and Jeremiah 29:14; 30:3; 33:7.) The expression aptly describes Job's severe affliction in terms of a captivity as he sat outside the city alone except for the few visitors who could only scold him. But now the Lord restored his fortunes—indeed, he made him doubly prosperous.

As we read verse 10 we might get the impression that the change in Job's life was instantaneous, that little or no time passed between the end of his ordeal and the full possession of his prosperity. Such a conclusion is hardly justifiable. Rather, verse 10 is a summary statement of his return to prosperity. Verses 12 to 15 suggest that those material blessings from God were acquired over a period of time rather than immediately.

Before his affliction Job had been a generous and hospitable man. Now again, after his restoration, he made people feel welcome at his table. Verse 11 informs us that his brothers and sisters (probably including also cousins and other relatives) as well as other acquaintances came to eat with him and comfort him.

The question naturally arises, Why didn't those people visit Job and console him when he was in such sore need of their company and comfort? During his terrible affliction he had complained, "He has alienated my brothers from me; my acquaintances are completely estranged from me. My kinsmen have gone away; my friends have forgotten me. My breath is offensive to my wife; I am loathsome to my own brothers. All my intimate friends detest me; those I love have turned against me" (19:13,14,17,19). Were his relatives and acquaintances only fair-weather friends? It seems as if they would hardly qualify to be included in Benjamin Franklin's description of a true friend: "A friend in need is a friend indeed." When Job was in need, they weren't there.

And yet we would do well to refrain from judging those people hastily and uncharitably. A number of considerations might explain, if not justify, their reluctance to visit Job at the time of his great suffering.

1. We live in a different society from theirs. It's difficult for us to understand or appreciate the customs of those people who lived about four thousand years ago on the other side of the world.

2. Job's relatives and acquaintances might have been horrified at the idea of looking at a friend whose physical

appearance had became so ugly and grotesque as a result of his afflictions. Their feelings for Job might have been strained to the limit.

3. Nowhere in these verses does the inspired writer mention that God criticized or reprimanded those people for their failure to visit Job during his period of affliction.

4. Job's loneliness was an important aspect of his affliction and suffering. During those difficult days no one gave him true sympathy and comfort. His three friends only scolded him. Elihu spoke of God's love, but he himself showed no sympathy for the sufferer. Their presence must have added to his discomfort. To prove that Job was his true child, the Lord put Job through a very severe test, but by God's grace Job passed that test.

Even though their absence may seem heartless to us, we would do well to suspend passing judgment on the relatives and acquaintances for their failure to visit Job during his suffering.

After his restoration, Job's relatives and acquaintances came in large numbers to dine with him and sympathize with him. They realized that he had lost all his property and children. Each also gave him a piece of silver and a gold ring. The Hebrew word translated as "piece of silver" apparently refers to a coin with a high value. The word is found only here and in two other passages in the Old Testament. In Genesis 33:19 we are informed that Jacob bought a plot of ground for one hundred pieces of silver. In Joshua 24:32 we read that the Israelites buried Joseph's bones in that plot of ground at Shechem. Since the word is not mentioned elsewhere in the Old Testament, we can conclude that it was a unit of money used during the days of the patriarchs but probably not in later times. The gold rings were worn by men as well as women in ancient times. The rings could be worn in the ears, as we can infer from what is stated in Genesis 35:4 and Judges 8:24. In the latter passage Gideon requests the Israelites to give him the gold earrings that they had taken from the Ishmaelites.

Verse 11 mentions that "all his brothers and sisters and everyone who knew him before" came to see Job. That must have been quite a gathering! Since each of his visitors gave him a piece of silver and a gold ring, the value of the gifts was undoubtedly very great. But those gifts were only a small part of his wealth, as we learn from verse 12.

In the opening chapter the sacred writer informed us that God blessed Job by giving him seven sons and three daughters. Then he adds that Job owned seven thousand sheep, three thousand camels, five hundred yoke (that is, one thousand heads) of oxen, and five hundred donkeys, as well as a large number of servants.

Job was a wealthy man! Now after his affliction God restored Job and *doubled* the number of his livestock: 14,000 sheep; 6,000 camels; 1,000 yoke (or 2,000 heads) of oxen; and 1,000 donkeys. No mention is made of his servants in this chapter, but we can be sure that he needed even more servants than at first, probably twice as many. We can only speculate about how many servants he had.

It's interesting that in chapter 1 his children are mentioned *before* the livestock, whereas in this closing chapter they are mentioned after the livestock. There is probably no significance in the order except possibly because the number of livestock was doubled and the number of children remained the same—seven sons and three daughters.

It has been suggested that in a sense the number of Job's children was also doubled, the first ten children having been taken to heaven at their death, so that Job really had twenty children. That theory is rather far-fetched and reads too much into the text. One Bible scholar suggested that Job's ten children who were killed in a mighty storm (1:19) were miraculously restored to life after Job's ordeal had ended, and that they were the same children mentioned in the closing chapter. He based his theory on a slight difference in the Hebrew text between 1:2 and 42:13. Literally, 1:2 reads "and *there were born* to Job seven sons and three daughters," whereas 42:13 reads "and *there were* to him seven sons and three daughters." The NIV translates both verses "he *had* seven sons and three daughters." Although that theory is interesting, it seems to press the distinction between the two passages in the Hebrew text too much. Moreover, there is no indication that a miracle of physical resurrection took place on this occasion.

One person who is not mentioned in this chapter is Job's wife. Neither is she mentioned in chapter 1. She briefly appears in the middle of chapter 2 when she urges Job to curse God and die. Job mentions her only twice in his speeches, in 19:17 and 31:10. The fact that Job's wife isn't mentioned in this concluding chapter raises a few problems. Was this wife the same person as the one mentioned earlier in this book? The vast majority of commentators maintain that she was. For example, in his book *The Word Becoming Flesh,* Horace Hummel states that "she does obviously again become the mother of his children in the restoration at the end of the book" (page 474). We would agree with that opinion. The sacred writer doesn't say that Job's wife had died and that Job had remarried. It would also be entirely out of character for Job to divorce his wife. We must, then, assume that the mother of the ten children mentioned in this closing chapter was the same person as the one who spoke those ill-advised words to Job in chapter 2.

And yet there remains a problem. After having borne the ten children mentioned in chapter 1, would she be able to bear ten more? Even if we assume that there may have been multiple births in some instances, wouldn't Job's wife have been well beyond the normal childbearing age? When Abraham's wife Sarah bore Isaac at the age of 90, the Bible pronounces it to be a miracle (see Genesis 18:12; Hebrews 11:11). Although Job's age at the time of his affliction and restoration is not given in the Bible, we get the distinct impression that he was a mature man. There is a tradition that Job was 70 years old when disaster struck. His wife was probably not much younger. Perhaps the best solution is to assume that God worked a miracle in giving ten more children to Job and his wife. Whatever the solution to the problem may be, we accept as God's Word what the text tells us: "He also had seven sons and three daughters."

In most passages of the Old Testament in which names of children are given, the names of the sons are listed and the names of the *daughters* are *omitted.* That is evident in Genesis chapters 5, 10, 11, and 46, as well as in other passages. In this closing chapter of the book of Job, the opposite is the case. The names of Job's three daughters are also interesting. His first daughter was named *Jemimah,* which means "dove." In the Song of Songs, Solomon addresses his beloved with the words "my dove" (2:14). The name of Job's second daughter was *Keziah,* meaning "cassia" or "cinnamon bark," suggesting pleasing fragrance. The third daughter, *Keren-Happuch,* had a name meaning "horn of eye paint," indicating facial beauty enhanced by eye shadow. (They used cosmetics in ancient times too!) All of those names suggest beauty, and the sacred writer states that no women in the land were as beautiful as Job's daughters. Beauty is also a gift of God.

Not only were Job's daughters beautiful; they also were given an inheritance along with their brothers. That fact indicates that women held a high status in the patriarchal culture at the time of Job. It also suggests that Job lived at about the time of Abraham. Special mention is made of the beauty of Sarah (Genesis 12:11) as well as Rebekah (Genesis 24:16) and Rachel (Genesis 29:17). All three women also exerted considerable influence in their households, as was probably the case with the three daughters of Job. During the time of Moses and the Israelites, the general rule was that only the sons in a family received an inheritance. The daughters had no share in it. An exception to that rule is recorded in Numbers 27:1-11, which mentions that a man named Zelophehad had no sons. His five daughters appealed to Moses, who sought a solution from the Lord. In response to his request the Lord instructed Moses to divide the father's property among the five daughters.

The equal distribution of Job's property to his ten children gives evidence of the harmony and peace that prevailed in his household again as at the beginning of this remarkable book. The agony and pain that Job had suffered was at an end. Ahead lay a long life of contentment and joy. In only a few words, the two concluding verses summarize the last and longest part of Job's life—140 years, two full ordinary lifetimes. We aren't told how old Job was when he began that long final portion of his life. If he was 70 at the time, as tradition relates, Job reached the age of 210 years— a longer lifetime than that of Terah (205), Abraham (175), Isaac (180), or Jacob (147). If he was 60 when disaster struck, he lived to be 200. We can't say for sure, but it seems he must have lived at least 200 years.

We read that Job saw his children and their children to the fourth generation. What does that mean? If we count Job as the first generation, he saw his great-grandchildren. If we count his children as the first generation, he saw his great-

great-grandchildren. In either case, he must have seen many descendants, particularly since he had ten children. Psalms 127 and 128 declare that children are a great blessing from God. Job enjoyed that blessing.

The book of Job concludes with a short verse: "And so he died, old and full of years." The Bible similarly describes the death of Abraham (Genesis 25:8) and Isaac (Genesis 35:29). The expression indicates a life that was long, successful, satisfying, and rich in God's blessings.

This concludes our study of the book of Job, a truly remarkable book. It is a book that expresses profound thoughts in beautiful language. In a dramatic manner, the book comes to grips with the problems of human suffering and God's governance of the world. It reveals Job as a man subjected to intense suffering for reasons of which he was unaware. Although he was tested to the limit and at times complained bitterly, by God's grace he clung to faith in his Lord and Redeemer.

What can we learn from the example of Job? The popular opinion is that we can learn patience in suffering. Of course, we need to learn that. But was Job always patient during his ordeal? Didn't he at times display impatience not only with his friends but also with God? As great a man as he was, Job also had his weaknesses. Had he trusted in himself, he would have failed completely. It was only when he placed his full trust in the Lord that Job found his true strength.

With the eyes of faith Job looked toward his Redeemer, the Lord Jesus Christ, whose afflictions and sufferings were even greater than those of Job. He suffered for Job, for you, for me, and for all people, that we might be spared eternal suffering in hell. By his suffering and death our Savior took upon himself the punishment for our sins. The afflictions we suffer as Christians are no longer punishment administered by an angry God but tender discipline given by a loving heavenly Father. Job learned that lesson. May we learn it also.

When troubles come, and we are tempted to complain or even despair, then may we turn to our Savior and receive the strength we need. In one of his hymns the great Lutheran hymn writer Paul Gerhardt has expressed that truth beautifully:

> Why should cross and trial grieve me?
> Christ is near with his cheer;
> Never will he leave me.
> Who can rob me of the heaven
> That God's Son for my own
> To my faith hath given?
>
> Though a heavy cross I'm bearing
> And my heart feels the smart,
> Shall I be despairing?
> God, my Helper, who doth send it,
> Well doth know all my woe
> And how best to end it. (TLH 523:1,2)

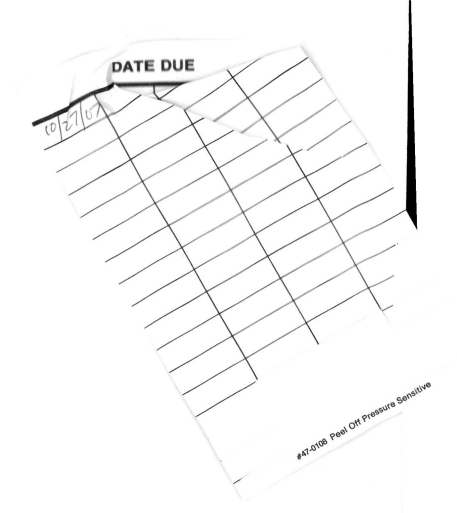